THE IDENTITY TRADE

CRITICAL CULTURAL COMMUNICATION

General Editors: Jonathan Gray, Aswin Punathambekar, Adrienne Shaw
Founding Editors: Sarah Banet-Weiser and Kent A. Ono

The Identity Trade

Selling Privacy and Reputation Online

Nora A. Draper

NEW YORK UNIVERSITY PRESS
New York

NEW YORK UNIVERSITY PRESS
New York
www.nyupress.org

References to Internet websites (URLs) were accurate at the time of writing. Neither the author nor New York University Press is responsible for URLs that may have expired or changed since the manuscript was prepared.

Library of Congress Cataloging-in-Publication Data
Names: Draper, Nora A., author.
Title: The identity trade : selling privacy and reputation online / Nora A. Draper.
Description: New York : New York University Press, [2019] | Series: Critical cultural communication | Includes bibliographical references and index.
Identifiers: LCCN 2018021495 | ISBN 9781479895656 (cl : alk. paper)
Subjects: LCSH: Internet industry—United States. | Privacy—United States. | Data protection—United States. | Consumer protection—United States. | Information technology—Social aspects—United States.
Classification: LCC HD9696.8.U62 D73 2019 | DDC 381/.142—dc23
LC record available at https://lccn.loc.gov/2018021495

New York University Press books are printed on acid-free paper, and their binding materials are chosen for strength and durability. We strive to use environmentally responsible suppliers and materials to the greatest extent possible in publishing our books.

Manufactured in the United States of America

10 9 8 7 6 5 4 3 2 1

Also available as an ebook

CONTENTS

For my grandparents—Joyce, Rich, Frank, and Eleanor

Introduction

Framing the Consumer Privacy Industry

From PRISM and the Edward Snowden scandal to the arrival of Google Glass, 2013 was the year that the desire to be seen and heard was turned on its head. Consider the following: in January, the TSA scrapped airport body scanners that produce near-naked images of travelers; in June, Edward Snowden revealed the widespread global-spying program, Project PRISM; in October, Google announced new privacy policy plans that allow the company to incorporate user data into advertisements. The discussion of privacy—what it is and what it isn't—embodies the preeminent concerns of 2013. For this reason, privacy is Dictionary.com's Word of the Year.

selfie noun, informal (also *selfy*; plural *selfies*). A photograph that one has taken of oneself, typically one taken with a smartphone or webcam and uploaded to a social media website.

Today Oxford Dictionaries announces *selfie* as their international Word of the Year 2013. The Oxford Dictionaries Word of the Year is a word or expression that has attracted a great deal of interest during the year to date. Language research conducted by Oxford Dictionaries editors reveals that the frequency of the word *selfie* in the English language has increased by 17,000% since this time last year.

In 2013, I came across several social media posts juxtaposing the selections of *privacy* and *selfie* as words of the year by Dictionary.com[1] and Oxford Dictionaries.[2] The posts pointed out a perceived paradox: the term privacy, often conceived of as freedom from observation, was seemingly at odds with practices of capturing and sharing personal images. While the cultivation of privacy is supported by careful efforts to manage information, popular discourses about selfies often reference an indiscriminant or even pathological desire to share. In fact, opinion pieces and news stories occasionally point to the rise of so-called selfie culture among young people as indicative of a generation of narcissists, unconcerned about privacy.[3] The selection of these terms in the same year, therefore, raises a question: how can a society that is deeply implicated in cultures that encourage self-promotion and information sharing be simultaneously preoccupied with anxieties about overexposure and unwanted observation?

This tension—between impulses to share and anxieties about losing control over personal information—was highlighted in 2014 when an illegal hack of Apple's iCloud servers resulted in the publication and circulation of a trove of personal photographs. Although successful hacking efforts often receive news coverage, the inclusion among the stolen images of selfies taken by female celebrities, some of which depicted the women without clothing or in revealing outfits, generated immense public interest. The incident—known alternately as "celebgate" and "the fappening"—provoked public debate about the responsibility of image sharing platforms that were trafficking in these stolen photos.[4] Public comments by the affected celebrities, some of whom condemned the hack as an assault on their right to a private life, raised additional questions regarding the ethics of viewing and sharing stolen images.[5] The resulting conversations contributed to ongoing debates about where and how to allocate responsibility and blame for failures to properly safeguard personal information in the digital age.

The celebgate incident clarifies the intimate connection between the cultural trends that resulted in privacy and selfie being selected as lexical exemplars in the previous year. Although selfies are visual artifacts—defined in part by their circulation through digital networks—not every selfie is intended as a public document. Expectations about the visibility of images stored on private servers or circulated in a specific network are informed by assumptions about the boundaries of those spaces. Taking a picture does not confer consent for that image to be viewed by others, just as sharing an image with a person or group does not grant rights for unlimited public visibility. Although we may not consider selfies circulated among friends or posted on social network sites to be private, we may nevertheless wish to limit how these images are accessed and by whom.

Read in this way, the selections of selfie and privacy as words of the year frame simultaneous investments in visibility and obscurity as entirely sensible. It is too simplistic, as social theorist Michael Warner observes, to suggest that a desire for privacy means forgoing public engagement. "Public and private sometimes compete, sometimes complement each other, and sometimes are merely parts of a larger series of classifications," Warner writes.[6] Rather than representing social confusion, the word of the year selections reveal a tension residing at the core of contemporary digital culture: a pressure cultivated by increasing social and economic incentives for visibility coupled with concerns about the consequences these forms of exposure may have on an enduring need for the intimacy and autonomy afforded by privacy. Implicit in both is a desire for agency: not a preference for invisibility, but a wish to be able to control when, how, and to whom we are visible.

This complex relationship between our desire to be social and, at the same time, to maintain personal space, is not unique to interactions mediated by digital technologies. As media scholar Zizi Papacharissi observes, sociality necessitates the voluntary abandonment of some of our privacy. "In order to become social," Papacharissi writes, "we must give up some of our private time and space, so as to share it with others."[7] As has occurred with the introduction of other communication technologies, digital media's growing ubiquity has disrupted the normative and practical barriers that inform this balance. As celebgate illustrates, the same tools that introduce opportunities to extend material practices of information sharing, identity construction, and community building, challenge existing norms of privacy by complicating social practices and norms related to disclosure and visibility. Technologies that facilitate the capture, replication, and distribution of content complicate assumptions about who gets control over how information is collected and used.

While celebgate raises questions about how we consider images shared without subjects' consent, other news events encourage reflection on how information shared willingly can, nevertheless, be misused. On Valentine's Day 2012, Nick Bergus shared a social media post that resulted in a brief and unintentional stint as a spokesperson for bulk personal lubricant. After seeing a tweet about a fifty-five-gallon drum of Passion Natural water-based lubricant available for purchase through the online retailer Amazon, Bergus decided to post the link on his Facebook wall accompanied by his own comment: "For Valentine's Day. And every day. For the rest of your life."[8] Soon after he made the post, Bergus, who later wrote about the incident on his personal blog, began hearing from friends that his comment was showing up as an advertisement for Amazon in their Facebook news feeds. The promotion was the result of Facebook's sponsored stories advertising strategy—a program the company has since abandoned—in which users' likes and posts, content they shared voluntarily, were repurposed as advertising copy for companies.[9] What had been intended by Bergus as a joke was being sold by Facebook as "organic" promotional content becoming, in the process, an uninvited part of Bergus's online presence.

The digital platforms that make up the contemporary online media landscape—including social network sites, search engines, online shopping platforms, and self-tracking technologies—offer features that encourage us to reveal more of ourselves as we seek the conveniences and pleasures of digital life. In building digital profiles through which to connect with others, we open ourselves to unique systems of observation. The distinctive forms of visibility facilitated by platforms in the digital ecosystem combine visible content—the information available to those with access to our social network profiles or who complete an online search for our names—with the data produced through our interactions with digital interfaces. By enabling surveillance systems that track and record online behaviors, the digital environment facilitates the construction and circulation of profiles that are sometimes invisible to us but are, nevertheless, influential. The integration of digital tools into our everyday lives, therefore, has forced a reexamination of what we mean when we assert expectations of privacy. Although we may assume that a selfie posted to a social network site such as Facebook, Instagram, or Snapchat will be visible to friends and followers, do we accept that it may be taken from our profile and reproduced endlessly across the web? Do we agree that it may be used as part of a promotional campaign for a product? Do we expect that the metadata attached to the image will reveal information about our location? Do we recognize that later efforts to delete or remove the image may be complicated by its presence on company servers or on the devices of others?

Selling Privacy as a Service

The inclusion of privacy in the zeitgeisty word of the year annals has the potential to obscure the importance of enduring conversations about the significance of this value. Ongoing debates through which we clarify what we mean when we assert a desire for privacy do more than shape practices of engagement or declare legal rights. Debates about the nature of privacy provide a language through which we evaluate the risks and responsibilities of being visible and make claims regarding the autonomy we have over our public image. Consider, for example, how the conversations sparked by celebgate and Facebook's sponsored stories engaged with questions about ownership and raised ethical issues regarding the access and use of personal information. Consider, too, how these incidents highlighted the sense of violation that accompanies the publication of content one expects to be private. In the 1990s, several entrepreneurs predicted that privacy concerns and identity management would be vital in the emerging online world. Based on assumptions that ordinary people would hesitate to adopt technologies that threatened their ability to control their personal information, these entrepreneurs designed tools and services targeted at safeguarding individual privacy online and giving control over personal information to the user.

Through their pioneering efforts to sell privacy as a service, these companies reflected and shaped cultural expectations about identity management in the emerging digital world. In promotional campaigns and educational efforts, the companies discussed in the following pages—those with names like Zero-Knowledge Systems, iPrivacy, Reputation.com, and BrandYourself—have encouraged consumers to think of their digital image as an extension of their offline identity and offered products and services to aid in its protection. *The Identity Trade* traces the history of these companies to understand their complex and evolving approaches to privacy over the first two decades of the commercial web.[10] By focusing on key moments in the industry's development, this book considers how the distinct but related responses of companies working to sell privacy online reveal the shifts in momentum that take place in the persistent struggle between efforts to control the circulation of personal information and demands that information be shared as a condition of participation in the digital world. Based on interviews with entrepreneurs and policy experts as well as textual analysis of policy documents, promotional materials, and news stories, this book considers how a group of tech start-ups have influenced the ever-shifting politics of visibility and the resulting implications for digital cultures.

Throughout this book, I use the term "consumer privacy industry" to describe the collection of companies that sell privacy-enhancing tools and image management services directly to consumers. Distinct from enterprise companies, those that sell privacy and security solutions to businesses, and designers building tools for niche populations with advanced interests and skills regarding information security and data privacy, this book considers companies united around a goal of building a *mass market* for privacy online.[11] Businesses in this industry include anonymizers and infomediaries—companies that emerged in the 1990s with products that allowed users to surf the web unobserved by government officials, advertisers, and other users. The industry also includes contemporary companies that encourage clients to optimize, rather than hide, their digital identities. Instead of seeking opportunities for invisibility and obscurity online, these companies, which include online reputation management firms and the companies behind the creation of a personal data ecosystem, help clients to understand, influence, protect, and leverage their personal information and public image. Despite their varied approaches, the companies across this proto-industry[12] share a belief in privacy as an essential component of personal autonomy. Moreover, they collectively endorse the use of technological, market-based, user-centric solutions to address concerns about perceived threats to identity and reputation exacerbated by the proliferation of digital tools and their corresponding cultures.

The consumer privacy industry includes firms backed by venture capitalists as well as small start-ups. It is embedded within a socio-industrial context that includes online publishers, search engines, social network sites, digital advertisers, data brokers, and policy makers. The research presented here, which explores the industrial discourses surrounding the risks and rewards of digital visibility, is the outcome of a combination of methodological approaches. This includes a comprehensive textual analysis of popular and trade press articles and publicly available industry documents including press releases, advertisements, websites, and company blogs. This textual analysis, which focuses on how the industry constructs itself internally and presents itself externally, helped identify key industry players. I also conducted semi-structured interviews between 2013 and 2014 with over two dozen representatives of the online privacy community as well as informal discussions and observations of presentations and roundtable discussions at select industry events. The research presented in this book focuses on the United States, where cultural approaches to privacy are informed by the country's unique political, legal, and social context. As with any study of digital media, however, networks transcend national borders. Consequently, my research has included formal interviews and informal discussions with people from several Western countries, including Canada and the United Kingdom.

Embracing Industrial Failure

In examining the evolution of the consumer privacy industry, this book follows several companies as they intervene in a socioeconomic climate where the stakes for digital privacy and online reputation are under continual negotiation. To understand the market for privacy, it is necessary to examine how social, political, and commercial forces have shaped this industry's development. I trace the efforts of companies across this industry as they provide individuals with strategies for balancing the challenges and opportunities of online disclosure. To this end, the book's early chapters describe the experience of several tech start-ups that emerged in the 1990s alongside a series of high-profile privacy violations. As they began to develop and sell tools to shield users' identities from commercial and governmental surveillance, these companies attempted to cultivate a market for selling digital privacy directly to individuals.

An approach that places contemporary companies in historical and sociopolitical context must also embrace industry failure as an important and fruitful site of inquiry.[13] While avoiding narratives that privilege companies that have been commercially, politically, or culturally successful, studies of failure allow for the examination of paths not taken and encourage a denaturalization of the status quo.[14] Based on interviews with entrepreneurs whose companies experienced declining financial success in the wake of the tech boom, *The Identity Trade* interrogates the perception that the economic failure of companies seeking to sell privacy-enhancing technologies at the turn of the twenty-first century can be fully explained by a lack of consumer concern about the security of their digital data or a tendency to choose convenience over privacy. Challenging the popular notion that people will not pay for privacy, the entrepreneurs behind these failed companies offer an alternative explanation for the challenges they faced: they cite sociopolitical and economic changes occurring in the United States at the start of the new millennium as having fostered an increasingly inhospitable environment for companies offering anonymous and pseudonymous channels for accessing the web.

Studying industrial failure in this way creates opportunities to examine the implicit and explicit negotiations between competing technologies, the results of which have played an important role in identifying the cultural and political boundaries in which conversations about privacy, identity, and reputation take place. In later chapters, I ask if and how contemporary companies consider their predecessors when they articulate their own visions for safeguarding privacy online. Juxtaposing the first-generation companies—those who pioneered digital privacy services for a mass consumer market—with more recent entrants to the field, allows for a careful examination of the shifting stakes in the negotiation of visibility online. It is a comparison that reveals how the ideological position shared by industry pioneers—that verifiable, unified, and consistent identity markers need not function as a primary organizing principle of the internet—was slowly replaced by a pragmatism on the part of an industry that often positions identity as a valuable strategic asset.

A research agenda limited to observing successful companies that command economic and social resources in the digital space misses out on much of the nuance embedded in a complex digital ecosystem. Rather than forgetting failed digital projects, the approach pursued in this book stresses the value of examining these enterprises. Such reflection is an essential component of a holistic understanding of the factors that have contributed to the current tension between a desire for meaningful control over personal information and the pressures that demand the cultivation and maintenance of a well-crafted online image.

Technological Solutions and Cultural Consequences

One of the central assertions of this book is that to grasp the cultural tension that informs contemporary practices of digital self-presentation and expectations of privacy, it is essential to understand the industrial forces that shape these ideas. Each of the chapters explores how companies at various moments in the development of the consumer privacy industry have defined the threats of unwanted exposure online and introduced tools and strategies designed to empower individuals to manage their online presence by balancing opportunities for obscurity with the requirements of visibility. Throughout these chapters, I explore how discourses about the consequences of online disclosure shift according to the industry's assumptions about consumer preferences and their corresponding strategies for enhancing user autonomy. I examine how industrialized approaches to consumer privacy shift from a strict focus on anonymity and pseudonymity to embrace techniques that offer individual empowerment through managed visibility and the cultivation of a self-brand. I detail how industry-endorsed options for managing personal information and image have expanded as companies identify and embrace a growing demand for online visibility and redefine the function of digital reputations.

Significant scholarly attention to the complexities of privacy in a digital environment has included research on the role of the commercial sector in shaping regulatory approaches and cultural norms around online visibility. Those studies that examine institutional influences, however, have tended to focus on the dominant industry players, including search engines, social network sites, advertising platforms, and commercial database companies, which are generally presented as threatening privacy.[15] Research on privacy advocates, on the other hand, has focused on the work of public sector organizations including those in government[16] and civil society,[17] largely leaving out the contributions of private sector players.[18] This book extends these discussions by examining the role of commercial forces in the promotion and sale of privacy services to understand how industrial constructions of the risks and benefits of visibility relate to the changing norms around self-presentation and image management online. By placing industry voices and scholarly discussions in conversation, this research reveals how the entrepreneurs behind the consumer privacy industry articulate their own interventions around important social problems, often operationalizing academic theories in the process.

The companies in this industry situate themselves at the intersection of culture, policy, and technology. To provide people with the agency to define and present their identities, they offer socio-technical tools and services designed to empower individuals to control both the collection of their digital data and the visibility of their online image. Through implicit and explicit education efforts, companies in the consumer privacy industry have engaged in public pedagogy campaigns[19] to promote both the value of digital data and the importance of online image management. As a result, these companies have popularized the language—the definitions and narrative terms—that informs broad conversations about the rights and responsibilities around information privacy online. The tools offered by these companies at different points in the industry's evolution demonstrate how ongoing efforts to exercise autonomy over one's own visibility extend beyond the companies themselves to inform collective approaches for understanding the stakes for digital identities more broadly.

Despite the diversity of approaches represented within the industry, these companies share a concern regarding the risks of losing control: both over the production and collection of personal information as well as over the ability to determine how this information is used to define and communicate one's identity. In contrast to definitions of privacy that suggest a desire to withdraw or hide from public view, those in this industry tend toward a definition that considers visibility as a necessary component of social, economic, and political participation. Based on a presumption that autonomy stems from the ability to manage the necessary balance between opportunities for obscurity with the visibility that supports social and economic engagement, the companies in the online consumer privacy industry frame privacy in relation to personal choice. This approach—one that relies on context and relationship management—is consistent with academic definitions that remind us privacy is rarely about being invisible, but is based on an ongoing process of boundary management. It is a definition of privacy that is not, as philosopher of technology Helen Nissenbaum writes, about "simply *restricting* the flow of information but ensuring that it flows *appropriately*."²⁰ The practical implementation of this definition, however, can be complicated by the socio-technical networks designed to identify and reveal patterns and connections that threaten to undermine efforts at self-determination.

The research in this book engages critical media industry studies as a framework through which to examine "the complex interplay of economic and cultural forces"²¹ within the consumer privacy industry. This approach is concerned with the interaction between *industrial* approaches to identifying and addressing digital privacy, and the corresponding *cultural* understandings of the risks and responsibilities of self-presentation online. By emphasizing the role of power and ideologies inherent in everyday practices, this approach observes the relationship between industrial and social processes to offer insights into the "ways in which economic, regulatory, and institutional forces influence cultural output."²² Consider, as I do in chapters 2 and 3, how entrepreneurs' different ideological assumptions regarding the role of personal information in the digital economy resulted in the concurrent introduction of two distinct technological solutions for consumer privacy in the 1990s. Influenced by countercultural ideologies and a cypherpunk ethos, the companies behind a set of products known as anonymizers encoded into their tools a belief that strong encryption was essential for ensuring a free and open web. While the anonymizers believed the emerging digital economy, which relied on the invisible collection, analysis, and use of personal information, was exploitative, another set of companies known as infomediaries sought solutions for what their inventors saw as the inefficiency of a system that failed to adequately compensate consumers for their personal data. The juxtaposition between these two models reveals the material consequences of the divergent ideological positions that inform the construction of technological systems.

Or consider, as I do in chapters 4 and 5, how the way a problem is defined can result in solutions that fail to meet the needs of all users. In these chapters, I explore the practical and ethical challenges facing approaches that rely on the cultivation of a public image to secure opportunities for digital privacy. For those who cannot or wish not to be visible online, practices that create spaces for private identities through the public presentation of an alternate image remain out of reach.

Moreover, these chapters consider how efforts to control the visibility of certain aspects of one's identity can be undermined by socio-technical systems that act to reinscribe cultural assumptions about connectivity and authenticity onto digital profiles.

The research for this book included conversations with CEOs, policy officers, product developers, communication staff, industry representatives, and regulators. My interest in speaking with people from various parts of the industry reflects a desire to avoid privileging one set of voices and, instead, to reveal a holistic sense of the industry culture.[23] This diversity is, however, limited in important ways. For example, the interviews cited in this book and the content included from press material and news articles tend to privilege male voices. This disparity, in part a consequence of the lack of gender diversity in the technology industry generally,[24] was compounded by a methodological approach that focused on companies identified in mainstream media coverage between 1996 and 2014. The extent to which those sources themselves favored certain voices shaped my initial pool of respondents.[25] Opportunities to speak with women occasionally revealed a relationship between representation and practice. At one industry event, for example, I sat in on a session that considered whether women might bring a different set of expectations, values, and preferences to the emerging personal data ecosystem. During the conversation, a small number of participants discussed how assumptions about what women want from personal information technologies often missed the mark. As I will return to, the homogeneity in this industry—which includes class and race in addition to gender—provides an important context through which to understand how companies define the problems and solutions surrounding digital privacy.

These chapters explore the consequences of shifting industrial approaches to privacy, from opportunities for anonymity and pseudonymity offered by the field's early participants to strategies that operate in a contemporary environment that seemingly demands visibility. I analyze how the reshaping of definitions of privacy at various stages in this industry's history have facilitated the reconsideration of online visibility from an option to an opportunity and, eventually, to a responsibility. This book maps the changes in the mass market for privacy as they reflect and shape shifting cultural understandings about what it means to have privacy in the digital world. Telling the story of this industry in this fashion runs the risk of presenting its history as if it has followed a linear narrative: one that moves from a preference for anonymity to a celebration of radical visibility and self-promotion. This is not, however, a book about the steady erosion of privacy as we move further into the digital age. The privacy-enhancing technologies presented here do not replace one another, nor does the emergence of a new tactic necessitate the end of an existing approach. Consider the availability of tools such as virtual machines, live operating systems, and virtual private networks, all of which can support anonymity online. Consider, too, apps such as Wickr and Signal that have received mainstream media attention more recently for their encrypted messaging services, or the increasing popularity of ad blockers. In fact, the circulation of ideas and the resurrection of strategies is an important part of this history.

Instead, this is a story about the process through which expectations of privacy are negotiated and challenged. I consider how identities—both those considered vulnerable and those celebrated for the value they provide—become a central feature of these debates. I also reflect on how mass markets for anonymity and strong encryption technologies receive less attention as consumer approaches to privacy focus on finding a balance between acceptable surveillance and individual rights. In studying companies in their historical, social, economic, and political contexts, this book examines how the reflections of an industry on individual, corporate, and legal responsibilities have consequences for defining and protecting privacy. Indeed, the story of this industry fits most comfortably with approaches that define privacy as an ongoing set of negotiations rather than as a static achievement. I argue for the importance of integrating industry studies—including those of failed companies—into communication research to understand the professional, practical, and ideological conditions under which information is produced and the discursive patterns through which these practices inform and are informed by the cultures in which they reside.

PART I

Selling Privacy to the Masses

1

The Consumer Privacy Space

Building an Industry

In the summer of 1997, on newsstands across the United States, *Time* magazine pronounced "The Death of Privacy." Published between an issue promoting a *Time* exclusive on a deal between "cyberlegends" Bill Gates and Steve Jobs to save Silicon Valley and an issue featuring a retrospective on Princess Diana following her death earlier that year, the August 25 edition contained an eight-page spread detailing the threats posed to privacy, reputation, and identity by digital media. In these pages, Joshua Quittner warned about the role of new technologies in chipping away at existing privacy protections.[1] Recently the target of a six-month campaign to hack his online accounts, Quittner warned that "our privacy—mine and yours—has already disappeared, not in one Big Brotherly blitzkrieg but in Little Brotherly moments, bit by bit."[2]

This casual erosion of privacy, the article continued, was alarming precisely because its seeming innocuousness had helped to foster a cultural ambivalence about the consequences of technologies that demanded access to personal information. By way of illustration, Quittner pointed to the myriad ways people were routinely and voluntarily, but not always knowingly, providing detailed records to third parties about their location, interests, and habits. Automated bank machines, cell phones, credit cards, and supermarket scanners all generate traces of information that could offer unique insights into individuals' attitudes, preferences, and behaviors. Perhaps of most concern to Quittner were emerging strategies to track, quantify, and analyze web-browsing patterns to better understand consumer behavior. Marketers, for example, had begun using small files called "cookies" stored in computer browsers to track individuals' online activities. The result of these efforts to collect and examine newly available information, Quittner wrote, was that data once hidden, obscured by the fact that they were tricky to find and difficult to interpret, were being made accessible and meaningful.[3]

The article offered strategies for avoiding these increasingly pervasive forms of digital surveillance. Consumers, for example, could give up online shopping and forgo the use of credit cards, choosing instead to shop in person and pay in cash. Drivers could get rid of their E-ZPasses and other electronic toll collection systems and opt instead to use cash at tollbooths. Internet users could continuously clear cookies from their browser or surf the web from behind a "privacy curtain" so marketers could not keep track of their online behaviors or website preferences. These strategies, however, highlighted the onerous task facing those who wished to avoid digital surveillance. Moreover, Quittner anticipated that most people did not think about privacy in these terms. He presented efforts to opt out not only as ineffective strategies for becoming invisible to surveillance apparatus, but as encouraging social alienation. "Only the Unabomber," Quittner wrote, "would seriously suggest that we cut all ties to the wired world."[4] Few people, he argued, would waive the unique opportunities created by digital technologies in favor of total obscurity.

This balance between the risks and opportunities of online engagement has become a hallmark of stories about life in the digital age. It reflects the tension revealed by the juxtaposition between the word of the year selections—selfie and privacy—that began this book. Digital infrastructures that support online shopping and social networking offer immense efficiencies while simultaneously supporting an environment characterized by information asymmetry in which data collection and use by public and private organizations is ubiquitous and, often, invisible. Building online profiles through which to connect with others opens unique possibilities for social engagement at the same time as it can introduce reputational risks if, for example, information is accessed by unexpected audiences or circulated out of context.[5] Quittner's strategies for avoiding persistent forms of surveillance highlight that doing so often means giving up significant social and economic benefits. Privacy solutions that demand individuals choose whether to opt in or out of digital life are unsatisfying due to their treatment of engagement in all-or-nothing terms.[6] Few people live at these extremes; rather than seeking to be virtual hermits or online exhibitionists, most people pursue options that allow them to toggle between controlled visibility and intentional obscurity. One of the core principles uniting companies in the consumer privacy industry is a belief that all-or-nothing approaches to visibility fail to capture personal preferences or the realities of life online. The companies introduced in the following chapters have built tools and services that attempt to allow people to navigate the surveillance ecosystem even as they enjoy the conveniences and pleasures of digital tools.

Broadcast Online: The Risks of Being Seen

I first read about Nick Bergus's experience as an accidental spokesperson for personal lubricant when I was researching online reputation and consumer culture as a graduate student. I was drawn to the story because it illustrated a fundamental anxiety about communicating and sharing information online. "In the context of a sponsored story," Bergus wrote in the final paragraph of his blog post, "some of the context in which it was a joke is lost, and I've started to wonder how many people now see me as the pitchman for a 55-gallon drum of lube."[7] When it was repurposed as an advertisement, Bergus's post went from a single entry on his social media timeline to a piece of promotional content that was popping up repeatedly in his friends' social media feeds. In this transition the post was stripped of the context that would encourage Bergus's friends to read his comments as satire rather than as an endorsement. Part of the anxiety surrounding online privacy comes from an appreciation of just how easily this decontextualization can occur—the ease with which digital pictures and messages shared in public and semipublic forums can be taken out of context, circulated, and used in unexpected and unintended ways. The persistence of the resulting profiles—both those that are visible and those created through the aggregation and analysis of data—introduces a sense of permanence that can make digital reputations feel inevitable and inescapable. Anxieties about the death of privacy tap into a sense of powerlessness that stems from a feeling we have little control over how others see us.

By altering the spaces and conditions in which people encounter one another, new media technologies provide a platform on which and through which individuals negotiate the changing conditions and contexts of self-presentation and identity construction. Perhaps the most famous response to a new media technology's challenge to expectations of privacy comes from lawyers Samuel Warren and Louis Brandeis. In an 1890 *Harvard Law Review* article titled "The Right to Privacy," the authors argued that a growing public appetite for salacious news stories in the late nineteenth century was being fed by journalists who, capitalizing on innovations in photography, were capturing and publishing private images of public figures.[8] Warren and Brandeis worried that, in the hands of journalists, the camera would circumvent physical boundaries that had established the privacy of particular spaces and activities. The pair's definition of privacy as the "right to be let alone"[9] has become the foundation for modern notions of privacy in the United States.[10]

While these authors were concerned about access to portable cameras to produce forms of visibility that contributed to unwanted exposure, similar concerns regarding the erosion of privacy have accompanied the introduction of other media technologies. Responses to the introduction of telephones into private homes generated unease about the division between domestic and social realms and produced fears that family secrets would become public spectacles.[11] Even the implementation of the U.S. Postal Service generated concerns that letters would be intercepted and opened or shared beyond their intended recipients.[12] It is through this capacity to challenge the physical and normative boundaries that divide public and private life and regulate behavior that new technologies routinely prompt anxieties about the erosion of privacy.

Long before I learned about sponsored stories or even Facebook, however, another story introduced me to the complicated nature of identity construction in online spaces. As a high school student in Toronto, and later a university student in Ottawa, I followed closely the murder trial of a twelve-year-old Canadian boy, initially known in the media only as "Johnathan." The details of this case have stuck with me in part because of their tragic nature, but also as an exemplar of the complex realities, and profound consequences, of engagement and self-presentation in virtual spaces. The facts of the murder are gruesome and need not be repeated in detail here.[13] Rather, what is pertinent is how the case—which eventually concluded in the conviction of two young men—initially ended in a mistrial. At the center of the Crown's case in the first trial was the testimony of the girlfriend of one of the co-accused. Alarmed by a phone call she had received from her boyfriend on the day of Johnathan's death, she called the young man back later in the day and recorded their conversation—one in which he shared his intention to join a plot to murder his friend's brother and stepfather.

The defense for the young man explained the phone call as an attempt by its client to show off for a girl who was losing interest in their nascent relationship, reportedly describing the conversation as "the musings of one vampire enthusiast to another."[14] When she took the stand, however, the witness undermined the defense's argument by claiming no interest in vampirism. While the jury was deliberating, a journalist uncovered and published posts from a vampire-related website reportedly made by the witness. In these posts the young woman appeared to contradict claims made in court that she found talk of vampires childish and unexciting. Although the witness's page on the site had been deleted months before the trial, a "cached" version was located through a search for her screen name.[15] According to reports, the defense lawyer introduced the posts as a strategy for discrediting the young woman's dismissal of arguments that she shared her boyfriend's interest in vampires: "This seems to be some sort of chatroom . . . she includes among her 'likes' blood, pain, cemeteries and darkness . . . there may well have been semi-nude photographs."[16] These details, including the seemingly irrelevant point that the young woman may have shared nude images, were used to weaken the Crown's efforts to present the witness as a poised and responsible young woman who secured evidence and alerted police to the crime.

Although the trial eventually concluded with a guilty verdict, the details of the mistrial continued to resonate with me. As a high school and university student, I was used to communicating with friends online—using instant messaging, visiting chat rooms, and writing in online journals—with little thought about how the information I shared in these spaces might be understood if encountered by others. Although it was not the same as the anonymous and fractured identity play described by social psychologist Sherry Turkle in her seminal research on early online communities—those in which socio-technical features supported the multiplicity and fluidity of identities that often differed from those assumed offline[17]—my online interactions did provide opportunities to engage in forms of self-presentation that were less informed by the structural realities of my offline life. My friends and I were, as I now understand it, engaged in what media scholar danah boyd has described as a form of identity exploration and relationship building that takes place across online and offline spaces.[18] The Johnathan trial, however, caused me to reflect, for the first time, on my own online identity. How might others read the messages I sent to friends online? Could my own digital image be used to tell a story about me? Would that story be different than the one I told about myself?

Social theorists recognize self-determination as a unique feature of modern life. Sociologist Anthony Giddens, for example, has described the late modern self as a "reflexive project" in which one's narrative biography is articulated, revised, and signaled to others through the adoption of a cohesive set of practices called lifestyles.[19] The relative freedom to select between these lifestyles provides individuals with a range of options through which to consider, construct, and reconstruct their own biographies.[20] Although this freedom is a widely celebrated part of modern life, the risks associated with choosing between preferred versions of ourselves have been well attended to by theorists. When modern identities become untethered from community traditions—as occurs, for example, when individuals are freed from the constraints of familial station that are calcified in more traditional societies to craft their identities[21]—they are also faced with the consequences that accompany those decisions.

Sociologist Ulrich Beck used the term "industrialized individualism" to refer to an environment in which the construction of identity is treated as a personal responsibility.[22] Like Giddens, Beck described the dissolution of traditional social and economic structures that constrain self-narration as enabling the construction of "elective" identities or what he called "do-it-yourself" biographies.[23] Alongside the freedom offered by self-determination, however, are the responsibilities associated with these choices. The "do-it-yourself biography," Beck concluded, must simultaneously be understood as a "risk biography."[24] Individuals, moreover, do not experience this risk equally. The narratives of freedom and choice that characterize discourse about self-presentation are bound by social constructs that limit how those freedoms are accessed. To assume that an undesirable public image can be attributed to a lack of personal responsibility or poor choices around self-presentation ignores the ways that social factors that include race, gender, ethnicity, sexuality, and class shape available opportunities for identity construction.[25]

In his classic definition of self-presentation, sociologist Erving Goffman drew on theatrical metaphors to describe individuals as actors who exert control over their image.[26] For Goffman, social interactions are purposeful, motivated by a strategic goal, and informed by a broader narrative agenda. Through performances in which the conditions and content of interactions are carefully managed to appeal to a specific audience, individuals construct a personal image with the help of those around them. Since, as Goffman observed, not all audiences expect us to behave in the same way, risks are introduced when we are forced to perform for multiple audiences at the same time. Digital platforms that allow individuals to craft a profile and define an intended audience closely mirror the deliberate strategies of self-presentation articulated by Goffman—a perspective that implies social interactions can be successfully managed through a comprehensive awareness of audience and carefully constructed performances. By allowing individuals to draw on text and images to build a preferred version of themselves and negotiate responses to this image, social network platforms present opportunities for the careful crafting of what Goffman called an idealized version of the self.[27]

At the same time as they provide tools for strategic self-presentation, however, digital platforms complicate the knowledge and control one can exert over their audience, a practice Goffman described as essential for impression management. As illustrated by the persistence of the chatroom messages highlighted in the Johnathan case, the possibility for information to be replicated, stored, and searched means that content can be stripped of its context and exposed to unintended audiences without the original poster's knowledge or consent.[28] Interactive tools, which create opportunities for the digital production of self, simultaneously support an environment where content is easily aggregated, searched, and retrieved, making it possible that a piece of information intended for a discrete audience or context may disrupt an otherwise carefully calculated performance. The result is what boyd refers to as context collapse: the experience of being confronted simultaneously with multiple social situations each with a different set of normative expectations.[29] While context collapse can occur offline—imagine, for example, a party with an invite list that includes friends, family, and employers—boyd argues the characteristics of digital media make these challenges more likely in a mediated environment. The persistence of digital content across platforms not only means it can be more easily discovered, but also that these reproductions lack the context that defined the original. Privacy is eroded, therefore, not necessarily at the moment when information is shared, but when control over the contexts in which that information is encountered is lost.

Social media platforms have helped habituate internet users to the norms of visibility and self-disclosure that characterize the contemporary online environment.[30] Many of us readily reveal information online as we post pictures to Instagram, like products on Facebook, and tweet pithy comments about current events on Twitter. Acceptance of current norms that support online visibility does not necessarily minimize concerns about the publicness of these activities. The same technological affordances that empower individuals to make strategic decisions about their digital identities simultaneously intensify the risks when narratives fail to conform to cultural expectations. Consequently, fears persist that, at any moment, a comment or picture could surface, out of context, to disrupt one's digital identity and ruin their online reputation. And while these narratives and reputations may originate in digital platforms, the erosion of boundaries between online and offline spaces mean their consequences often reach beyond the virtual world. The notion of control—over personal narratives and the audiences with whom they are shared—is an integral component of theories of identity and privacy. One objective of this book, however, is to consider how we understand claims to autonomy and empowerment when control is compromised.

Hidden Online: The Risks of Being Invisible

Recent years have been characterized by an abundance of media stories detailing the consequences of undesirable public scrutiny regarding the details of one's digital life. Take, for example, the 2015 Ashley Madison data breach in which information about users of a website catering to those seeking extramarital affairs was made public.[31] The construction of a searchable database provided easy access for people looking for the names or email addresses of those who may have used the service. Or take the public outrage registered that same year over an online picture posted by a game hunter in which he was posed beside a lion named

Cecil he'd killed during a safari in Zimbabwe.[32] The hunter became such a popular online target that he was forced to close review pages associated with his business. These stories, while different in their details, reflect a similar narrative regarding the potential consequences of unexpected or uninvited attention. The associated construction of privacy is one in which an individual or group has failed to achieve desired levels of seclusion. Indeed, these may be the types of privacy violations with which we are most familiar—the ones that get the most news coverage. Social psychologist Irwin Altman observes, however, the additional threats to privacy that are felt when a person or group experiences more seclusion or isolation than they desire.[33] This occurs when people's efforts to be viewed or read are undermined by conditions that render them invisible. Ideal privacy, then, "is a position on a continuum of desired interaction, with deviations in either direction being unsatisfactory."[34]

Feminist scholars have made similar observations regarding the harms associated with having too much privacy. In reference to the legal framework derived from Warren and Brandeis's "The Right to Privacy," Anita Allen and Erin Mack observe that "the privacy tort was the brainchild of nineteenth century men of privilege and it shows."[35] Social norms in American life, they argue, have made the achievement of ideal privacy difficult for women who find themselves constrained by expectations of modesty and chastity, confined by domestic isolation, and given few opportunities for the forms of autonomous individuality and decision making that privacy supposedly affords.[36] Further, a sharp distinction between the public and private spheres has long been employed as a way to avoid addressing behaviors—including intimate partner violence and child abuse—that tend to occur in domestic spaces.[37] Conversely, the sanctity of what Warren and Brandeis's referred to as the "sacred precincts of private and domestic life," which allowed policy makers to turn a blind eye to domestic abuse, was far less strict when, into the second half of the twentieth century, sodomy laws continued to be used aggressively to target consenting adult men engaged in sexual acts within the home.[38]

In an article titled "Gender and Privacy in Cyberspace," Allen revisits her earlier efforts to examine privacy through the lens of gender. After describing social improvements toward the end of the twentieth century that allowed women more access to the benefits of individual privacy, Allen notes that, online, women and men do not enjoy the same access to *desirable* privacy.[39] The disparity, she observes, is at least partially due to greater pressures faced by women to guard their conduct from public scrutiny. The consequences of these expectations are visible in the publication of the seemingly spurious detail that the witness in the Johnathan trial may have shared nude images. The inclusion of this information, likely intended to undermine the witness's credibility, plays on expectations of female modesty and responsibility, which Allen identifies as barriers to women's achievement of ideal privacy.

While following the Johnathan trial, which revealed the consequences of the unanticipated exposure of content shared online, I also became aware of the potential damages that could result from, to borrow Allen's language, too much of the wrong kinds of privacy.[40] Under Canada's Youth Criminal Justice Act, the names of minors accused of crimes cannot be published.[41] Since one of the accused in this case was the victim's older brother, releasing the murdered boy's name would have revealed his identity. As a result, publication of Johnathan's full name was forbidden throughout the trial, so publicly he was known only by his first name.[42] When the two young men were found guilty of charges relating to the boy's death and sentenced as adults, Johnathan's mother asked that the publication ban be lifted so that her son could be remembered properly. "In the process," she reportedly said, "I feel like we've forgotten Johnathan as a person."[43] In seeking to protect the young people at the center of this horrific trial, the system had rendered Johnathan invisible. Through the publication of his name, Johnathan's mother sought to openly celebrate her son's life—including through an online commemorative page—to prevent his story form being erased from public memory.

As is the case with self-presentation, cultural structures shape individual experiences of visibility. Those who are unable to "blend in" when they wish may find themselves all too visible in public spaces: their bodies and identities subject to uninvited and unwanted attention. Others may find themselves rendered invisible by systems designed to ignore or erase them. These two conditions—being highly visible and being invisible—often overlap.[44] Consider, for example, the experience of those with visible disabilities. In her essay "The Politics of Staring: Visual Rhetorics of Disability in Popular Photography," humanities scholar Rosemarie Garland-Thomson observes that the "history of disabled people in the Western world is in part the history of being on display, of being visually conspicuous while politically and socially erased."[45] This is the experience of simultaneously being looked at but not seen.

Digital architectures have come to play a decisive role in shaping the everyday experience of visibility in social life. Media scholar Tarleton Gillespie observes how the work of algorithms to collect, categorize, and rank digital materials for consumption operates to determine which forms of content are made visible and which are made invisible.[46] These choices are far from objective: they carry normative assumptions about the value, acceptability, and importance of content. As a result, they shape not only how information is organized and accessed, but also how it is understood. Scholars interested in the social consequences of technology have observed the work of invisible codes to define user interactions with digital platforms, which has a profound influence on opportunities for self-presentation. Digital media scholar Lisa Nakamura, for example, describes the ways online drop-down lists that offer a "menu" of racial categories define and delimit the range of available ethnic identities. Those who have what Nakamura calls "culturally ambiguous identities—such as those belonging to hyphenated Americans—are rendered unintelligible, inexpressible, and invisible, since they can't be (or rather, aren't) given a 'box' of their own."[47] Similarly, sociologist Rena Bivens describes how Facebook's decision to introduce flexible gender options to replace those that forced identification within a male/female binary was undermined by the company's own algorithms. Even as Facebook introduced nonbinary options for gender identification in the user interface, Bivens describes the platform's back-end database as reconfiguring users within a binary gender paradigm.[48] These decisions, made at the level of code, can radically curtail options for self-determination by imposing identity categories. For those struggling to achieve visibility—including those with nonbinary gender or hyphenated racial identifications—these technical decisions can be experienced as an assault on their identity.

While being seen is an essential component of self-expression, a lack of control over the context of that visibility can also work to undermine personal autonomy. Media scholar Larry Gross describes the gay rights movement of the 1960s as "founded on the importance of coming out as a *public* as well as individual act."[49] Despite the very real potential for harassment and persecution, visibility was positioned as a necessary step toward gaining civil rights. However, tensions surrounding demands made by some members of the movement that gays and lesbians—particularly those in prominent social and political roles—out themselves or face the threat of being outed, demonstrate the importance of autonomy in these decisions. What Gross calls the "politics of outing" raises important questions about the relationship between visibility, choice, and power.[50] Algorithmic technologies that presume to be able to ascertain the gender, race, or sexual preferences of users based on their behavioral patterns must, therefore, be understood as intervening in debates about the right to self-determination even while they claim objective neutrality.[51]

A further example of technological platforms insisting on so-called authentic self-expression is highlighted by the efforts of some social network sites to mandate the use of "real names."[52] Facebook, which has had some version of a "real name" policy in place since its inception in 2004, requires users to sign up under their name "as it would be listed on [their] credit card, driver's license or student ID." These efforts are, ostensibly, used to ensure civil discourse and to build trust online. In 2014, however, the profiles of several well-known drag queens—including Sister Roma and Lil Miss Hot Mess—became casualties of this policy when the performers' accounts were suspended for failing to comply with the platform's rules. Since Facebook does not actively seek out violators, relying instead on users to flag or report those whose profiles contravene company policy, the performers reported feeling as though their profiles had been targeted and their identities had been outed.[53] Writing in *Salon*, Lil Miss Hot Mess observed, "For many—including our LGBT community—digital platforms like Facebook have become part of how we end isolation and try out new identities."[54] The use of terms like "real" and "authentic" to deny members of this community access to the site, she continued, was insulting.

Although Facebook responded to the subsequent protest by promising to work with members of the drag community to help authenticate their stage names under the existing policy, the coalition that emerged to protest the platform's insistence on real names went beyond the drag community and its allies. The real name requirement was decried as harmful for other populations, including victims of domestic violence and stalking, undocumented immigrants, political dissidents, as well as gay and transgender people who were not out to all of their communities.[55] The concerns these groups have about the dangers associated with forced visibility demonstrate that being seen is not, in and of itself, empowering; rather, the ability to choose if and when to be seen and to the define the terms of that visibility is an essential component for achieving an ideal level of privacy.

You Are the Product: The Political Economy of Personal Information

Eulogies for privacy, such as the one penned by Quittner, often point to the capacity for new technologies to capture, aggregate, store, and access vast quantities of data—a combination that radically alters how we recall and use digital information. When the seemingly innocuous bits of information created when we incorporate digital tools into everyday tasks—such as reading the news, shopping, or connecting with friends— are combined to build multifaceted profiles, the results shape our digital environment. When the advertisements, search results, and news items an individual sees are based on conclusions about preferences drawn from analyses of their online behaviors—many of which would not be considered sensitive in their own right—we are forced to rethink how we categorize personal and nonpersonal information.[56] When invisible patterns embedded in these data profiles are used to predict future actions, the line between public behaviors and private information is further muddied.

The use of demographic and behavioral data to make assumptions about individual preferences and, increasingly, to predict future behaviors, is part of a broader practice of the commodification of personal information. In the *Political Economy of Communication*, political economist Vincent Mosco offers commodification as a framework through which to examine social reality.[57] Mosco, drawing on the writings of Karl Marx, defines commodification as "the process of transforming things valued for their use into marketable products that are valued for what they can bring in exchange."[58] From this perspective, commodification is inherently exploitative insofar as it requires workers to give up control over the means of production and fails to adequately compensate them for the value they produce. As a theoretical approach, political economy has been usefully applied to the production, analysis, and exchange of digital data.[59]

Practices of identifying and classifying individuals based on their demographic characteristics and consumer behaviors—and anxieties about those practices—predate the ubiquity of the internet. In the 1950s, the U.S. government turned to computers to administer and keep track of Social Security payments.[60] The practice raised concerns about how this newly digitized data would be stored, accessed, and shared. Public resistance encouraged the introduction of the Privacy Act of 1974, which set the conditions under which information can be released and also granted citizens the right to request access to their government records and correct errors.[61] The new law did not, however, cover the private sector, where privacy guidelines continued to be enforced by industry-specific policies.

The process of packaging consumer attention to sell to marketers was similarly established long before the introduction of home computers, let alone the internet.[62] Mass media industries, including newspaper, radio, and television, have long been in the business of creating content designed to deliver audiences to marketers. What computer databases added was a level of specificity that narrowed mass audiences into niche markets.[63] Mirroring the U.S. government's use of new technology to keep track of citizen data, marketers in the mid-twentieth century began to employ computers to track and classify consumer interests and priorities.[64] Marketers used this information to divide the population into homogeneous consumer segments and created customized marketing strategies that reflected the unique interests of particular consumer groups. The result, marketers argued, was the reduction of waste as a consequence of sending consumers undesirable or irrelevant content.[65]

While advertisers focused on the potential of database marketing to reduce inefficiencies by purging irrelevant content from consumers' media environments, communications scholar Joseph Turow argues that these practices marginalized those in markets deemed unworthy of advertising dollars.[66] Through expanding consumer surveillance apparatus, which communication scholar Oscar Gandy Jr. has called the "panoptic sort," marketers gathered information to monitor, identify, and classify citizens, to assist in directing communication efforts.[67] Concerns about the consequences of population segmentation have intensified with the entrenchment of an online economy based largely on the capture, analysis, and use of personal information to generate narrowly targeted or personalized communication experiences. The proliferation and sophistication of digital media technologies has extended strategies for consumer monitoring and allowed for more detailed audience parsing. Using interactive digital tools, marketers have developed an environment where consumers implicitly agree to submit to surveillance in exchange for highly tailored promotional content. The twentieth-century methods of consumer tracking and targeting described by Gandy relied on classification systems that organized individuals into types based on a set of shared characteristics. Although assumptions about characteristics shared by affinity groups still play an important role in contemporary advertising, digital technologies now allow messages to be personalized based on information about an individual.[68] These messages are then delivered through digital channels that facilitate the construction of a unique media environment.

Gandy's term—the panoptic sort—refers to a nineteenth-century prison imagined by philosopher and social reformer Jeremy Bentham in which the presence of a central but obscured observation tower encouraged inmates to behave as if they were under constant surveillance. In the twentieth century, philosopher Michel Foucault adopted the panopticon as a metaphor for contemporary institutions characterized by a pervasive threat of surveillance, internalized by citizens and resulting in docile, self-monitoring populations.[69] Although the panopticon—with its single point of observation—is insufficient for understanding contemporary digital environments where observation is distributed and uneven, the articulation of power in Foucault's model informs critiques of database marketing regimes in which consumers are routinely monitored, identified, and categorized and their behaviors disciplined by inclusion in or exclusion from consumer systems. The application of political economic theory to contemporary practices of data production, collection, and analysis is constitutive of what business scholar Shoshana Zuboff calls "surveillance capitalism": a "new form of information capitalism [that] aims to predict and modify human behavior as a means to produce revenue and market control."[70] This approach underscores the alienation individuals experience from the content, data, and resulting identities produced through their online activities. Not only are people denied access to the tools necessary to capture or analyze this information, they are also deprived of compensation for the value generated through its analysis, sale, and use.

Nick Bergus's brief career as an unintended spokesperson for personal lubricant illustrates this principle that privacy can be violated even in instances when the violation stems from information that was provided voluntarily and shared publicly. Bergus himself was miffed by his role. "I'm partially amused that Amazon is paying for this, but I'm also sorta annoyed," he wrote. "Of course Facebook is happily selling me out to advertisers. That's its business. That's what you sign up for when [you] make an account."[71] Bergus's response reveals an understanding and, perhaps, even an acceptance of the underlying agreement that drives the online economy: personal information in exchange for access. Many platforms that offer content and services without a paid subscription— news sites, social network sites, email providers—collect information about users that is sold to marketers. Facebook's experiment with sponsored stories is emblematic of how this works; however, the myriad uses of online data, sometimes referred to as "data exhaust" or "data trails," are not all this straightforward.

Although Facebook users agreed to have their likes turned into endorsements when they consented to the platform's terms of service, the company received backlash as individuals bristled at finding their clicks and comments turned into advertising copy. As legal scholar Daniel Solove writes, "It is one thing to write about how much one enjoyed a movie or album; it is another to be used on a billboard to pitch projects to others."[72] The comments under Nick Bergus's blog post range from questions about the legality of using a person's image in advertisements, to instructions on how to turn off sponsored stories, to advice on how to disrupt Facebook's advertising initiative by intentionally liking obscure or grotesque items. Many of the comments point out the privacy issues inherent in campaigns that use information provided for one purpose in unrelated contexts. But several comments point to another issue: Facebook's failure to adequately compensate Bergus for his efforts. Not only did Bergus write "quality content" for Amazon, commenters note, but he delivered an audience—his friends—who might be interested in his endorsement. These observations raise questions about the distribution of profits in an economic system where personal information and user-created content have become core economic resources, but they also point to a larger question: what happens to privacy when personal information becomes a commercial good?

Algorithmically Defined: The Construction of Online Identities

The proliferation of digital information and the corresponding construction of an economic system that relies on its capture and use has also fostered an extensive market for consumer data itself. Media scholar Mark Andrejevic writes that as such information is being collected and aggregated, companies are privatizing this so-called raw data and turning it into a packaged commodity.[73] With the help of database marketing services (those companies that aggregate information about individuals from a variety of sources), marketers create what Solove calls "digital dossiers": detailed profiles based on information about individuals' demographic and behavioral data.[74] When analyzed using proprietary algorithms, these data are used to predict interest in consumer products that inform the development of personalized advertising messages and customized deals, such as the sponsored stories for wholesale lubricant that appeared in the news feeds of Nick Bergus's Facebook friends.

Celebrated privacy scholar Alan Westin defines privacy as "the claim of individuals, groups, or institutions to determine for themselves when, how, and to what extent information about them is communicated to others."[75] Privacy, observes Westin, is essential for supporting personal autonomy: the ability to identify as one chooses.[76] Based on this definition, the cultivation of digital dossiers can be read not only as a violation of privacy, but as an encroachment on the right to self-determination. The practice of monitoring our online activities and mirroring them back to us in the form of targeted content creates what digital media scholar John Cheney-Lippold calls "algorithmic identities."[77] Informed by mathematic inferences designed to make assumptions about individuals and classify them accordingly, "the advertisements and content targeted to those categorizations effectively situate and define how we create and manage our own identities."[78] In other words, the content we see as the result of algorithmic inferences are not reflections of some "true self" manifested through our online behaviors; rather, they impose on us an identity whose power comes both from its invisibility and from the apparent objectivity of the algorithms on which it relies.[79]

The lack of transparency about the construction of these algorithmic identities coupled with limited opportunities to view and correct errors in these digital reputations or to opt out of commercial surveillance efforts altogether, undermine marketers' assertions that personalized messages benefit consumers by shielding them from irrelevant content. The fact that people do not experience the consequences of surveillance equally presents a further challenge to these claims. "The lived experiences of people subjected to surveillance," writes communication scholar Torin Monahan, "can vary widely along lines of race, class, gender, sexual orientation, age, and nationality."[80] While we may think of databases as receptacles of information passively collected as the result of digitally mediated interactions and analyzed by objective algorithms, the assumption that these tools are neutral can obscure the choices that go into their construction and their effects. Monahan observes that the biases and assumptions built into technologies mean they are more accurately characterized as social agents rather than neutral tools.

Take, for example, the algorithms that shape the digital environment. Gillespie writes that, in their capacity to select and recommend relevant content, identify important or trending information, and manage social interactions by determining the individuals from whom we receive updates, algorithms play a critical role in social life.[81] While commercial platforms take great pains to cultivate trust in their algorithms by indicating their neutrality, rhetorics of technological objectivity are troubled by the reality that these systems are designed to make choices. They rank, rate, and return information that shapes how we assess importance and relevance. These invisible "patterns of inclusion" play a fundamental role in determining what is knowable and who is visible.[82] Consequently, Monahan writes, "new surveillance systems often amplify existing social inequalities and reproduce regimes of control and/or exclusion of marginalized groups in societies."[83] Practices of identifying people in terms of their consumer value and structuring communication based on such labels only deepens the disenfranchisement already experienced by those at the social margins. With limited regulation in place to curtail these surveillance activities, justifiable concerns are raised about the unbounded and unsanctioned use of personal data by third-party organizations.

Efforts of the consumer privacy industry focus on these critical tensions between individual empowerment and institutional control over personal information. Over the past two decades, the entrepreneurs in this industry have participated in debates about who has the right to own this information. Rather than choosing between arguments that the creation and use of personal data *either* empowers individuals *or* reinforces existing power dynamics, many of those in the industry consider the possibly that both positions may be true. The consumer privacy industry taps into a persistent optimism that celebrates the democratic potential of emerging communication technologies to facilitate access and knowledge through distributed networks. It is a perspective on the digital economy that represents neither a complete triumph of individuals nor the absolute retrenchment of industrial hierarchies. Instead, it highlights a continuous dialectic process in which consumers and producers struggle over how digital information will be used, shared, and monetized.

"Death" of Privacy: Birth of an Industry

As digital media technologies have grown ubiquitous, strategies for avoiding surveillance, such as those described by Quittner, have become increasingly inadequate and opportunities for opting out completely, nearly impossible. In the years since Quittner's article, laments about the role digital technologies have played in killing privacy have become routine.[84] And yet, as communication historian Josh Lauer usefully reminds us, privacy is a value that has died many deaths.[85] These casualties tend to occur at the hands of new technologies, which introduce novel opportunities for creating, storing, organizing, and accessing information. In a 1969 book titled *The Death of Privacy*, Jerry Rosenberg described how the use of computers by government agencies to collect and store information about citizens would challenge individual autonomy. "Under the surveillance of a national data bank or center, most of our actions could be documented, put into a permanent dossier and stored on tape along with other vital data about us," Rosenberg wrote.[86] "Here it would always be available at the push of a button. We would never escape in time or distance the bureaucratic machinery keeping tabs on us."[87]

A new medium's capacity to "remember" or "see" information that would have otherwise been "forgotten" or "invisible" puts pressure on established boundaries between the spaces, information, and behaviors understood to be public and those expected to be private. The concerns raised by Rosenberg parallel those experienced today as people wonder how the information produced as a consequence of their online activities will be accessed and used. By challenging the constraints that divide public arenas from private ones, new technologies have a history of instigating anxieties about the rise of surveillance, the introduction of new forms of evidence, and the loss of protected private spaces. Consequently, contemporary assertions that digital systems have rendered the term "privacy" meaningless must be situated within a longer rhetorical history regarding the threats of new media technologies.

In their analysis of newspaper articles published between 1980 and 2016, communication scholars Nicholas John and Benjamin Peters identified over a hundred stories that remarked on the death of privacy.[88] The most commonly identified killers, the authors note, were technology, institutions, and culture. Rather than treating these repeated obituaries as the product of journalistic convention or professional laziness, John and Peters suggest it is the construction of privacy itself that ensures its continual mortality. "Modern privacy discourse is endist," they write, "because unlike other rights, the modern right to privacy was born out of the conditions for its violation, and not its realization."[89] In other words, when Warren and Brandeis defined privacy as the right to be let alone—to be free from unwanted observation—they not only placed privacy rights at the center of modern debates about communication technologies, but ensured those rights would never be fully realized.

In view of this legacy, contemporary observations about the "death of privacy" at the hands of new media technologies may seem hyperbolic; however, concerns that the internet and mobile devices are facilitating massive changes in how society grapples with privacy and identity should not simply be dismissed as either overly anxious or mundane. As John and Peters suggest, assertions that privacy is dead "should be taken as a sort of public service announcement about the deleterious impacts that ongoing emerging alliances of information technologies and institutional powers may have."[90] These fears mark an important moment in the cultural renegotiation of norms as established boundaries governing shared space and communications shift to accommodate new technologies and their associated practices. As I stated in the introduction, this is not a book about the end of privacy; rather, it considers ongoing conversations that inform the cultural organization of privacy and the role that power plays in these conversations. More specifically, it explores the role commercial interests have played and continue to play in these discussions through an analysis of how the versions of privacy sold by companies in the consumer privacy industry shape how people experience the rewards and threats of visibility online.

The role of the consumer privacy industry in the renegotiation of normative expectations of privacy over the past twenty years has been largely unexplored in accounts of privacy online. In recognizing the challenges to image management introduced when people began to use digital channels to communicate and share, the industry has responded by promoting strategies that allow individuals to oversee their data, identity, and reputation. Together, the companies in this industry have attempted to secure private spaces for self-presentation and experimentation while managing the activities that become part of a public image. They also aim to reorganize the existing relationship between producers and consumers around digital data by providing individuals with the capacity to access, understand, and even leverage their digital profiles.

Through efforts to provide their clients with power over how their data and image are used, these companies aim to disrupt hierarchies of knowledge and value that define the digital economy. By creating tools that allow users to produce, manage, and promote their online image, they sell the promise of online privacy through strategies of information control. Companies in the consumer privacy industry seek to empower their clients by encouraging them to access and leverage the reputations produced by their online activities. At the same time as these companies reveal economic systems built on a foundation of digital surveillance, they embrace a political economic system that normalizes privacy as a consumer good.

This tension between expectations that one have a compelling digital image and the associated risks of a public identity is reflected in the mission articulated by members of this industry. These companies intervene to address consumer concerns by offering strategies that balance a socially constituted need for connectivity and visibility with a desire to control how this visibility functions in the digital environment. Representatives from this industry describe a persistent risk that digital profiles will be used in ways that conflict with an individual's expectations or preferences. Even the most well-crafted image, they warn, can be undermined by unwanted exposure. Through their products and services, the industry responds to assertions that the cost of online engagement is an acceptance of the risk of losing control over one's image by offering strategies and tools that defend against the threats of unwanted exposure, thereby helping clients to obtain ideal privacy. As the following chapters will demonstrate, however, these efforts rarely challenge the economic structures and cultural conditions that create different rewards for visibility and different experiences of surveillance. Moreover, industry efforts may at times do as much to cultivate anxieties about overexposure as they do to quell those fears.

If we take the term "industry" to refer to a set of companies that have regular interactions and an enduring presence around the production, distribution, and exhibition of a product or service, is it not clear that those invested in selling privacy to individuals constitute an industry. Many of the entrepreneurs and company representatives I spoke with in what I came to think of as the consumer privacy arena did not talk about themselves as part of a broader industry. While they acknowledged sharing the space with other companies, with whom they occasionally cross paths at industry events and with whom they appear in news stories, with a few notable exceptions most of the people I spoke with preferred to talk about what *distinguishes* them from other companies rather than what *unites* them.

Despite their apparent disconnectedness, the companies in the consumer privacy industry share several core ideologies and practices. First, they adhere to a definition of privacy that focuses on individual control over personal information and self-presentation. Whether they see privacy-enhancing technologies as a supplement to or an alternative for government regulation, these companies share a commitment to technology-driven and market-based solutions that provide individuals with the tools to manage how their data, images, and reputations circulate. The companies engaged in selling privacy as a service also share a complicated political economy. Through the provision of commercial services that help people manage their digital image and personal data, companies in the privacy industry have what some respondents described as a "double bottom line"—a corporate goal that combines a profit motive with a desire for social change. Those I spoke with exhibited varying levels of comfort with that position. Some distanced themselves from the ethical dimensions of their services, describing their companies' primary goal as the creation of a business model that would solve an economic inefficiency rather than addressing a moral issue.[91] Others foregrounded their companies' social mission, describing profit motives as a secondary, albeit necessary, consideration. Some also articulated ethical concerns about being in an industry that benefits from the unwanted disclosure of information that fosters practices of digital shaming and also expressed ambivalence concerning their position as arbiters over decisions about which reputations deserve protection.

The notion of an industry and its boundaries is often taken for granted when dealing with media and technology companies. In media industry research, companies that occupy a similar geography,[92] operate in a single medium,[93] or share collective rituals, are defined as industries.[94] Often these industries are identified by a shared system of ethics, formalized in industry codes of practice, which foster "moral communities."[95] The malleability of the term "industry" itself has strategic power. How the players in the consumer privacy industry imagine themselves and their relationships with others in this field is a central concern of this book. Looking at the similarities and differences—in beliefs, in tools, and in practices—across the field, reveals a common approach to privacy that is performed through a type of cross talk around a set of ideologies about the politics of information ownership and the importance of self-presentation online.

As the dynamics of digital cultures have shifted over the past two decades, there have been corresponding changes in how this industry has constructed narratives about the risks and rewards of online visibility. While early entrants in the field tended to focus on visibility as an unwanted result of institutional privacy abuses, there have been more recent attempts to reframe publicity and promotion as a preferable alternative to concealment. By designing, controlling, and leveraging a carefully crafted digital image, these companies stress the possibilities for personal empowerment. As the political and economic climates in which digital cultures are embedded have evolved, sociological constructs such as reputation, identity, and authenticity have been redefined alongside privacy in inconsistent and often antithetical ways. These shifts, evident in the products and services offered by companies throughout this industry's history, tell an important story about the evolution of the commercial web and the corresponding cultural changes in digital visibility.

2

Digital Privacy Goes Mainstream

Selling an Anonymous Web

It was during his time working on a Ph.D. in astrophysics at the University of California, San Diego that Lance Cottrell first became interested in cybersecurity. Although the internet was still in its infancy, Cottrell's relationship with UCSD meant that he had direct broadband access to the campus network from the remote workstation where he was conducting his research. When we spoke in 2014, Cottrell described a period in the mid-1990s when he was spending a lot of time in the mountains with astronomers who were devising encryption strategies to protect their equipment and findings. Cottrell, too, started to explore encryption for securing his own work. As he was designing strategies for personal use, Cottrell heard that the United States government was working on its own initiative for telecommunication security. Introduced in 1993 by the Clinton administration, the Clipper Chip initiative proposed to provide encryption technology certified by the National Security Agency to protect communication over telephone lines, including wireless phones, computers, and fax machines.[1] The approach was simple enough: when two people wished to engage in a private conversation mediated by one of these technologies, each party would activate their Clipper Chip encryption. Using the participants' encryption keys, the messages would be encoded at one end and decoded at the other, thereby facilitating secure communication between the two authorized parties but making the conversation unintelligible to others.

Although the Clipper Chip's explicit goals addressed some of Cottrell's concerns about the privacy and security of digitally enabled communication, there was a catch in the program that concerned him. Since the government would provide the technology, authorities planned to keep a copy of each chip's encryption code in "key escrow." This "backdoor" would provide the government with access to encrypted messages, which could be used to facilitate wiretaps and other forms of government-authorized surveillance.[2] Although the program was presented as a voluntary standard, there were public suspicions that it was being designed for eventual mandatory implementation for all telecommunication technologies.[3]

Critics challenged the Clipper Chip initiative citing technical, social, and legal flaws in the proposed program.[4] While some argued the encryption could be vulnerable to hacking, others expressed concerns that government officials holding the keys could be bribed to give them up. Still others suggested the program violated protections afforded by the U.S. Constitution. These critics were concerned that it could violate free speech protections guaranteed by the First Amendment, protections against unreasonable search and seizure enshrined in the Fourth Amendment, and the right to due process guaranteed by the Fifth Amendment. It is possible, however, that the program's assault on privacy—the right to be let alone and the right to personal autonomy—provided the most compelling public case for its eventual abandonment.[5] Based on his concerns about the path signaled by the introduction of the Clipper Chip initiative, Cottrell became involved with a group of techno-activists known as the cypherpunks. During his involvement on this community's newsgroups and mailing lists Cottrell ran an anonymous remailer, an email service that helped disguise the sender's identity by forwarding the message through a series of channels.

In addition to his concern about the government's Clipper Chip program, Cottrell was skeptical about the privacy protections offered by websites and online retailers. He felt, however, that existing encryption tools used by those in the hacker and cypherpunk communities did little to protect ordinary people from threats to their online privacy. "I sort of realized," Cottrell told me, "that the problem with almost all of the cypherpunk built tools is that they were by geeks for geeks only, really." At the time, access to the internet was expanding beyond universities, research labs, and government departments, creating a new cohort of users who lacked the expertise enjoyed by those in tech communities. As Cottrell observed, for "the tools that were out there, the first steps in the instructions were 'Go and torrent this and then run the makefile and compile it on your UNIX workstation,' which rules out most people who actually need a tool like this." By 1995, Cottrell's dissertation research had stalled and he decided to focus full-time on consumer privacy services, eventually founding the company Anonymizer.

Cottrell was an early entrant into an industry identified in a 2001 *Atlantic* article by Toby Lester as the "privacy sphere."[6] The people and companies behind this effort sought to introduce privacy-enhancing technologies (PETs) to a consumer population with limited technical experience or expertise.[7] Although they came from different backgrounds, those in this new industrial space shared a common concern about the use of digital technologies by government and industry to encroach on individuals' rights to privacy and autonomy. As a result, they were skeptical that either efforts by the online marketing and retail industries or interventions by government would result in the robust privacy protections necessary to support a free and vibrant cyberspace. Together, those in the privacy sphere identified the possibility of a middle way—between the efforts of marketers and government—to empower individuals to make choices about their own level of disclosure and involvement in the information economy developing online. They advocated for the use of strong encryption technologies to protect individuals from having their online activities monitored while allowing for access to the conveniences and pleasures of the digital world. By allowing individuals to choose how, when, and with whom to share information, those promoting consumer privacy tools sought to empower users by letting them set parameters for visibility and disclosure that were consistent with their personal preferences. These entrepreneurs viewed themselves as providing an alternative approach to digital privacy—one that did not rely on government action or retail industry efforts at self-regulation. In fact, it was the tension between these two positions and the resulting inaction that created the space for this industry to emerge.

The companies that made up the consumer privacy industry in the 1990s were in a unique position to influence how privacy would be defined and protected in the context of an emerging technological system that threatened to disrupt existing legal, structural, and normative boundaries. By offering technologies that would mediate the interactions between users and websites, thereby limiting the ability of third parties to collect data about people's online activities, these commercial services aimed to give individuals control over the flows of digital information. Before turning to an examination of the anonymizers, a collection of companies that incorporated countercultural ideologies into their privacy tools, this chapter examines how rising public anxiety about the safety of digital information introduced a unique opportunity for the sale of privacy online.

Through the Policy Window: Capitalizing on Privacy Concerns

The Netscape web browser, introduced in 1994, changed the face of the internet.[8] By allowing designers to include color images on their sites and embed hyperlinks in pictures, Netscape transformed the internet from a universe of code into the World Wide Web—a virtual space that was comprehensible to the average user.[9] Netscape's intuitive interface helped to expand access to the internet beyond communities of scientists, academics, and hobbyists. As a result, the percentage of adult Americans who used the internet grew from just 14 percent in June 1995, immediately following the browser's introduction, to 46 percent in March 2000.[10] This flood of new users meant people with a vast range of technical skill and expertise began using the web for everything from communicating with friends and strangers to booking vacations. By March 2000, 48 percent of adult American internet users had purchased a product or service over the internet.[11]

Even as they migrated many of their daily activities online, however, people worried about the privacy and security of their information in the new digital environment. In 2000, an overwhelming majority of adult American internet users—84 percent—expressed concern about the ability of businesses and strangers to use the internet to access information about them and their families.[12] Regulators expressed similar anxieties about how new digital tools would be used to capture and share personal information. At the end of the twentieth century, the U.S. government was looking carefully at how digital data was being collected, stored, and used. These efforts took place amid a debate regarding the most appropriate strategies for ensuring privacy in the online environment.

On one side of this debate were the privacy advocates—those concerned about rising efforts by public and private organizations to track individuals' online behaviors. On the other side were those representing a new class of digital professionals who feared government regulation would stifle innovation. They argued that government intervention would foster uncertainty about the boundaries of legitimate online business practices and introduce unnecessary limits regarding acceptable uses of personal data. Where some privacy advocates favored regulatory intervention to control the collection and use of personal information gathered online, this second group preferred industry self-regulation. Concerned with the consequences of slow-paced government action, they argued for the use of voluntary, industry-driven standards to ensure user rights were respected. This conflict over desirable levels of regulatory intervention often accompanies the emergence of new fields. "Infant industries," writes legal scholar Saul Levmore, "often make claims for special treatment, and the evolution of law is in part the story of lawmakers' coming to terms with claims of novelty."[13]

Occasionally, when public and political attention coalesces around an issue, there is swift and decisive action to address the problem. In regulatory circles, this is known as a policy window—a brief opportunity for those invested in a particular issue to push through regulation that might otherwise receive limited support.[14] Some policy windows are predictable, such as the annual renewal of a specific program; however, other windows open unexpectedly, often because of a shift in the composition of an administration, a change in public mood, or the emergence of a new issue that captures the attention of government officials.[15] These types of policy windows do not open often and can close quickly.[16] A case can be made that, prompted by media coverage of troubling corporate and government practices and fueled by popular concern about the security of digital information, a policy window for online privacy was flung open in the United States in the last decade of the twentieth century. As advocates for consumer privacy rights moved quickly to capitalize on attention to this issue, so, too, did industry players hoping to stave off regulatory intervention.

The Government Approach: Empowering Individuals through Regulation

In his *Atlantic* piece, Lester pointed to several attempts in the late 1990s and early 2000s to enact legislation that would limit the ways private sector businesses could collect and use personal information gleaned from online interactions. During this time, several bills with bipartisan support were introduced in the U.S. Congress. Richard Shelby, a Republican senator from Alabama, drafted the Freedom from Behavioral Profiling Act of 2000. This bill would have amended the Gramm–Leach–Bliley Act, which governs how financial institutions share information, by limiting the distribution of marketing and behavioral profiling data.[17] That same year, Democratic representative Raymond Green introduced the Consumer Online Privacy and Disclosure Act, which proposed to "require the Federal Trade Commission to prescribe regulations to protect the privacy of personal information collected from and about individuals on the Internet, to provide greater individual control over the collection and use of that information."[18] Both of these bills—and several more like them—received initial bipartisan support but died after being referred to committee. Despite these setbacks, the turn of the twenty-first century seemed poised to become a bellwether moment for online consumer privacy protections. Observers reasoned that impending regulation coupled with limited consumer faith in online retailers would force those engaged in digital commerce to change their relationship to consumer information to be successful.

Indeed, the threat of regulation concerning the collection and use of digital data spurred online marketers and retailers to action. Industry representatives appeared before Congress to make the case that hasty regulation could have the unintended consequence of suppressing innovation. During a Senate hearing in 2000 considering the need for regulation governing the collection and use of personal information online, former FTC commissioner Christine Varney voiced the marketing industry's preference for self-regulation over government intervention. Speaking on behalf of the Online Privacy Alliance (OPA), an industry group made up of digital retailers and marketers who shared a preference for internal actions to protect consumer privacy online, Varney argued against government intervention. "What we need is to make the promise of meaningful choice and control over personal data real. . . . What we do not need," Varney noted in her testimony, "are sweeping regulations governing the collection and use of data, the conditions and methods under which that data use can be consented to, the dimensions of access that must be provided to data and the level and design of web security."[19] Broadly, the OPA argued that privacy efforts should focus on empowering individuals through a framework of data self-determination rather than creating new regulatory powers for government. By empowering individuals to make their *own* choices about online privacy, industry representatives argued, self-regulatory solutions would offer consumers adequate protections and hold online retailers and marketers accountable without limiting the potential for commercial growth.

Several regulators agreed that consumer concern would serve as a more effective incentive for companies to curtail their use of personal data than would government regulation. There were also those who shared industry concerns that ill-considered or hasty efforts by legislators had the potential to throttle private sector growth. These regulators supported options that would empower individuals to make their own decisions about how personal information would be used. For example, New Jersey senator Robert Torricelli, who sponsored the Secure Online Communication Enforcement Act of 2000, emphasized the value of minimally invasive regulation to encourage direct negotiations between consumers and companies. Torricelli stressed that his "legislation is not a final product" but was instead aimed at establishing "a national dialog first to educate ourselves about the privacy problem in cyberspace" and then to "begin collecting ideas of how to enhance privacy."[20] The bill proposed an opt-in regime for the use of personal information so that citizens could control if and how their data were used. Torricelli stressed that this would keep government regulation and oversight to a minimum, describing the bill's "twin pillars" as citizen choice and citizen enforcement.[21] Torricelli's bill was designed to be "self-enforcing," with individual citizens, rather than government watchdogs, initiating legal action in the case of privacy violations.[22]

The Industry Approach: Self-Regulation and Individual Choice

Although proposed legislation favored only minimal intervention, online advertisers, marketers, and retailers continued to lobby against *any* regulatory oversight. In the face of mounting public concern regarding online privacy that foretold a seemingly inevitable wave of regulation, industry representatives took several steps to indicate that information privacy and data security were top concerns. Some companies, for example, hired chief privacy officers (CPOs) to act as internal watchdogs for the enforcement of existing regulation and work with industry groups on the development of best practices around user privacy.[23] In 2000 Jules Polonetsky was appointed CPO by DoubleClick, an early leader in online banner advertising. Soon after, he described the importance of this new position for building a strong relationship between consumers and business. "In this difficult market, businesses that lose consumer trust find it very hard to operate," he said in 2001. "You can't afford to lose business customers or have consumers not come to your site when times are slow. So you're seeing businesses taking more aggressive steps to police each other."[24]

Another industry initiative designed to placate fears about the misuse of digital information by commercial websites was the introduction of privacy policies. These statements, which have become a familiar feature of the digital landscape, describe the ways websites collect, use, and share consumers' personal information. Although these documents were introduced as a strategy to minimize consumer and government concerns, privacy policies have faced skepticism from privacy advocates since their inception. Far from offering users protection, critics argue, privacy policies authorize business practices that are based on the default exchange of consumer data for access to content and services.[25] Analyses have found that the language used in policies is overly complicated, which obscures rather than clarifies how personal information is used.[26] This includes research finding that people incorrectly believe that the presence of a privacy policy itself offers robust protections.[27] The length and complexity of the documents also places a heavy burden on internet users to take the time to read and understand their contents.[28] As Lance Cottrell observed, "It really takes several years of college education to even understand most privacy policies."[29] The result is that many users simply skip over them, implicitly agreeing to whatever terms are listed without a thorough reading.[30]

This skepticism notwithstanding, privacy policies have been useful for online retailers and marketers, who discuss the documents as a valuable first step toward ensuring privacy online. Given their proliferation on websites in the final years of the twentieth century,[31] several initiatives were presented to strengthen existing privacy policies. Authentication services were created to audit websites and assess compliance with stated policies. The Council of Better Business Bureaus introduced a privacy seal program called BBBOnline. The organization, known for issuing grades to companies based on consumer reviews and acting as an arbiter in disputes between consumers and retailers, issued a CBBB "stamp of approval" to websites that met their standard for user privacy protection and consented to audits of their practices.[32] A similar program called TRUSTe provided a seal to participating sites, which were required to post a privacy policy and submit to monitoring and auditing by the organization to ensure compliance. Advocates of the authentication programs argued the BBBOnline and TRUSTe privacy seals worked by providing users with a shorthand to assess websites' privacy protections.[33]

Authentication programs were, however, criticized by some privacy advocates who argued that far from protecting consumers, the programs revealed just how ineffective self-regulatory approaches are for guaranteeing user privacy online. For one thing, these programs offered substantial leeway in the content of privacy policies. As a result, they failed to enforce the minimum standards introduced by the Fair Information Practice Principles, which are the Federal Trade Commission directives that set out a framework for ensuring individuals are informed about the collection of their personal information based on the principles of transparency, notice, choice, oversight, and security.[34] Critics concluded that the seal programs offered by BBBOnline and TRUSTe provided inconsistent standards for the protection of personal information.[35]

The World Wide Web Consortium (W3C), established in 1994 to help create standards for the web, attempted to improve on these initiatives by offering a more robust authentication program that turned privacy policies from static documents into a set of actionable principles. Although the W3C program relied on privacy policies, it advanced the privacy seal initiatives by integrating users' preferences into the process. The W3C's Platform for Privacy Preferences Project, known as P3P, called for machine-readable privacy policies that would enable computer-facilitated negotiations between the website and the individual regarding the amount of personal information a user was willing to disclose and for what purposes. The idea was that individual users would establish a set of privacy preferences. The browser, which would be able to read and interpret website privacy policies, would allow personal information to be shared only with websites that met a user's minimum standard for privacy protection.[36] Individuals would be alerted when they arrived at a website that did not meet their privacy requirements. If the individual wanted to proceed to the website, the program would allow for the negotiation of an amended policy.[37]

Tim Berners-Lee, a computer scientist commonly credited as the inventor of the web and a member of W3C, endorsed the initiative for its ability to make privacy policies useful. "P3P simplifies that process, so that your browser can read the privacy policies instead," he said. "Without this technology, there will always be this fine print."[38] Members of the cyber-activist community joined companies such as Microsoft and America Online to endorse P3P as an "elegant solution" to the growing concerns about the lack of protections for personal data online.[39] Others, however, were less optimistic about the program's likely success. One industry analyst predicted P3P would be the V-chip of the internet—a reference to the little-used television feature introduced in the late 1990s to allow parents to block content rated violent or sexual.[40] Others critiqued the program's reliance on privacy policies because of their inherent limitations.[41] Perhaps most important, P3P, like other authenticator initiatives, failed to provide recourse to those who elected not to visit a website that lacked adequate privacy protections. Of course, people could signal their preferences by simply avoiding those websites, but the result would be to forgo the benefits and pleasures those sites offered. Many critics remained unconvinced that any form of industry-driven self-regulation would be adequate to protect and promote privacy online. Rather than giving individuals legally enforceable privacy rights, critics saw these initiatives as last-ditch efforts to avoid having external standards imposed.[42]

These industry-backed efforts promoted self-regulation as the ideal approach for balancing technological innovation and consumer privacy. While there were those who continued to advocate for government intervention, the Federal Trade Commission expressed its commitment to industry-led efforts in a 1999 report, writing that "self-regulation is the least intrusive and most efficient means to ensure fair information practices, given the rapidly evolving nature of the Internet and computer technology."[43] Many of those behind early privacy-enhancing technologies—the first entrants into the consumer privacy industry—joined industry representatives in their assertions about the slow pace of government regulation. However, they also registered concern about industry efforts that did more to protect the interests of business than those of consumers. Situating themselves between languid government regulation and ineffective industry self-regulation, these entrepreneurs imagined consumer tools that would allow people to interact with websites of their choosing in ways that were consistent with their unique and contextual privacy preferences. The focus of the consumer privacy industry was the development of products and services that supported this more robust option to allow individuals to opt out of commercial tracking while still experiencing the benefits of cyberspace.

Privacy Is Not Secrecy: Technologies of Selective Exposure

In his *Atlantic* article, Lester pointed to "A Cypherpunk's Manifesto," published in March 1993 by Eric Hughes, which describes the ideological commitments of a community dedicated to building anonymity into internet architecture through cryptography. The importance of privacy for achieving Hughes's vision is evident throughout the document. Hughes makes clear, however, that his definition of privacy is not synonymous with invisibility. "Privacy is necessary for an open society in the electronic age," Hughes writes. "Privacy is not secrecy. A private matter is something one doesn't want the whole world to know, but a secret matter is something one doesn't want anybody to know. Privacy is the power to selectively reveal oneself to the world."[44] Through the development of tools that provided individuals with the ability to control when and how they were visible online, those behind the first-generation consumer privacy-enhancing technologies embraced and operationalized this perspective. The term "privacy-enhancing technologies" describes communication systems that "strengthen the protection of an individual's private life in an information system by preventing unnecessary or unlawful processing of personal data or by offering tools and controls to enhance the individual's control over his/her personal data."[45] Encoded in these products was a definition of privacy that promoted personal control and autonomy.

Some of the earliest companies in this space were the anonymizers, offering products that allowed users to interact with a website without revealing their IP address or receiving cookies from the site, thereby

providing the option of remaining anonymous. Some of the early anonymizer companies, such as InterQuick, downloaded webpages to their
own servers and then displayed the webpage when the user typed in the
associated URL.[46] Others, such as IDZap and SafeWeb, used encryption
to mask URLs and HTTP data, which allowed the user to surf the web in
stealth mode without needing to continually download versions of the
site to the host server or to their computer.[47]

When Lance Cottrell turned from his Ph.D. to focus full-time on
consumer privacy protection, the company he founded, Anonymizer,
advanced existing approaches through the introduction of the service's
"mixmaster system," which routed messages through a series of remail-
ers, making their origins nearly impossible to trace. Anonymizer, which
launched in 1995 as Infonetics, was based in San Diego and supported
Cottrell's efforts to translate the privacy tools used by those with sophisticated technical backgrounds to the mass public. The company's
original product included anonymous email accounts and web-hosting
services. The result was identities that were so difficult to track that even
Anonymizer administrators would have had difficulty tracing and identifying a single user.[48]

In response to the rising popularity of the World Wide Web, Cottrell
reoriented the company in 1997 toward products focused on web-based
privacy rather than on services to encrypt email. The services Anonymizer offered prevented websites from being able to access information
about a user visiting their site. For example, if an Anonymizer client
engaged the company's cloaking software while visiting a website, they
would be identifiable to the site only as "Anonymizer.com."[49] By cloaking the user's identity, Cottrell's company ensured that a website looking
for information would only be able to access data about the company
rather than information about the individual, thereby obscuring any reference to personally identifiable details.

Zero-Knowledge Systems (ZKS) was an anonymization service based
in Montreal. The company's founders, brothers Austin and Hamnett Hill,
were veteran tech investors who had made a significant profit through
the sale of a previous company. They began ZKS in 1997 with the goal
of providing products to help individuals maintain their privacy online.
Like Anonymizer, ZKS offered a range of services to support online anonymity. The company's first consumer product was called the Freedom

Network. This tool, also known as Freedom 1.0, was a software program that allowed users to surf the web anonymously and exchange encrypted email. The software also allowed users to associate their online activities with a series of pseudonyms—or what ZKS called "nyms"—to segregate their online activity into different profiles.[50] Significantly, communications over the Freedom Network could not be decrypted by ZKS, which meant the company, like Anonymizer, could not connect users to their online activities.

Although the services allowed for complete anonymity, privacy for this community was not defined strictly in terms of secrecy. Recognizing the importance of being able to communicate under a consistent persona to build relationships and communities online, the anonymizers provided the option to use persistent but pseudonymous identities. By offering tools that allowed users to toggle between anonymity and pseudonymity, anonymizers—including ZKS and Anonymizer—offered a continuum of privacy that supported a range of disclosure practices. While anonymous services would generate a new identity for each interaction, pseudonymous options allowed users to develop persistent identities that they could return to again and again. According to Cottrell, "Being able to post anonymously or pseudonymously allows you to have an identity and interact with people, so they recognize and get to know you, [without] hav[ing] to suffer the dangers inherent to applying a real name to it."[51]

Despite the name for these tools—anonymizers—their products were not exclusively targeted at those seeking the most extreme forms of privacy online; rather, they focused on the appropriate and limited exchange of necessary information. Take, for example, two follow-up products introduced by ZKS that were intended to have broader market appeal. In December 2000, the company introduced Freedom WebSecure, or Freedom 2.0, which was a variation on the original product design.[52] The primary difference between the products was the level of anonymity each offered to users. Whereas Freedom 1.0 rerouted communication through a series of networked computer servers to make it nearly impossible to track user activity, Freedom 2.0 used only one server run by ZKS. Consequently, ZKS would have access to the identities of those using the Freedom 2.0 product. The company could, therefore, respond to requests from law enforcement to track an individual's future web traffic.[53] A third product, Freedom 3.0, offered similar services but featured further-reduced cryptographic protections. This product was introduced to help users address the "more benign day-to-day threats to privacy," including banner advertising and virus protection, without offering encryption technology that would prevent surveillance by law enforcement or government.[54] These products were not about ensuring absolute secrecy online; rather, they were intended to stem unnecessary exposure by limiting the exchange of information to include the details pertinent to a specific interaction.

These companies recognized that, while some people were interested in maintaining complete anonymity online, others wished to build relationships based on a consistent if unrecognizable identity. Moreover, users who wanted total anonymity for some aspects of their online lives may wish to maintain a persistent identity in other digital spaces. A user participating in a chat room, for example, might prefer to use a consistent, pseudonymous persona to develop their reputation as a reliable and valued member of the community. That same individual, however, may prefer complete anonymity when visiting news sites or browsing for health-related information.

The distinction between anonymity and pseudonymity gets at one of the core principles motiving companies such as ZKS and Anonymizer: privacy is neither binary nor one-size-fits-all. This approach parallels academic theories which argue that treating privacy as a choice between complete visibility and complete anonymity obscures its real value. As legal scholar Anita Allen notes, "privacy" acts as an umbrella term for other concepts—including seclusion, solitude, anonymity, confidentiality, secrecy, intimacy, and reserve—each of which denotes different degrees of inaccessibility.[55] From this perspective, privacy is a process, rather than an endpoint. While products that facilitate anonymous surfing may resonate with definitions of privacy that privilege solitude and seclusion, the opportunities offered by ZKS and Anonymizer to create persistent, pseudonymous identities, and even to "uncloak" when desired, demonstrate a more nuanced approach to privacy that seeks to balance opportunities for anonymity with the periodic desire or need for the visibility that supports sustained social interaction and companionship.

A central concern for privacy advocates is the indiscriminate production, collection, and observation of information that accompanies everyday encounters. Although most interactions require the exchange of some personal data, individuals are often asked to reveal information that is immaterial to the transaction. Imagine, for example, that a bartender must request identification to verify that a patron is of legal drinking age before selling them alcohol.[56] By looking at a government-issued driver's license, the bartender can access a picture and date of birth, both of which are necessary to verify the cardholder's age and to confirm that the license holder is indeed the purchaser. By looking at the license, however, the bartender also gains access to a plethora of information that is not germane to the sale of alcohol, including the cardholder's name, address, height, and weight. The extraneous exchange of information as part of everyday communications is exacerbated in digital interactions, where the production and collection of this information is often built into taken-for-granted infrastructures and rendered invisible.

Researchers in the University of Toronto's ID Lab, interested in the consequences of unnecessary information production and collection, developed data-minimization solutions that they call privacy-enhancing identification models.[57] As part of the Proportional ID Research Project, they aim to restrict the information exchanged in everyday interactions to include only the necessary details.[58] One version of these efforts is the team's "ID Covers": translucent sleeves for various forms of government-issued identification. The sleeves reveal the information necessary to, for example, determine whether someone can legally purchase alcohol; however, by blacking out information found on the license that is irrelevant for proving the cardholder's age, the cover minimizes the visibility of extraneous data.[59] By recognizing that identity was unnecessary to facilitate most online interactions, anonymizers applied a similar logic of data minimization to the digital world. While an email provider needs to know where a message is being sent, it does not need to know the identity of the recipient or the content of the message.[60] Concerned with infrastructures that mandated the inclusion of information regardless of its relevance to the interaction, these privacy-enhancing technologies sought to create strategies to block unnecessary visibility: the digital equivalent of a transparent ID sleeve.

Good Privacy Is Good Business: Selling Trust in the Online Environment

Those in the consumer privacy industry were not the only ones to view public concerns about privacy as a business opportunity; rather, they were part of a larger group of companies that saw the potential profitability of selling privacy as a service to a population anxious about the safety of their digital data. The possibility for consumer information generated through online interactions to be mishandled was illustrated by several news stories at the end of the twentieth century, each of which revealed business practices that triggered questions about the collection and use of consumer data by online retailers and vendors. One such event occurred in 1999 when Toysmart, a company that sold educational toys for children, filed for bankruptcy. The company attempted to sell its consumer database as a valuable commercial asset despite language in the website's privacy policy indicating that personal information would never be shared with third parties. As an online retailer, Toysmart had collected personal information from website visitors to create consumer records. The resulting profiles contained names, billing information, shopping preferences, and family profiles, including the names and birth dates of children.[61] The Federal Trade Commission brought a lawsuit to stop Toysmart's sale of consumer information, ruling that the company was prohibited from selling the database as a "stand-alone" asset; however, the FTC allowed that consumer information could be sold as part of a package to a "qualified buyer" in a related market.[62]

In the same year, DoubleClick announced it would merge with an offline data collection company called Abacus Direct. Previously, Abacus had worked primarily with companies that distributed paper catalogs. The proposed merger with DoubleClick marked the company's first foray into online promotions. Privacy advocates raised concerns that the union would make it possible for DoubleClick to link anonymous online profiles with personally identifiable information captured and stored in the company's offline database. DoubleClick addressed this issue in its privacy policy, stating that the company had "no rights or plans to use Abacus' database information prior to the completion of the merger"; however, it continued, "should DoubleClick ever match the non-personally-identifiable information collected by DoubleClick with Abacus' database information, DoubleClick will revise this Privacy Statement to accurately reflect its modified data collection and data use policies."[63] Indeed, DoubleClick later revised its privacy policy to inform users that the company did plan to combine online tracking data with personally identifiable information supplied by Abacus.[64] After significant public backlash and an FTC investigation, DoubleClick reversed its decision and announced it would not merge the two databases.

In a story for the April 30, 2000, issue of the *New York Times Magazine*, legal scholar Jeffrey Rosen argued the DoubleClick controversy exposed the ways the new digital economy threatened privacy. "There are many fearful consequences to the loss of privacy," Rosen wrote, "but none perhaps more disquieting than this: privacy protects us from being misidentified and judged out of context."[65] Stories about Toysmart, DoubleClick, and others like them[66] contributed to mounting fears about the consequences of consumer skepticism for the future of an online market. Digital retailers worried that concerns about privacy and information security might stifle the growth of e-commerce.[67] These apprehensions were voiced by one business analyst who cited "growing concerns on the part of e-shoppers" who would avoid spending money online until they had "some indication, some kind of guarantee, some kind of rule out there saying how much privacy is mine, how much permission must I give before people can take my information and sell it to second and third and fourth parties."[68] Mark Schar, vice president of global internet ventures at Procter & Gamble, one of the world's largest advertisers, similarly warned that privacy concerns were undermining potential growth in the digital market. "If consumers don't trust what we do," he cautioned, "then none of our stories will make sense."[69]

As a response to consumer concerns, some companies began to think about the provision of comprehensive privacy protections as a strategic business opportunity. Ann Cavoukian, the former information and privacy commissioner of Ontario, is a longtime proponent of the argument that strong privacy protections can be profitable. As a champion of Privacy by Design—an approach that advocates for the inclusion of comprehensive privacy protections in the earliest stages of product design and development—Cavoukian argues that companies generate goodwill from business practices that respect their customers' personal information.[70] Those advocating for the commercial benefits of responsible information practices, which Cavoukian calls the "privacy payoff," maintain that privacy practices and commercial success are not mutually exclusive. Instead, they contend that companies with a reputation for sensitivity toward consumers' privacy concerns and strong data security can profit from the trust generated through responsible data-handling practices. "An increasing number of businesses," Cavoukian wrote in 2002, "realize that trust is a currency in the new economy, and profiting from this economy means proactively obtaining as much of this currency as possible."[71]

Indeed, some of the companies setting up shop in this new digital landscape turned privacy into a branding strategy, hoping the approach would appeal to consumer concerns and differentiate them from competitors. One example was the Atlanta-based internet service provider (ISP) EarthLink. According to a company press release, EarthLink had, since it was established in 1994, "aggressively pursued a policy of not selling individual subscriber data to its partners or third-party marketers" and "actively fought to protect its subscribers from unsolicited email and other intrusive marketing practices."[72] The company's chief privacy officer Les Seagraves, in a testimony before Congress, discussed the tempting business case for ISPs to supplement monthly subscription fees with revenue from the sale of client information. Seagraves, however, outlined the more compelling reason not to sell consumer data to advertisers. EarthLink, he explained, "decided to forgo additional revenue we could make from selling our customers' personal information in exchange for gaining our consumers' long-term trust by protecting their privacy."[73] In other words, he argued, "good privacy means good business" and "trust equals revenue."[74]

Through its promotional materials, EarthLink built a brand that promoted the company's commitment to comprehensive privacy practices. In a 2001 advertising campaign, the company drew attention to its privacy-conscious practices. A television spot titled "Privacy" blended together thirty actors to create the image of a single person going through a morning routine: getting out of bed, looking through a dresser, and washing in the bathroom sink. The voice-over stated, "They are watching you: compiling your information; invading your privacy; revealing your identity. At EarthLink, we would never do that. We just deliver the totally anonymous internet."[75] The commercial promoted

Figures 2.1 and 2.2. Stills from an EarthLink commercial showing a man being bombarded with offers and advertisements while walking down a city street. Screenshot by author.

EarthLink's practice of "obscuring" IP addresses to make content origins difficult to trace.[76] Describing EarthLink as "one of the most active privacy advocates in the ISP space," Claudia Caplan, vice president of brand marketing, said the company "created this ad to further illuminate the growing importance of Internet privacy and to let people know that not all ISPs or online services have the same level of commitment to privacy protection."[77] The message behind the ad—and, according to Caplan, "a key point of differentiation"—was that "EarthLink is not in the business of exploiting its subscribers' personal data."[78]

Another EarthLink television spot communicated a similar message. This ad showed a man walking down a busy urban street. As he walked, strangers who seemed to know him by name tried to interest him in a series of increasingly specific items: a morning newspaper, a wireless camera, a new job, and carpet cleaning. As the individual voices dissolved into a chorus of people demanding "look here" and "click here," the voice-over said, "Is your internet provider selling your personal information? That's not the way the internet was meant to be. Switch to EarthLink: the number one provider of the real internet."[79] This reference to the "real internet" was perhaps intended to invoke a nostalgia that had already begun to set in for a pre-commercial web.

The EarthLink campaign played on public anxiety by highlighting the ways online retailers, marketers, and service providers were violating consumer expectations of privacy. EarthLink added a guerilla-marketing component to its campaign to draw parallels between the assumptions we make about anonymity in public and semipublic spaces and the types of privacy we expect online. In one promotion, EarthLink hired "privacy protection teams" to place rearview mirrors above urinals in restaurant and bar men's rooms in Washington, DC, and Austin, Texas. Printed on the mirrors was the slogan "EarthLink protects your privates."[80] Toilet seat covers and toilet paper dispensers with the same message were placed in women's restrooms. Caplan explained the company's use of public restrooms as a strategy for highlighting the importance of social norms around privacy. "We call these places public restrooms—yet we have an expectation of privacy in them," Caplan noted. "There's a similarity to the Internet."[81] As part of this campaign, EarthLink distributed tens of thousands of free bags of chocolate chip cookies in six U.S. cities. Printed on the cookie bags was the question "Do you know where your cookies come from?"[82] The message referred to the small files dropped in internet users' browsers that allow websites to track their online behavior. The effect of being handed a bag of cookies with this message was intended to highlight the vulnerability of accepting a package from an unknown source.

Privacy advocates praised EarthLink's efforts to draw attention to the issue of online privacy and demonstrate that respectful data handling practices could also be good business practices. There were, however, concerns that EarthLink's advertising campaign overstated the actual protections the company offered. One industry analyst noted, "It's not really a solid promise to say that they're going to protect your privacy when all they're really protecting is stuff like names and addresses that can be gotten a million other ways."[83] And, despite their marketing campaign, EarthLink did not automatically block cookies. Instead, the company provided tips on how to manage cookies and made software available that would allow customers to selectively accept or reject cookies.[84]

Of significant concern to regulators and privacy advocates was the company's use of the word "anonymous" across their campaigns. Privacy experts argued that few ISPs could truly claim to offer anonymity because of the vulnerability of such services to government investigations and requests from law enforcement.[85] A 2002 investigation by the FTC that considered EarthLink's claims regarding its privacy and spam protection services focused on the company's use of this term. A statement from the FTC's Division of Advertising Practices questioned EarthLink's claim to provide a "totally anonymous Internet."[86] In response to the investigation, EarthLink pulled the TV spot and removed claims to anonymity from its website. Considering these actions, the FTC did not pursue its case. The regulator did, however, recommended that "Earth-Link be careful not to overstate the degree of consumer risk on the Internet from invasions of privacy, or the protections EarthLink actually provides against those risks, so that consumers are not misled."[87]

The EarthLink campaign is just one example of corporate attempts to capitalize on privacy as a strategy for securing consumer trust. The argument that strong privacy protection was essential for generating confidence in online businesses was becoming more accepted.[88] The prevalence of this position is exemplified by a series of comments from Scott McNealy, CEO of Sun Microsystems, who is responsible for the oft-cited quip that on the internet "you have zero privacy anyway" and should "get over it."[89] Less well-known, however, is McNealy's later discussion of the economic imperative for companies to understand and respect consumer concerns regarding privacy. In a *Washington Post* editorial two years after that statement, McNealy wrote, "Any company that doesn't properly safeguard people's personal information will suffer the same fate as a bank that doesn't safeguard people's money. It will go out of business."[90] Despite this revised position, McNealy can hardly be considered a privacy advocate. Rather, he was responding to the challenges presented by a consumer population worried about the risks of unauthorized information sharing. Chief among those consequences was that companies could miss out on a valuable commercial resource. "Most people" he reasoned, "would gladly reveal their personal preferences, as long as they feel certain the information won't be misused. On the Internet, even more than in other areas of our lives, trust is the real currency."[91] For McNealy, as for EarthLink, good privacy practices represented a way of generating consumer confidence in a new economic landscape. At a moment when the public was unsure of the security of information shared online, privacy was viewed by some as a profitable framework through which to differentiate themselves from competitors.

Selling Freedom through Privacy

In his book *Code 2.0*, legal scholar and political activist Lawrence Lessig described a sense of excitement taking hold in the mid-1990s as people began to consider the possibilities of the internet to foster a new social order. He wrote that the internet's architecture, which allowed for information to be widely shared, was fundamentally different from the hierarchical broadcast models that defined existing media. Cyberspace's design, Lessig observed, seemed to support a new social organization: "freedom without anarchy, control without government, consensus without power."[92] For those who saw the possibilities of this new society, it appeared clear that no government should regulate the internet, but also that no government could.[93] Unlike the position motivating the business community's anti-regulatory sentiments, which were oriented toward ensuring the internet was hospitable to corporate interests, the ideology described by Lessig—that cyberspace should remain free from government interference—was celebrated by a libertarian-minded coalition of hackers and cypherpunks who valued the freedom and prosperity afforded by the absence of state intervention and commercial interests.[94]

Nowhere is this ideology clearer, perhaps, than in John Perry Barlow's "A Declaration of the Independence of Cyberspace." In the 1990s, Barlow had joined adherents of the Free Speech Movement in their anticipation of the prospects and possibilities of the internet for redefining society.[95] This group was excited by opportunities for self-determination supported by a digital world that seemed to be unencumbered by the cultural and political limitations that restricted life offline. Despite impending concerns about the role of new technologies in destroying privacy, there was an excitement about the potential for digital media to empower individuals and groups. Barlow's "Declaration" provides an emblematic and enduring example of this optimism. Written in Davos, Switzerland, at the World Economic Forum in 1996, the essay describes a digital world where government and corporate interests could not be imposed. "Governments of the Industrial World, you weary giants of flesh and steel, I come from Cyberspace, the new home of Mind," the document begins. "On behalf of the future, I ask you of the past to leave us alone. You are not welcome among us. You have no sovereignty where we gather." Barlow went on to consider how the repressive cultural constructs that organized the offline world—including gender, race, and class—would have no place in the new online landscape. "We are creating a world," he wrote, "that all may enter without privilege or prejudice accorded by race, economic power, military force, or station of birth."[96] The resulting cyber-selves, distributed across jurisdictions, would be directed by enlightened self-interest and ungoverned by any single authority. In short, Barlow envisioned that lives lived online would reject external authority and experience pure autonomy.

That Barlow wrote his "Declaration" on behalf of "lovers of freedom and self-determination" is noteworthy. Freedom from authority—in the form of government, military, business, and prejudice—was a vital component of early internet culture, and privacy played a central role in ensuring that freedom. Theorists point to the importance of privacy for protecting a range of rights, including freedoms of speech, opinion, and association. In its absence, as philosopher Jeffrey Reiman argues, opportunities for autonomy are restricted.[97] The threat of constant visibility, he notes, exerts a subtle influence on behavior, which may make people vulnerable to external control. If a sense of continuous observation is internalized, as is the case in the panoptic environments famously described by Michel Foucault, the pervasive gaze can increase susceptibility to normative social pressures.[98] Such conditions, according to Reiman, create a state of psycho-political metamorphosis in which the complete visibility of actions infantilizes people and inhibits personal growth.[99]

Privacy was, therefore, essential for securing the utopian vision many shared for cyberspace: the chance to build a society that celebrated individual autonomy in the service of collective interests beyond the purview of restrictive and oppressive social and institutional forces. That the entrepreneurs behind the anonymizers used language related to freedom to promote their consumer privacy tools is, therefore, not surprising. When we spoke in October 2013, Stephanie Perrin was the president of a privacy consulting firm called Digital Discretion. Prior to founding that firm in 2003, Perrin had worked as ZKS's chief privacy officer. During our conversation, she recalled the profound influence ideologies of freedom and independence had on ZKS's product development. It was not a coincidence, she told me, that the company called its software "Freedom." The name reflected a commitment to the ideals of a free and open internet and a belief that preserving opportunities for anonymity was essential to supporting these principles. That the commitments of both Anonymizer and ZKS to obscure any record of its clients' online activities, thereby preventing the companies from coordinating with government or law enforcement to comply with subpoena requests, similarly speaks to this vision.

Although the subpoena-proof nature of these services captured much of the media attention, the companies' products were perhaps more broadly relevant for their ability to protect individuals from having their online interactions assembled as a permanent record of actions. The value of private spaces that facilitate identity exploration and discovery through opportunities to try out ideas and make mistakes are considered essential for the development of what the philosopher and ethicist Jeroen van den Hoven has called one's "moral biography."[100] Those opportunities are restricted if every action a person has ever taken becomes part of a visible, recorded, and enduring reputation. In a prescient description of concerns that would later be associated with the internet's so-called inability to forget, Anonymizer's Lance Cottrell observed in 1998 that while people often treat their online interactions the same as they might "a casual gathering of friends," they might not wish to be associated indefinitely with the information they share online. "Let's say while you're in college, you're experimenting and posting to sites like alt.drugs or alt.sex," he noted. "Several years later, you're trying to get a job at a stodgy law firm. Prospective employers are likely to go to a service like Deja News and pull up what you've been doing."[101] Although the forums and search tools have changed, Cottrell's sentiments reflect a familiar set of contemporary concerns. The ability to shield behaviors from public view not only allows people to segment their online personae but also generates opportunities for experimentation and discovery within those identities.

Media historian Fred Turner argues Barlow's contemporaries were concerned that threats to digital privacy could erode political freedoms. They also feared the colonization of cyberspace would threaten the collectivist ideals that animated its early communities, turning cyber citizens into "fuel for the engines of economic production."[102] Those developing anonymization technologies shared this concern that the economic structures taking root online made individuals susceptible to commercial exploitation. Perrin described her time at Zero-Knowledge Systems to me as "a race to get products out before we were overtaken by what actually did happen—namely, the monetization of the internet." In April 2000, ZKS launched an ad campaign in a dozen publications that was described by company president Austin Hill as "a consumer manifesto."[103] Each version of the ad showed a person with a barcode on their forehead. The copy read, "I am not a pair of eyeballs to be captured or a consumer profile to be sold. I am an individual and you will respect my privacy. I will not be bartered, traded or sold. On the Net I am in control." Part of being free, the advertisement suggested, is having autonomy beyond commercial influence: the right to be treated as a citizen and not as a consumer. Lance Cottrell voiced similar concerns about the persistent collection of information about online behavior that takes place without user knowledge. He described the threats associated with merging offline and online information to create a more complete picture of individual behavior: "I think the real issue is the amount of information gathering going on," he noted. "People underestimate the value of this information."[104]

Before she signed on as the chief privacy officer for Zero-Knowledge Systems, Stephanie Perrin had worked on crafting and implementing privacy legislation in Canada's public sector. Because of this experience, she described herself as having a generous view of the value of public policy for protecting privacy online. Although Perrin advocates for regulation that meets the needs of a rapidly changing technologi-

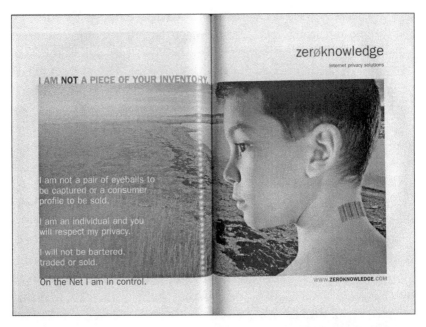

Figures 2.3 and 2.4. Zero-Knowledge Systems advertisements, which the company described as a "consumer manifesto." *Fortune* magazine, May 2000 and Summer 2000.

cal environment, she also pointed out the benefit of having commercially available technologies to support those regulatory initiatives. In describing her shift from the public to the private sector, Perrin told me, "I had been working on the impact of technology for quite some time and I felt that there's no point in having privacy law if we didn't find a way of controlling the information that was being released and emitted as metadata on the internet." She described an ideal mix of legislation, unique codes of practice, public education, and privacy-enhancing technologies as offering what she called a "toolkit approach" to privacy. Part of this toolkit involved educating people about the threats to privacy in this new digital world.

The entrepreneurs behind the anonymizer services faced a fundamental challenge in their attempts to sell digital privacy: although their consumer base was anxious about privacy online, many lacked the technological sophistication to fully grasp the problem or evaluate existing solutions. In fact, companies like Anonymizer and Zero-Knowledge Systems were not simply providing tools to address concerns about unwanted visibility online; they also tasked themselves with teaching the public about the value of protecting one's digital data and online image. Educating the public about the need for vigilant awareness regarding the production, collection, and use of digital information was a difficult task in the 1990s, when people were only beginning to understand what the internet was. Recalling bewildered responses to the company's early promotional efforts, Lance Cottrell described education as an important part of Anonymizer's strategic plan. "In 1995," Cottrell told me, "you go out and say, 'Hey, you need to worry about privacy on the internet,' and people would sort of go, 'Wow. Tell me about this internet thing.' And so we had to take a step back."

Because of these early conversations, Cottrell said public relations became an important way for the company to build awareness about the services they were providing and the problems they addressed. "PR was a big area for us," he shared with me. "We didn't have access to a lot of direct marketing, so working with the media, working with reporters, doing public speaking, was a significant aspect of this." Stephanie Perrin referred to similar promotional work at ZKS to educate the public about digital privacy. Perrin, who described herself to me as the company's unofficial "PR person," remembers going to conferences and talking about the need for digital privacy. Even at these events, she told me, a lack of awareness and technological sophistication made it difficult to convince people about the importance of protecting their privacy online: "There was such a huge steep uphill climb to get people to understand what was going on. That was thirteen years ago. People don't understand it today."

Unlike the companies that saw privacy as a brand, simply a feature that differentiated them from competitors, the anonymizers viewed privacy as at the core of their service—a right that was essential for maintaining a strong internet. Through the provision of services that allowed individuals to construct their digital identity, independent from commercial efforts and outside of governmental surveillance, the anonymizers aimed to support strategies for digital self-determination. While online retailers and advertisers advocated for self-regulatory measures to manage the collection and use of personal information, anonymizers sought technical solutions for data minimization that would protect user privacy even in the absence of robust regulatory intervention. Consequently, the solutions offered by the anonymizers were at odds with an emerging economic system that sought to exploit a newly available source of consumer data. Not everyone in this space, however, viewed efforts to protect consumer privacy as inevitably in conflict with a thriving online economy. The next chapter explores the efforts of a set of companies that sought to reconcile the economic interests of online marketers and retailers with consumers' desire for privacy online.

3

Opt Out for Privacy, Opt In for Value

The Introduction of the Infomediary

As an early website designer, Fred Davis is a self-described internet pioneer. Although he believed the internet was poised to change the world when it became more widely accessible in the 1990s, Davis joined many cyber-evangelists in a shared concern about the consequences of business incursion in the online space. He worried about the threat to privacy presented by commercial tracking tools and weak encryption. "I think privacy is the cornerstone of democracy," Davis told me when we spoke in the fall of 2013. "It's an individual liberty that people should not have taken away from them." For ordinary users to preserve their privacy online, Davis reasoned, they required a comprehensive and easy-to-use tool that would assist in the management of identity and reputation. Davis's belief in the value of privacy coupled with his confidence in the capacity for technology to address this issue provided the basis for Lumeria, a service designed to put individuals in charge of how the personal information they generated and shared online was captured and used.

Lumeria, one of the first efforts to build a user-centric online privacy management tool, closely followed a strategy introduced by business and management consultants John Hagel III and Jeffrey F. Rayport. In a 1997 *Harvard Business Review* article titled "The Coming Battle for Customer Information," Hagel and Rayport observed a rising public concern regarding the deepening collection of digital data by companies seeking to aggregate, analyze, and monetize consumer information.[1] Contrary to those who argued that individuals objected to corporate data collection because they saw it as companies encroaching on their privacy rights, such as those behind the anonymizers, Hagel and Rayport maintained that public concern was the result of feeling exploited at the hands of an economic model where personal information was the cost of access. "We are witnessing the growth of a 'privacy' backlash among consumers," they wrote, "which we believe has less to do with the desire to keep information about themselves confidential and more to do with the pragmatic assessment that the returns for the information they divulge are, simply put, unsatisfactory."[2] Consumers, they argued, were not worried about the circulation of their personal information; rather, they wanted to share in the profits of its use.

Hagel and Rayport's assertions parallel political economic critiques that see the commodification of consumer attention and information as unjust. Arguing that consumers would ultimately reject an economic model that exploited rather than engaged them, Hagel and Rayport anticipated a new type of company that would assist in this exchange— one that would help individuals collect and organize their information and bargain with third-party vendors for its sale. They called these consumer-focused data brokers "infomediaries." By the turn of the twenty-first century, several companies, including Lumeria, had adopted some version of the infomediary model as a strategy for addressing privacy online. Davis estimated that, as early as the mid-1990s, 80 percent of web-based companies were involved in the resale or rental of personal data as a source of revenue. The consequence, he said in 2000, was a brewing conflict between companies engaged in this type of data-gathering "free-for-all" and consumers who "want their privacy back."[3] Davis wanted Lumeria to "transfer control back to the individual," providing users with the tools to "profit from the sale of their attention."[4] The company's slogan, he told me, was "opt out for privacy and opt in for value." The infomediary model was built on a belief that people make conscious decisions about when to divulge personal information by weighing the consequences of disclosure with the benefits of sharing.

The assumption that people assess privacy risks as a form of tradeoff was popularized in the work of influential privacy scholar Alan Westin. Based on survey research conducted between 1978 and 2004, Westin developed a typology that placed Americans in one of three categories regarding their interest in personal privacy: the fundamentalists, the pragmatists, and the unconcerned. While those described by Westin as privacy fundamentalists place a high value on confidentiality and favor strong regulation to curtail the collection and retention of personal information, the unconcerned are described as readily providing information to public and private organizations and dismissing the need for government intervention.[5] The privacy pragmatists, who Westin consistently found make up over half the population,[6] have some privacy concerns but are occasionally willing to exchange personal information for other benefits.[7]

Rather than presenting the pragmatists' seemingly erratic behavior as resulting from uncertainty regarding their views on privacy, Westin described them as rational actors who make calculated decisions about when to disclose personal information. The pragmatist, Westin wrote, "weighs the value to them and society of various business or government programs calling for personal information, examines the relevance and social propriety of the information sought, looks to see whether fair information practices are being widely enough observed, and then decides whether they will agree or disagree with specific information."[8] Hagel and Rayport's infomediary model is built on assumptions similar to those that inform Westin's vision of the privacy pragmatist. Both consider privacy behaviors to be the outcome of rational decision making that weigh the risks and benefits of disclosure. Those behind the infomediaries aimed to provide user-centric tools that would support the execution of these contextual and evolving privacy preferences.

In advocating for the infomediary model Hagel described a "growing sense that we're providing more and more information and we're not getting tangible value, or that the information gets misused" but asserted that, for most people, apprehensions about privacy can be explained by economic logics rather than moral or ethical ideologies.[9] In other words, Hagel argued that the value of privacy stems from its role in ensuring the scarcity of information to enhance economic value rather than the provision of additional rights and freedoms. By placing privacy in an economic framework, the infomediary approach positioned personal information as a commodity that could be managed for individual benefit. This application of economic principles to personal information generated opportunities for people to exercise power in their role as consumers. In so doing, this approach shifted the landscape for discussions about privacy away from civic rights to focus on economics. Consequently, individual responsibility—rather than social good—has become a central framework through which conversations about digital privacy take place.[10]

By investigating the differences between the anonymizers and infomediaries—contemporaries in the consumer privacy space—this chapter reveals key distinctions in their industrial discourses. While those behind the anonymizers advocated for privacy as necessary to preserve the integrity of a free and open cyber world, the entrepreneurs behind the infomediaries tended to stress opportunities for individuals to own and leverage their personal information. Through alternative models of empowerment, the anonymizers and the infomediaries proposed different approaches for addressing digital privacy needs. An examination of the role these companies played in shaping regulatory discussions about privacy online reveals how the infomediary approach turned personal information produced through digital interactions into a consumer asset. This strategy was compelling for those seeking to reconcile privacy protection with the emerging world of e-commerce. By providing individuals with the opportunity to participate in and benefit from the emerging surveillance economy, this model offered a framework for optimizing one's online visibility.

Although neither the anonymizer nor the infomediary model enjoyed sustained commercial success in the twenty-first century, both ventures played an important role in shaping the discursive agenda around digital privacy. The conclusion of this chapter details how the entrepreneurs behind these initiatives understand the social, political, and economic conditions that precipitated the commercial failure of most companies in this industry's first generation. Their accounts provide a counter narrative to the belief that people are uninterested in protecting their privacy or unwilling to pay for tools and services that would help them do so. Rather, these entrepreneurs introduce the possibility that economic and political circumstances, rather than consumer choice, challenged the consumer privacy industry at the turn of the twenty-first century. Before evaluating the industry's decline, however, this chapter introduces the infomediary model and examines how the approach, which framed privacy as a consumer issue, helped to normalize the idea that digital privacy comes at a cost.

Building an Anonymous Web: Privacy from Surfing to Shopping to Shipping

Before he started the Colorado-based infomediary PrivaSeek,[11] Larry Lozon had been the head of online marketing at General Motors. From this position, Lozon witnessed an exponential growth in the amount of information that companies could collect about consumers by tracking their online activities. When we spoke in November 2013, Lozon pointed to the influence of the Hagel and Rayport model when he described the concerns that motivated PrivaSeek—the fear that consumers would turn their backs on a system that was exploiting their personal information for monetary gain. Uncomfortable with what he saw as a set of practices that cut consumers out of the benefits of this new information economy, Lozon decided to build a platform that would provide individuals with a more advantageous position. By giving them a say in who could access their data and how it could be used, he aimed to empower people who wanted to engage in the online economy without opening themselves to consumer surveillance.

Rick Jackson's introduction to the consumer privacy industry bears a striking similarity to Lozon's. Prior to being hired as CEO for an infomediary named Privada, Jackson had been working at a marketing company developing strategies for online behavioral advertising. When we spoke in 2014, Jackson told me the company he had been working for had no intention of mapping consumer behavior with personally identifiable information and was planning instead to target their digital advertisements anonymously. Nevertheless, he observed several other online advertising companies that were beginning to experiment with incorporating information about users' online behaviors into tailored advertisements—a practice that gave him pause. Jackson believed that the use of personal information to create tailored ads would prompt a backlash from consumers and privacy groups and saw Privada's services as a possible antidote. The company's approach, he told me, offered "an interesting intersection of helping consumers feel confident in their privacy and yet still allowing advertising companies and commerce companies to really be able to track things and map things and to do better, more targeted offers." This, he said, was what consumers really wanted. According to Jackson, Privada's tools merged an interest in preserving privacy with a desire to engage with online retailers and advertisers.

In their description of the infomediary model, Hagel and Rayport observed that, when it came to reaping the benefits of digital data, power sat firmly with corporations. They argued most people would jump at the opportunity to barter personal information for profit, and they imagined that infomediaries would act "as custodians, agents, and brokers of customer information, marketing it to businesses on consumers' behalf while protecting their privacy at the same time."[12] Infomediaries offered users tools to collect, manage, and exchange their personal information for deals. PrivaSeek's PersonaValet service, for example, would store information added by users to a secure online vault.[13] The company had developed relationships with online merchants and would use the information in users' vaults to serve them relevant advertisements when they visited partner sites.[14] PrivaSeek described this platform as a "personal datamart" that allowed individuals to take control of "a brand called me."[15]

Privada offered similar services that allowed consumers to protect and control the dissemination of their digital data.[16] The company's anonymous web browsing service, Web Incognito, and anonymous email service, Messaging Incognito, shared features with the services provided by anonymizers. Using these tools, Privada's clients could surf the web and exchange email while shielding personal information from third parties. When a Privada user went online, the websites they visited could see that they were a Privada client, but could not access information about the individual user. Unlike the anonymizers, however, Privada was interested in fusing privacy protections with commercial opportunities. This desire motivated the inclusion of additional features to facilitate relationships between consumers and retailers. Privada would, for example, accept website-issued cookies. Instead of being hosted on the user's browser or computer, however, these tracking tools would be stored in the users' profile on the Privada network. By masking these "convenience cookies"—those tracking tools used to improve a website's functionality—Privada allowed consumers to enjoy the benefits of websites and maintain a consistent identity online without requiring they reveal personal information.

To further support users' engagement in digital commerce, Privada created private channels for shopping and shipping. A partnership with

American Express, which Jackson described to me as a central component of Privada's plan, provided clients with anonymous, single-use credit cards. These cards allowed Privada clients to shop online without the requirement they reveal their name or other personally identifiable information. Additionally, Jackson told me Privada had acquired a company that had an existing deal with Mail Boxes Etc. Through the partnership with this chain, which is now the UPS Store, Privada intended to provide its clients with the option for anonymous shipping. Jackson described the mailing company as "a delivery vehicle for all of these privately purchased items." After a purchase was completed with a single-use American Express card, Jackson explained to me, the item would be packaged and shipped to a local Mail Boxes Etc. store, where the client could pick up the package using a physical credential like a driver's license. The combination of anonymous shopping and shipping, Jackson said, "kept the circle of complete privacy."

Anonymous shopping and shipping may seem like an extreme response to concerns about digital surveillance. After all, even when we use cash to buy items in brick and mortar stores there are witnesses to our purchases. These precautions, however, do not only respond to concerns about the observation of any single purchase, but also to the emergence of digital profiles that consider consumer behaviors in aggregate rather than as discrete transactions. When combined, individual purchases can paint a holistic picture of shopping habits that may invite assumptions about the consumer. Similar to networked cameras that allow for pervasive observation across time and space, interactive digital technologies that support the creation of a persistent consumer identity allow purchase records to be stored, combined with additional records, and analyzed to reveal insights.[17] The consequences of these activities become evident when, for example, a bank reduces a client's approved credit limit because their purchase patterns feature similar indicators to those of clients who have failed to pay their debts.[18]

Another infomediary, iPrivacy, developed a similar approach to ensuring anonymity for those who wanted to take advantage of opportunities for online shopping without being required to sacrifice their privacy. Started by a group of former Citibank employees, iPrivacy described itself as an "identity-filtering" company. From its headquarters in New York City, the company defined its mission as the creation of tools that would allow for anonymity online in everything from surfing to shopping to shipping. iPrivacy's platform was designed to act as a blind intermediary that would facilitate online interactions without revealing its clients' identities to retailers. Providing what it called one-way mirror technology, the company aimed to put consumers in control of online economic interactions. Like Jackson's assertion that economic engagement should not come at the cost of privacy, iPrivacy's goal was to enhance consumers' control over their personal data without undermining the conveniences offered by online shopping. By providing clients with single-use identification tools, iPrivacy obscured individual consumers' purchasing habits. To make a purchase, iPrivacy clients would access the company's platform through a trusted provider such as a bank or credit card company, after which they would be granted a single-use email address, an iPrivacy number, a single-use credit card number, and a fake address.

Salvatore Stolfo, a computer scientist and one of the company's cofounders, told me during a 2013 conversation about a partnership that iPrivacy had forged with the United States Postal Service. Through this relationship, iPrivacy could ensure packages were delivered to the client's preferred location without requiring they provide online retailers with a valid address. When iPrivacy clients purchased a product online, the retailer would be given a proxy address for shipping. When the package arrived at the post office, USPS would recognize the incorrect address and create an address label marked with the proper destination. This process, Stolfo told me, would be similar to what happens when you register to have your mail forwarded after a move. The idea behind this approach was that the retailer would know what was in the box, but not where it was going. Conversely, the post office would know where the box was going, but not what was inside. If the consumer decided they wanted to carry on a relationship with a retailer after their transaction was completed, they had the option of using a consistent proxy email address through which the selected company could reach them. Similar to partnerships Privada had with American Express and Mail Boxes Etc., this relationship was designed to ensure that the cycle of privacy remained intact from purchase through delivery.

iPrivacy's clients also had the option of joining what Stolfo referred to as a "selling circle." Like PrivaSeek's personal datamart, this service would allow consumers to identify the types of products they were interested in. iPrivacy would collect this information, anonymize it, and sell it to retailers, who would use the information to shape the coupons or discounts those retailers would distribute to members of the selling circle. This approach was designed to reward individuals for their participation in the data economy while at the same time preserving their privacy. iPrivacy would use its strategic partnerships with banks to authenticate consumer identities, thereby assuring retailers they were dealing with verified consumers without revealing any personal information to the companies. Stolfo described this process as an opt-in service that offered a win-win situation for consumers and retailers. The consumers win, he noted, because they are not required to give up any personally identifiable information but are still able to engage with online retailers. The retailers win because they are given insight into the preferences of consumers whose credit worthiness has been certified by a reliable third party.

Efforts to ensure privacy online often resort to binary tools that ask users to select between two options: opt out to remain anonymous or opt in to access services. Websites, for example, ask visitors to accept or reject cookies and other tracking tools. Opting out offers users protections from the unwanted collection of their personal information, but makes many websites unusable. Opting in allows for access to a fully functioning website, but also allows information about the user to be collected even after they leave the page. Positioning privacy as a tradeoff between two options is not only a common feature of technological systems, but also a common rhetorical strategy—one which Ontario's former information and privacy commissioner Ann Cavoukian refers to as a zero-sum paradigm.[19] Approaches to privacy that offer binary solutions—either you're in or you're out—help to normalize surveillance by suggesting that decisions to opt in are the result of careful calculations and personal choices. The infomediaries complicated this dichotomy by offering users opportunities to opt in to some forms of economic participation while obscuring details about their identity. They also provided tools that allowed users to move between anonymity and visibility in ways that more closely aligned with privacy preferences that are contextual and fluid rather than static.

In addition to sharing Hagel and Rayport's concerns about the lack of fairness in an online economic system where the data subjects who produce value are prevented from sharing in the rewards, the entrepreneurs behind the infomediaries also expressed frustrations about the system's inefficiencies. Online advertisers, they argued, were failing to reach consumers with appealing and persuasive messages. While digital media allows for addressable content, advertisers were using strategies designed for a mass media environment. Lumeria's Fred Davis described the prevailing approach of online advertising as "interruption marketing," in which messages were sent to "break into your attention when you are paying attention to something else and shoving something in front of you that you may or may not be interested in." Not only are many of these advertising dollars wasted on uninterested audiences, Davis contended, but the practice of disrupting individuals when they are reading or watching something is fundamentally rude.

Several people I spoke with described the interruption marketing model as being simultaneously annoying and ineffective. When the technology exists to ask people about the products they are interested in seeing advertised, why, many of my respondents asked, would companies pay to send mass messages to consumers who are indifferent to their products or services? To explain the inefficiencies in this approach, Davis gave the example of car advertising. "How many ads for how many different cars do you see on your TV or in your paper and how often do you buy a car?" he asked me. "Once every five years? So the wastage in that market is just mind-boggling." Based on his experience in online marketing, Larry Lozon had insight into the industry's strategies, but expressed a similar set of frustrations. "Maybe I'm tired of seeing the sneaker ads just because I did a Google search on Nike," he noted. "Maybe I can say, 'Hey guys, I already bought the sneakers. You don't need to do that. Stop wasting those bits, throw me something else.'" By failing to engage consumers in the process, those behind the infomediaries warned, advertisers risked alienating potential consumers and missing out on the unique communication opportunities enabled by digital media.

By engaging consumers in a conversation about the promotions they are interested in, a practice Davis called permission-based marketing, infomediaries argued that advertisers and retailers could improve consumer relations and minimize inefficient spending. Despite these advantages, they had difficulty convincing others involved in online retailing that this type of consumer-centric marketing was consistent with the needs of a growing digital economy. Davis reported concerns from his venture capitalist friends that a model that asked consumers about their marketing preferences—an approach journalist and blogger Doc Searls has called vendor relationship management[20]—would damage the other companies already in their portfolios. Lozon said friends told him that the infomediary model would destroy the ability of the online advertising industry to continue behavioral targeting. Despite their reputation for "disruptive technologies," those I spoke with described their colleagues and friends in the technology industry as reluctant to engage any approach that might threaten existing digital advertising strategies. Lozon maintained, however, that the infomediary model would not have destroyed behavioral advertising; rather, it offered a more finely calibrated method of targeting promotions through the cultivation of consumer consent. By creating a two-way dialogue, he told me, this model introduced interactivity and sociality to improve marketing messages.

Lozon and Davis's perspectives mirror Hagel and Rayport's presentation of the infomediary as a disruptive technology—one that would challenge the economic model that was taking root online by shifting power from companies to consumers. Through their information management platforms, infomediaries would offer individuals tools of control in an online ecosystem where the data saturation threatened to devalue information about any single individual. Allowing individuals to opt out, Hagel and Rayport argued, would increase the value of consumer data through the introduction of market scarcity. The infomediaries could respond to this scarcity by giving individuals the power and the tools to set the price for their personal data. Although they differed in where they located ideas about data ownership, the infomediary entrepreneurs shared with companies in the emerging online economy a belief that valuable consumer information could be used to support new commercial initiatives. This is where those behind the infomediaries diverged with their counterparts who were promoting anonymization services. Although the anonymizer and infomediary projects both engaged in the sale of privacy online, a comparison between these clarifies a divergent set of ideologies.

Invisibility versus Marketability: Comparing the Anonymizers and Infomediaries

Unlike the other infomediary entrepreneurs I spoke with, Fred Davis did not have a background in banking or marketing. In fact, during our interview, Davis told stories and articulated positions that tracked more closely with those told by entrepreneurs behind the anonymizers. Moreover, his ideas drew heavily from cypherpunk ideology. Because of Davis's unique background, Lumeria provides a clear illustration of the similarities and differences between two of the dominant consumer privacy-enhancing technologies being launched at the end of the twentieth century. Like anonymizers, infomediaries positioned themselves as a shield that protected consumers from unwanted observation; however, when users wanted, they could opt in by allowing for the release of their data to specified third parties through secure channels. Like anonymizers, Lumeria allowed users to visit websites through a proxy server, which obscured information that would identify the user, including IP address, Ethernet address, and geographic location. By constantly swapping IP addresses and other identifying information, Lumeria complicated data collection and tracking efforts.

Lumeria also followed the practice, common to anonymizers, of not keeping a record of users' passwords, which Davis said made the service "subpoena proof." If Lumeria was issued a request for access to a user's profile or record of communication, the company would be unable to comply. This level of security introduced a possible problem: if a user forgot their login details, they would lose access to their account. To help users recover their passwords safely, Davis told me, Lumeria had agreements with financial institutions that would provide safety deposit boxes for users' profile keys. Since people already trusted banks with many of their most valuable assets, Davis reasoned, these institutions provided a perfect safeguard against password amnesia. For those with heightened security concerns, Davis noted, there was the opportunity to split their key between financial institutions to offer further protection. The practice of distributing decryption keys at different banks mirrors the framework for security that informs the internet itself—a network with a distributed infrastructure that is much less vulnerable to attack than one that is centralized. This solution, which Davis referred to as a "key escrow service," was designed to provide individuals with full control over their accounts.

Davis also shared with those behind the anonymizers a perspective that, far from being inauthentic or elusive, the construction of multiple identities was a unique benefit offered by the digital world. Lumeria, he decided, would offer a centralized "identity management" tool that would help people keep track of those discrete identities and manage the flow of information between them. One benefit of this approach is that it would not privilege one identity over another; rather, it would help support the management of online profiles crafted for different audiences and in diverse contexts. In a democratic society, Davis told me, there is an "individual right to chronicle your life through whatever means you feel is appropriate, [which] should not be interfered with nor spied on." Lumeria's "Super Profile"—like Zero-Knowledge Systems' "nyms"— offered tools to facilitate the careful construction, management, and visibility of various online identities. Moreover, by giving clients the ability to segment information and create various profiles, these services provided opportunities for the audience-specific performances, which assist in the creation of identities that are consistent, credible, and authentic.[21] At the same time, they addressed concerns about information being unknowingly revealed to invisible audiences online.[22]

Up to this point in the narrative, the services Lumeria was developing sound similar to those provided by the anonymizers. Davis's company, however, provided an additional set of features that mean Lumeria is, perhaps, more appropriately categorized as an infomediary. What differentiated Lumeria from the anonymizers was the extent to which its services were integrated into the digital economy. "The crux of this whole [online privacy] issue," Davis noted, "started with the tension between people wanting customization and personalization but not [being] willing to give up the information that was necessary to get that level of personalization and customization." Through the incorporation of consumer tools into privacy-enhancing services, Davis believed Lumeria could solve this problem. In addition to cloaking services that facilitated anonymous and pseudonymous surfing, Lumeria's Super Profile would provide clients with a centralized identity management tool populated with personal details, including information about demographics, financial status, and consumer behaviors. Lumeria customers would have access to all this information and could "organize it and prioritize it and divide it amongst personas." That these features, according to Davis, would allow users to manage their identities in an environment that had been tested and endorsed by both hackers and major businesses illustrates Lumeria's position as a bridge between the anonymizer and infomediary services.

Central to the infomediary model was the ability to leverage the personal information collected and stored in user profiles for economic advantage. When a Lumeria client was interested in purchasing something, the company would become their agent, negotiating with online retailers and advertisers for deals and discounts relevant to their interests in exchange for information that the company could not match directly to the individual. Davis referred to this as the "MeBay" platform. Using this system, people could engage in a form of "identity commerce" through which they would be compensated for their attention and their willingness to disclose personal information. The model offered by Lumeria's MeBay platform positioned personal information as a form of currency from which individuals could extract a profit.

This approach, which recognized attention as a resource that retailers and advertisers were willing to pay for, was consistent with existing practices that treated audiences as a commodity. In 1977, Canadian political economist Dallas Smythe argued that the primary role of the mass media was to construct audiences, which could then be sold to advertisers.[23] Smythe stressed that audiences pay for content by attending to and internalizing advertisers' messages. In this respect, audiences do work when they consume media.[24] Smythe was highly critical of the mass media model that capitalized on audience attention. Although Davis articulated similar skepticism regarding the mass media, he described mechanisms that allowed individuals to participate in this exchange as turning exploitation into empowerment. Lumeria's MeBay platform operationalized a belief that individuals could profit by working with advertisers and retailers to commodify and sell their attention and personal information.

The blending of privacy protections with a commercial agenda distinguished the infomediaries from other privacy-enhancing technologies available in the late twentieth century. Jackson identified Privada's consumer-based approach as setting it apart from companies in the consumer privacy space that he characterized as having an "anti-business, anti-commerce, anti-government bent to them." He described Privada's approach as one that embraced the possibilities of e-commerce. "Our view," Jackson told me, "was really one of being pragmatic, which was, we were not trying to serve the consumer who says 'I want to be off the grid.'" Based on the assumption that not everyone would want the level of comprehensive anonymity offered by the anonymizers, Privada targeted a different consumer group: "We were trying to serve the consumer who actually says, 'I appreciate the web and e-commerce for what it can offer, but I'd like to maintain control over my personal privacy.'" In line with what Jackson called Privada's "conservative" and "pragmatic" approach to internet privacy was a commitment to cooperating with government-issued subpoenas—a stance that was different in important ways from the services offered by companies Jackson referred to as the "off-the-grid crowd."

By embracing the possibilities of digital commerce, the infomediaries offered consumers and policy makers an option for online privacy that did not conflict with the increasing corporatization of the web. In fact, they aimed to empower their clients to engage in the online marketplace from a position of strength. In Jackson's view, the collective sentiment of the privacy movement had "started becoming very anti-commerce and anti-advertising on the web." He believed that an anti-commercial approach would "be the death of the Internet because if you don't allow vehicles for monetizing content and if you don't allow e-commerce to really bloom the way it has, it's just not nearly as useful a medium." The founders of iPrivacy took a similar approach. Press releases described the company's privacy tools as a strategic business opportunity for retailers and marketers looking to mitigate consumer concern about the safety and security of their personal information. iPrivacy did not describe its mission in ideological terms, nor did it use language about rights or ethics to talk about the maintenance of private spaces online. In 2000, iPrivacy president Ruvan Cohen noted, "We don't look at ourselves as solving an online *ethics* problem. We see this as a big *marketing* opportunity."[25] While the voices behind the anonymizers talked about the need to address social concerns around rights of self-determination and personal autonomy, those in the infomediary business discussed their efforts as ensuring these rights by facilitating the growth of the online economy.

It's Your Data: Applying Ownership Rights to Digital Information

The commodification of personal information marked an important divide in the approaches motivating privacy-enhancing technologies. Whereas the infomediaries were informed by the principle that engagement in an information economy could be empowering as long at the individual was in control, anonymizers were committed to challenging the rise of a marketplace for personal data. Austin Hill, co-founder of the anonymizer Zero-Knowledge Systems, commented on the dangers of "enticement-based" approaches to online privacy. By treating information as a currency, Hill argued in 1999, these efforts provided a short-term incentive to surrender control of personal information that could have negative consequences.[26] "What really makes me nervous," he warned, "is the 'Trust me' approach. . . . Bad security sold as good security is worse than no security."[27]

Hill's concerns were echoed by some academics and activists. Writing about the consequences of the commodification of personal information, privacy advocate Simon Davies described digital privacy as having "metamorphosed from an issue of societal power relationships" to be "recast as a legal and consumer-rights issue."[28] As communication scholars John Peter Campbell and Matt Carlson observed, by placing privacy rights within a free market framework, privacy becomes an expensive add-on to existing systems rather than a right based on shared social values.[29] Even among those who allowed for the potential of a privacy marketplace, there were concerns about the limits of applying economic logic to personal information. Communication scholar Oscar Gandy Jr. suggested the possibility of a marketplace for consumer data if "property rights in personal information are formally established" allowing individuals to "trade these rights against goods and services."[30] Even so, he warned, a fair exchange in such a market is unlikely since the monetary value of personal information reflects its value to the company and not to the individual. This imbalance, Gandy wrote, is likely to result in individuals being consistently underpaid for their information. Moreover, economic systems that assign value to personal data will likely place more worth on information about "high value" individuals.[31] Although it may benefit some people, it is an approach that has the potential to reproduce systematic inequalities by offering more for personal data from individuals whose identities already provide them with social and economic advantages.

For infomediaries to give consumers a seat at the table to negotiate how their personal information would be collected and used by marketers, there had to be some agreement that users themselves have ownership claims on their data. For those behind the infomediaries, there was a general agreement that this could be accomplished through the application of property rights to personal information. While working in marketing, prior to founding PrivaSeek, Larry Lozon was conflicted about companies' proprietary use of information to which he believed the consumer might have a claim. He wondered who really owned the information generated in interactions between consumers and companies. "One can argue that, well, the corporation that is collecting the data . . . believes that they have some ownership over that information," he noted. "And the other side says, 'Yeah, but it is information about me.'" Lozon settled on a position that individuals should share some ownership and control over the use of their information. Salvatore Stolfo referenced a similar set of ownership rights as a central piece of the iPrivacy approach. "When you as an artist . . . generate a piece of art or piece of music, that's your property, that's your intellectual property," Stolfo reasoned. "Your behavior with all of your financial relationships, and your financial transactions, you're generating that. In my view," he told me, "that should also be your intellectual property." Repositioning personal data as property, Lozon noted, opens a "very rich set of laws, rights, and notions around personal property," including rules around buying, selling, lending, and trespassing.

The application of property rights to personal information is an established framework through which to understand privacy.[32] Ann Cavoukian, writing with Don Tapscott, describes the possible benefits of such an approach. "With respect to the commercial uses of our personal information," they write, "a property right to personal information, which in turn would ensconce the right to control our property, might be a good idea."[33] The authors propose a framework for thinking about personal information as a commodity with associated value. This framing allows for the application of a royalty system under which individuals would be compensated for the commercial use of their data. As will be discussed in later chapters, however, there are limits to the market's ability to address the social and moral issues surrounding digital privacy through strategies of information ownership.[34]

Despite their differing approaches, those behind anonymizers and infomediaries shared the goal of minimizing the availability of personal information to third parties. As described in the previous chapter, data minimization in a commercial context refers to the principle that organizations limit their data collection to that which is necessary for a transaction.[35] By building an environment in which a "real" identity is not necessary for authentication in commercial transactions, all of these companies offered tools that supported principles of data minimization. While developing the iPrivacy platform, Salvatore Stolfo says his team "looked very deeply at what identity was actually used for" and concluded that, in the digital landscape, identity was simply being used as a marker to collate the pieces of information necessary to engage in economic transactions. If identity is a social rather than an economic construct, the question for Stolfo was "why do you need a truthful identifier, like your name, address, Social Security, and so forth, when you can be given a unique identifier that hides your true identity and that you are in control of?" By offering tools that allowed for commercial and social interactions untethered from one's offline self, these entrepreneurs were advocating for an internet that did not rely on identity as a central component of its architecture.

Technologies of Choice: Privacy as Control

Those behind companies in the first-generation consumer privacy industry tended to reject the operational definition of privacy as a tradeoff between visibility and anonymity. They recognized that people's privacy preferences could be altered based on factors such as time, context, or audience. They realized that people do not always think about their identity as a unified or cohesive entity, preferring to share different parts of it, with different people, at different moments. They built tools that reflected these understandings by offering strategies to cloak or uncloak, to be anonymous or pseudonymous, to engage in commercial systems or to avoid them. In pushing back against logics that suggest privacy is an all-or-nothing decision, those behind these first-generation consumer privacy products embraced perspectives that imagined digital privacy as a function of personal choice optimized through tools that enabled control.

Those behind the anonymizers and infomediaries both believed in the possibility for digital tools to empower individuals to manage how their personal information was collected and shared. Their services offered a practical solution to a pressing problem in the emerging online economy: a need for authentication strategies to generate trust online coupled with concerns about the consequences of unchecked consumer surveillance and fears about insufficient data security. Through their insistence that online interactions—economic and social—did not necessitate the use of "real" or persistent identities, the infomediaries and anonymizers reflected academic and cultural perspectives that situated strong privacy protections as an important feature of cyberspace. Seeing the introduction of online platforms that relied on the use of centralized identities as a move that threatened privacy and autonomy, they offered solutions aimed at building online architectures that operated without reference to specific identity markers.

The identity management tools built by companies in the consumer privacy industry relied on a version of ideal privacy as achieved through decisions made by individuals. Despite the countercultural rhetoric that informs some of the companies in this space, this is a view of privacy that sits fairly comfortably within existing government regulation. Existing privacy provisions in the United States tend to rely on a framework of notice and choice in which an informed individual makes decisions that reflect their own self-interest, "opting in" when services meet their privacy needs and "opting out" when they do not. The goal of this approach, which legal scholar Daniel Solove refers to as "privacy self-management," is to "provide people with control over their personal data, and through this control people can decide for themselves how to weigh the costs and benefits of the collection, use, or disclosure of personal information."[36]

As previously noted, solutions that consider privacy in terms of a single opportunity to choose between secrecy and disclosure tend to overlook the compounding significance these decisions have. Privacy violations are just as often the result of information that is spread, combined, or misrepresented—occurrences that are rarely anticipated when decisions about information disclosure are made. Philosopher Jeffrey Reiman writes that "privacy results not only from locked doors and closed curtains, but also from the way our publicly observable activities are dispersed over space and time."[37] As a result, he continues, if "we direct our privacy-protection efforts at reinforcing our doors and curtains, we may miss the way in which modern means of information collection threaten our privacy by gathering up the pieces of our public lives and making them visible from a single point."[38] By allowing for more granularity in decisions about when the information alluded to by Reiman is publicly available, the anonymizers and infomediaries push beyond a blunt binary between visibility and invisibility.

Nevertheless, the focus on individual choice risks ignoring the larger social context in which decisions about privacy are made. Moreover, the tools offered by the infomediaries in particular encouraged individuals to see data as an asset, teaching them to think about their personal information as a good that could be traded and sold for profit. By providing individuals with tools to support personal options about the disclosure and use of personal information online, the infomediaries offered a pragmatic response to concerns about the ways digital data were being collected and sold to create profiles of online behavior. In disseminating such tools to allow individuals to participate in that exchange, the infomediaries reasoned, consumers would be empowered rather than exploited. As media scholar Mark Andrejevic observes, however, the recruitment of individuals to take part in their own observation may create more precise profiles, but fails to empower the individuals who remain the targets of observation.[39] Although these strategies allow individuals to share in the economic rewards that result from consumer surveillance regimes, Andrejevic argues that they do little to change broader political economic systems that support asymmetries of power by ensuring that opportunities to collect and make use of information are reserved for those already in authoritative positions.

Despite the enduring power of this consent-based model, there are problems inherent in the treatment of privacy primarily as the consequence of individual decisions and actions. Framing privacy as an informed choice makes individuals uniquely responsible for completing the assessments and calculations to determine the conditions under which they wish their information to be shared, and then correctly identifying and using tools that support those preferences. In environments where information is routinely shifted from one context to another to be used for unanticipated purposes and in unexpected ways, it is nearly impossible for any person—even one who is highly informed—to make rational decisions about the risks and benefits of information disclosure. There is, however, an even more fundamental problem with the treatment of privacy as a function of personal choice. By suggesting individuals signal their privacy preferences through a series of discrete decisions, the individual choice model mistakenly isolates privacy from the broader contexts in which it resides. Surveillance scholars Jennifer Whitson and Kevin Haggerty observe this process in the related field of identity theft.[40] As people are encouraged to protect themselves through responsible actions and consumer choices, they argue, the roles and responsibilities institutions have for risk mitigation are obscured. As a result, individuals become unduly burdened with the task of self-protection and penalized when their efforts fail.

The construction of privacy as the result of individual decision making also provides limited protection against creeping forms of surveillance. By providing people with options about when and how to share personal information, choice-based privacy regimes can normalize visibility by disregarding the ways digital environments are built to incentivize disclosure. In a surveillance society, we are continually subjected to the problematic idea that, by allowing ourselves to be known to governments, businesses, and one another, we are becoming safer citizens, savvier consumers, or more social community members. Disclosure options that conceal mechanisms that encourage visibility support what Simon Davies has called an "illusion of voluntariness" in which the presentation of choices makes us *feel* empowered without offering *legitimate* options for avoiding persistent surveillance.[41] Further, Davies notes, by presenting options using the discourse of individual empowerment, choice frameworks help neutralize concern about privacy violations by facilitating feelings of control and autonomy. As feminist scholar Ellen Riordan observes, empowerment rhetoric can inadvertently undermine motivations for challenging powerful social and economic systems by promoting a belief in individual entitlement.[42]

Using the language of consumer empowerment, infomediaries suggested their platforms would help the market respond to consumer preference, resulting in ideal levels of privacy. This approach is characterized by a belief that market-based solutions offer an effective strategy for responding to inequality through the integration of individual preferences. This faith in commercial systems to address social problems is a hallmark of neoliberal thinking. In his book *A Brief History of Neoliberalism*, David Harvey offers the following definition: neoliberalism is "a theory of political economic practices that proposes that human well-being can best be advanced by liberating individual entrepreneurial freedoms and skills within an institutional framework characterized by strong private property rights, free markets, and free trade."[43] The data ownership framework proposes a set of rights around the collection and use of personal information. This approach encourages policies that focus on efforts to empower individuals by promoting self-determination operationalized through consumer choice. Technical tools that provide opportunities to opt out without fundamentally challenging the conditions that incentivize opting in exemplify what Andrejevic has observed as a practice of enlisting individual concerns about privacy as a form of discursive resistance that ultimately fails to undermine pervasive and invisible methods of surveillance.[44] As we will see in subsequent chapters, however, policies grounded in thinking that privileges personal choice over collective action produce a system of personal responsibility where achievements and failures are intrinsically tied to individual decisions.

Reconciling Regulatory and Technological Solutions

When it came to dealing with privacy online at the end of the twentieth century, policy makers were faced with a challenge. They were wary of introducing regulation that might create barriers for online commerce or stifle innovation in the tech industry. Moreover, they were confronted by unpredictable consumer behaviors that challenged the rationality of a one-size-fits-all policy for dealing with personal information online. A consumer handbook issued by the U.S. Senate in 2000, titled *Know the Rules, Use the Tools: Privacy in the Digital Age*, described this seeming inconsistency. "Although consumers indicate they are concerned about the possibility of their private information being traded to third parties" the report stated, "research shows a continued trade-off by Internet users between privacy and security on the one hand, and utility and price on the other."[45] Reference to this so-called privacy paradox[46] made legislators weary of introducing any regulation that could be framed as paternalistic and instead encouraged them to seek opportunities that would allow individuals to decide for themselves how their information should be used. This dovetailed with Alan Westin's claims that most people were not confused about their privacy preferences; rather, they were seeking opportunities to make informed choices about how to exercise their personal preferences. Westin was optimistic about the infomediaries' role in helping regulators and businesses balance consumer privacy concerns with growing economic incentives to share personal information online.[47] "The struggle over privacy today," he told Toby Lester in 2001, "is the struggle over the minds and hearts of the privacy pragmatists."[48] Through their flexible approach, the infomediaries were positioned as enabling exactly this kind of consumer choice.

Thanks to a framework that integrated individual choice into disclosure decisions without undermining e-commerce, the infomediaries enjoyed support from policy makers. Those behind the infomediaries tended to share the position advocated by politicians, including senators Orrin Hatch and Herb Kohl, that self-regulation would be an essential component for achieving robust protections for consumer privacy without strangling innovation.[49] However, while regulators were enthusiastic about industry approaches that would *supplement* government oversight, those in the consumer privacy space sometimes spoke about consumer technologies as *replacements* for ineffective policy measures or as a strategy for avoiding government intervention. Lumeria's Fred Davis, for example, expressed dissatisfaction with the ability of existing privacy laws to protect individuals. Lumeria's contribution, according to Davis, was to offer a solution to privacy and security concerns that did not rely on what he saw as insufficient regulatory protections for consumer privacy.

Others saw infomediaries as working alongside existing regulation to protect consumer privacy without requiring additional regulatory measures. Unlike Davis's assertion that Lumeria would work *despite* laws that were ill-suited to support consumer privacy online, Larry Lozon and Salvatore Stolfo saw their companies, PrivaSeek and iPrivacy, as offering technological support to *strengthen* existing legal infrastructure. Stolfo described iPrivacy's efforts to brief staffers and congressional representatives on their products. iPrivacy was viewed by regulators, he remembered, as the "darling" of privacy-enhancing services because its products complied with existing regulations in the financial sector, thereby making it unnecessary to change policy or develop new regulatory strategies. Stolfo told me about discussions with regulators in which he would emphasize the flexibility of the iPrivacy approach, stressing that "we don't need new policy, we just need new technology."

Technological solutions that place control in the hands of individuals offer a compelling alternative for those skeptical of regulation. The pervasive belief that technology is well suited to address complex social problems is referred to as techno-fundamentalism, which media scholar Siva Vaidhyanathan describes as a "blind faith in technology."[50] Those who take this position support a shift in responsibility away from companies and governments to provide solutions and onto individuals armed with technical tools that allow for choices consistent with their individual preferences and needs. Media scholar Tarleton Gillespie observes a preoccupation with technological solutions can offer seductive fixes that "abrogate the responsibility of both the people involved in the problem and the designers of the technology themselves."[51] By developing new technical tools to address existing challenges, technological approaches that put control in the hands of the individual offer a convenient workaround to regulation. Harvey describes how the fetishization of technology to provide simple solutions to complex problems—an important component of neoliberal thinking—works with market fundamentalism to support a vision of policy making that prefers "consumer choice" or the aggregation of independent consumer decisions as the defining metric for what constitutes a public good.[52]

There are those, however, who support the idea that policy and technology can work in tandem to establish solutions to social problems. Ann Cavoukian describes the importance of commercial technologies that operationalize existing regulation and policy. The Privacy by Design approach, introduced in the previous chapter, is predicated on the idea that new technologies must consider how to build robust privacy protections into products beginning at the design phase. By embedding privacy safeguards in technologies from the outset, Cavoukian argues designers can ensure regulatory compliance through features that facilitate, rather than inhibit, user experience.[53] Despite her long-term role as a regulator, when we spoke in her Toronto office in the fall of 2013, Cavoukian described herself as "respectful" of business interests and positioned herself as a champion of contributions made by those in the consumer privacy space. "In the future" she told me, "regulatory compliance as the sole means of enforcement will not be sufficient." A comprehensive approach, she argued, must make use of technologies and laws that work in tandem to protect user privacy.

At least one infomediary explicitly positioned its services as supporting industry self-regulation. As companies tried to figure out how to engage with consumers online, PrivaSeek suggested that its products created transparency in consumer preferences. Steve Lucas, PrivaSeek's chief information officer, predicted consumers would "walk away from companies that don't respect their privacy."[54] In sharing this concern during a House committee meeting in 1999, Lucas praised the self-regulatory measures taken by online retailers and marketers to safeguard consumer privacy. He offered infomediaries, such as PrivaSeek, as tools to support self-regulation through the provision of technological mechanisms to facilitate user choice and strengthen the regulatory measures already in place. Despite concerns about the value of self-regulatory programs, some of which came from the entrepreneurs behind other infomediary services, Lucas argued that the self-regulation implemented to that point had been effective and simply needed more time to develop before the government introduced additional regulation that could suppress industry growth. He concluded his testimony by noting, "In light of the emergence of viable and innovative technological solutions, as well as the increasing adherence by Web sites to self-regulatory programs, PrivaSeek believes that a legislative mandate governing online privacy protection would be premature at this time."[55] Some representatives on the Senate Judiciary Committee agreed with this assessment and pointed to infomediaries as an example of a technological solution for helping people "assert greater control over their personally identifiable information."[56]

This preference for individual control responds to a disenchantment with government regulation and a trust in free market mechanisms to solve social problems. However, an approach based on the aggregation of consumer choice, Harvey points out, presumes that by recasting something as a commodity, we can rely on the supremacy of market signals to determine how it is most appropriately allocated.[57] The application of ownership rights to personal data demonstrates how susceptible beliefs about privacy are to this way of thinking. The result of this characterization is the reconstruction of individuals, not as citizens, but as consumers and privacy, not as a right, but as a product.[58]

Privacy-Enhancing Technologies: The Unfinished Revolution

In 2000, Anonymizer's Lance Cottrell was optimistic about the future of consumer privacy services, predicting that "in the next five years, the majority of Internet users will be using some form of privacy-enhancing technology."[59] Although Anonymizer did continue to succeed into the 2000s,[60] many other consumer-oriented privacy companies struggled to recruit users or attract venture funding. When the Silicon Valley bubble burst in the early 2000s, privacy-enhancing services joined companies from across the technology sector in a struggle to remain economically viable. The experience of the Canadian anonymizer company Zero-Knowledge Systems (ZKS) at the start of the twenty-first century provides an emblematic case. Despite being lauded by technologists, gaining a following among hackers and privacy advocates,[61] and raising at least US$55 million in venture capital,[62] ZKS's Freedom 1.0 software reportedly sold fewer than fifteen thousand units.[63] In the wake of the dot-com bust, the company reduced the size of its staff from 275 to 50.[64] The company also abandoned plans to take up residence in offices leased in Silicon Valley and cancelled an initial public offering scheduled for late 2001. In response to changes in the sociopolitical environment, ZKS introduced less comprehensive privacy solutions—Freedom 2.0 and Freedom 3.0[65]—to appeal a broader range of consumers, but in 2002 the company abandoned its user-facing technology to focus on privacy solutions for businesses.[66]

Less than a year after Lester's *Atlantic* article about the future of privacy space, several companies he profiled were struggling. Lumeria's Fred Davis remembered having about $15 million invested in his company at the time of the dot-com bust. Davis found that, after the bust, people shied away from making investments in technology; however, he believed he would be able to invest enough of his own assets into Lumeria to keep the company going until the economy recovered. Davis joined others I spoke with in pointing to the effects of September 11, 2001, as the real nail in the coffin of the consumer privacy industry. These entrepreneurs reported that in the aftermath of the four coordinated terrorist attacks by al-Qaeda, investors were hesitant to contribute to services that would facilitate opportunities for anonymity or secrecy online. When the stock markets reopened a week after the attacks, Davis told me, people unloaded tech stocks and Lumeria could not sustain the resulting losses.

Salvatore Stolfo related a similar story. Prior to the 9/11 attacks, he described iPrivacy as having lined up deals with a major U.S. bank and the United States Postal Service. The company had also reportedly recruited about thirty thousand people in Silicon Valley for a pilot test that was scheduled to take place on September 13 or 14. Stolfo said that the crash following the events of September 11 caused their financial partners to pull back temporarily; however, the real damage, he believed, was caused by the introduction of the Patriot Act, which expanded the powers of the U.S. government to engage in surveillance efforts. The legislation, which received near-unanimous support in the Senate and overwhelming support in the House, exemplifies Daniel Solove's thesis that security and privacy are often positioned as conflicting values. Privacy rights, Solove argues, tend to be devalued when weighed directly against a need for security.[67] Many of those I spoke with in the consumer privacy industry recalled seeing support for their products evaporate as political investments shifted toward the physical protection of Americans. Stolfo told me that the passage of the Patriot Act "basically put a chill down the spine of all the lawyers" who did not want to be involved in the provision of private online spaces.

Privada's Rick Jackson shared similar memories regarding the consequences of a change in the political climate around online privacy after the September 11 attacks. Jackson also identified a dramatic shift in the legislative environment as a Republican government took over in 2000 and privacy bills fell off the agenda. "So there was really kind of almost a governmental shift," Jackson told me. "And what we saw with that shift was literally every privacy bill that was looking so promising, that was going to come through, actually went off the floor. I've never seen a legislative agenda just do a 180 turn so quick." According to the former Privada CEO, this shift in attitudes amplified the effects of the dot-com crash on the consumer privacy industry. The result, he said, was that "people became less interested in or less committed to those business deals and so it just became a very unfavorable environment for continued investments in a company like that."

Lance Cottrell offered a slightly different take on how the September 11 attacks influenced public interest in consumer products to support online privacy. He described the attacks as producing a "bifurcation" in the climate around technology, surveillance, and privacy. Although Cottrell agreed with others I spoke with who saw an increase in concern about opportunities for anonymity online, he also described the government response to those events as having spurred a countervailing set of anxieties. "On the one hand," Cottrell told me, you had "the Patriot Act and everyone worrying about terrorism exploding, but at the same time you had this huge number of people who were very concerned about the government's potential to outlaw privacy tools, to crack down on them and all that. We actually saw a spike in users following that."

Since several of these companies were still in beta (or test) mode at the time of the dot-com bust, it is difficult to assess how economically successful they would have been had their growth not been cut short by new political and economic realities. When we spoke over a decade after the tech bust, Ann Cavoukian used the phrase "ahead of their time" to describe the companies in the consumer privacy space at the end of the twentieth century. ZKS's Austin Hill offered a similar rationale in 2001 to account for the company's failure. The company's consumer software, he said, "pushed the boundaries and the envelope in the science of privacy, but at this point it's ahead of its time in terms of market acceptance."[68] There were also those, however, who were skeptical that the public would have paid for services to protect their privacy. Stephanie Perrin remembered asking during her interview prior to taking the job at ZKS, who else was going to buy the product once the cypherpunks had all purchased it. Cavoukian suggested that convincing individuals to pay for privacy-enhancing add-ons may not be the way to build the market for privacy. "Demand is going to go up" she predicted during our discussion, "but the market for it will be on the part of the expectation of the consumer to have businesses offer them privacy protective services as the default."

One possible conclusion is that the market for consumer privacy services failed because people were unwilling to or uninterested in paying to protect their digital privacy. This view supports the privacy paradox: that people say they care about privacy, but are rarely willing to take the extra steps to protect it, particularly if those steps are costly or onerous. Another version of events, however, is the narrative provided by those entrepreneurs I spoke with—a story that suggests changes in the economic and political climate created an inhospitable environment for companies selling digital privacy. One might also be tempted to write off these companies as having little influence due to their limited economic success. A compelling counter narrative, however, is that through efforts to educate the public about the threat of online surveillance, the voices behind these products helped introduce internet privacy as an important social issue and shaped the conversations around the subject. In addition to raising awareness about the importance of privacy online, these companies advanced the argument that individuals were uniquely suited to make decisions regarding the collection and use of their personal information and promoted an economic framework for thinking about the value of digital data—both positions that continue to dominate discussions about online privacy today.

Despite their differences, those behind the anonymizers and infomediaries were united in their belief that the internet did not need to rely on "real" identifiers. These companies shared a perspective that the economic model emerging online—one in which personal information was exchanged for access to "free" content and online identity was tied to individuals' offline identities—was unsustainable. By offering technologies that empowered individuals to control when, how, and with whom their personal information would be shared, anonymizers and infomediaries articulated the importance of reserving space for privacy in a digital economy that was quickly becoming defined by opportunities for consumer surveillance.

The resonance of personal choice with themes of individual freedom and self-determination was attractive to a range of stakeholders, including regulators and marketers. Moreover, opportunities to solve privacy problems through the introduction of new technological platforms and tools were appealing both to those who felt the government had no authority online and to those who believed government interference could stifle economic innovation. As active participants in policy debates, some members of the privacy industry encouraged regulators to seek technological solutions to the problem of online privacy as a strategy to enhance individual self-determination and reduce restrictions on digital retailers and advertisers. By locating individual autonomy in the choices enabled by user-centric technologies, these services alleviated the burden on government and industry to invest in systematic solutions for controlling the use of personal information in the digital environment.

When the political imperative to seek solutions to digital privacy concerns waned at the start of the twenty-first century, much of legislation that had been introduced to address concerns about the security of personal information online expired and privacy slipped from the congressional agenda. The shift in the sociopolitical climate around privacy reduced the attractiveness of privacy-focused businesses to investors, making it difficult for these companies to find funding. After reflecting on the social, political, and economic environment, some entrepreneurs in the consumer privacy industry decided the market for services that helped people manage their privacy, identities, and personal information online was gone. It is possible that as these companies closed shop, their absence left a space in the landscape of voices advocating for consideration of digital privacy and calling attention to the ways in which personal information was being collected and used online.

In the meantime, the political economy of the digital world continued its trend toward privileging visibility over anonymity. The demise of these models—the anonymizer and the infomediary—foretells the emergence of a digital economy where personal information is treated as a form of currency and empowerment is tied to individual choices. The next few years saw the reemergence of companies offering consumer tools and strategies to combat the consequences of unwanted online visibility. The second-generation of the consumer privacy industry, however, was responding to a digital environment with a different set of expectations around visibility. The next chapters explore the challenges facing a new crop of companies trying to sell privacy as a service. When they began to emerge, in the years following the dot-com crash, these companies were facing a different sociocultural context from the one that had given rise to the anonymizers and infomediaries at the end of the twentieth century. The changes in the digital culture meant commercial privacy companies—their presentation of the risks facing individuals online as well as their proposed solutions—took on a distinct form.

PART II

Privacy Goes Public

4

Reputation Defenders

Selling Privacy in Public

In 2009, I began hearing stories that parents were hiring professionals to scrub the social network profiles of their teenage children who
were in the process of preparing college applications. Parents, I was told,
were worried about what admissions officers and, eventually, potential
employers would find when they searched for their children's names
online. Distressed about the possible implications of digital material for
their children's prospects, these parents were rumored to be seeking the
assistance of a new class of web professional to find, cleanse, and rebuild
their kids' online images.

As I sought out individuals and companies who might be doing this
kind of work, I spoke with the head of a firm in the then relatively new
field of online reputation management. He confirmed that his company
occasionally received this type of request from parents; however, the services his company offered, he explained, tended to be too expensive for
the average parent looking to have a few online posts deleted or pictures
removed. The bulk of his clients, he told me, were high-powered professionals, celebrities, athletes, and politicians. At the time of our conversation, the winter of 2010, several politicians were already beginning to
test their feasibility as candidates for the 2012 U.S. election cycle. An
individual considering running for office, the online reputation management professional told me, had sought his company's advice about the
possibility of removing some online content that might hinder a successful bid. After looking at the potential client's case, he told me he had
reported to the client that while burying the offending content might be
possible, it would take a lot of time, effort, and money.

During our conversation, I did not ask who the would-be candidate
was, nor did I attempt to verify the company's client list after we spoke.
The specific details were less interesting to me than what the client's re-

quest and the company's response suggested about the power of online image and the strategies available for its management. For years, large online search platforms such as Google, Yahoo! Search, and Bing have presented themselves as neutral conduits that match people with the digital information they seek. For the vast quantity of digital information contained on the web to be organized and presented in an intelligible manner, these systems evaluate and rank content on factors such as quality, popularity, relevance, and freshness.[1] Algorithms—a general term for the processes and rules through which computational problems are solved[2]—are largely responsible for these calculations. Online reputation management strategies aim to identify and exploit those algorithmic assumptions to help individuals manipulate the information search engines return, effectively allowing them to control their digital image.

Online reputation management—known in the trade press by its shorthand ORM—has grown quickly from a digital cottage industry to a well-funded enterprise.[3] Like the anonymizers and the infomediaries discussed in previous chapters, online reputation management firms address a persistent tension between the rewards and risks of online visibility. Where the first-generation privacy-enhancing tools were embedded within a culture that embraced opportunities for invisibility and anonymous self-expression, the online reputation management industry developed in response to a different set of assumptions regarding the value of being seen online.[4] Following the rise of social network sites, which have altered both the expectations and consequences of online disclosure, these companies respond to a digital culture deeply invested in the benefits of social sharing.

Approaches to privacy predicated on opportunities for anonymity are challenged by norms that treat disclosure as a requirement of participation. Rather than adopting a construction of privacy that negotiates movement between spaces that allow for anonymity and publicity, the online reputation management industry embraces a perception of the internet as a public space. Industry approaches, therefore, offer "managed visibility" and "strategic transparency" as tactics for facilitating privacy in a world where the threat of unwanted exposure can feel inescapable. By exploiting the technological assumptions in online search tools, these interventions use the production and promotion of positive content to bury negative materials deep in search results where they are less likely to be found. The result, the industry argues, is that people can have effective, though not perfect, control over their digital image. In other words, by creating an identity for public consumption, people can carve out opportunities for privacy online.

Through a sustained public pedagogy campaign, this industry has promoted a logic about the necessity of digital image management as a practical response to the seemingly inevitable privacy threats that accompany digital life. In so doing, they have supported a language and a culture of self-promotion as an essential component of contemporary social life. In the next chapter, I focus on the thin line between identity protection and self-promotion to emphasize how the logic and strategies employed to repair and protect a negative online reputation are also used to promote and capitalize on a valuable public image. I begin here, however, by describing how the online reputation management industry emerged to respond to the unique threats introduced by social and interactive media through an approach to privacy that relies on strategies of controlled publicity.

The Threat of a Negative Online Image

In his book *So You've Been Publicly Shamed*, journalist and author Jon Ronson describes the plight of individuals whose lives have been ruined because of a poor online reputation.[5] A culture of outrage supported by tools for the dissemination of digital content, he observes, has encouraged widespread participation in online shaming campaigns. Although some of Ronson's stories are about people whose reputations have been destroyed due to major social or professional indiscretions, he also relates stories where relatively minor misbehaviors are magnified and distorted under the glare of social media. In an interview, Ronson described how the mutual surveillance culture enabled by social media supports the disproportionate punishment of these social transgressions.[6] The personal and professional consequences of digital shaming are woven throughout Ronson's book. In many of the stories he tells, the targets of digital shaming not only face job loss, but also experience social alienation coupled with mental health issues.

Although we often think of privacy breaches as the unwanted publication of otherwise private information, Ronson's most poignant stories focus on incidents that occurred when public information, voluntary supplied, spreads beyond its original context and becomes visible to a broad audience. When a tweet, a post, or a picture shared in a public or semipublic forum goes viral, it tends to be stripped of its original context and deprived of nuance. When reading the stories of reputations destroyed by the unintended and unwanted circulation of digital information, it is hard not to reflect on one's own flippant email exchanges or ill-considered jokes texted to friends—fragments of private conversations whose materiality persists even after the context has faded.

At the end of the twentieth century, the first generation of consumer privacy tools offered protection in part by supporting online identities that were fragmented and fractured. It was an approach that corresponded with a concept of unrestricted identity experimentation fostered by the unique technical affordances of cyberspace. As online social spaces developed, however, scholars began to question the universality of this experience of cyberspace as a world apart.[7] Although many online communities in the 1990s promoted anonymous or pseudonymous participation, some encouraged and even mandated participation under a persistent persona that included information about the user's offline identity.[8] The emergence and popularity of social network sites in the first decade of the twenty-first century further normalized the performance of consistent and coherent identities online.[9] While contemporary platforms such as 4chan, Reddit, and Tumblr embrace anonymous and pseudonymous participation, the creation of digital profiles that reproduce recognizable elements of one's offline self now hold a prominent place in digital cultures.[10] As a result, companies invested in helping clients protect their online image in the contemporary landscape rely on an operational definition of privacy that varies in important ways from the one adopted by their predecessors.

Commentators often point to social network sites as evidence of a cultural moment deeply invested in (over) sharing. These platforms are credited with introducing a unique set of impulses that compel us to reveal more of ourselves in more public ways. For example, Mark Zuckerberg, founder of the social network giant Facebook, connects the rising popularity of social media with corresponding changes in social norms around sharing.[11] Although social media does not create the desire to share—exchanging personal details is a well-worn strategy for establishing intimacy and building social bonds[12]—the cultural dominance of these networking platforms has helped normalize rituals of sharing in public forums. As a result, such platforms have altered the contexts, and thereby the stakes, of information disclosure.

Although social network sites can be used to find new friends and make new connections, these platforms are more popularly used to support existing relationships.[13] Common characteristics of social network sites—such as biographies, profile pictures, and "friends" lists—encourage the construction of a cohesive and recognizable profile.[14] Not only does the inclusion of identifiable information make people findable on social media, but those behind social network platforms often credit the practice of using of "real names" with curbing antisocial behaviors such as trolling, flaming, and cyberbullying.[15] And while the creation of hospitable social environments is a laudable goal, there is limited evidence that restricting anonymous participation is itself sufficient to ensure good behavior.[16] Moreover, consideration of their funding structures suggests social network sites have additional motivations for promoting the use of a consistent identity within and across digital platforms. By tracking and attributing online behaviors to an individual, social network sites can target ads within their platforms or can sell user profiles to digital marketers.[17] The economic value of social media sites depends largely on their ability to capture this information and connect it to a unique profile.[18]

Regardless of the motivations, social network platforms have helped normalize practices in which the publication and sharing of information under a consistent and recognizable identity is more than a convention; it is a social expectation. And while interactive platforms allow users to design carefully crafted, reflexively developed profiles, the sense of control one may feel over these online identities is largely an illusion. When concealed tracking tools allow third parties to capture, aggregate, and analyze online behaviors to create identity profiles that inform the content individuals receive, it is difficult to argue that the user is in command. When content shared with a small group of friends can be stored, copied, and accessed beyond the audience for which it was intended, assertions of autonomy based on control are undermined.[19] Strategies of engagement supported by social media heighten the risk that, when used in ways that ignore individuals' intentions and preferences, the visibility of digital content can lead to undesirable consequences. The results can be as dramatic as a ruined reputation or as seemingly mundane as an advertisement that reappears across the web. Both, however, demonstrate how personal information is being accessed and interpreted without individuals' explicit consent.

Digital venues often do double (or triple) duty as spaces where individuals craft professional profiles, engage with friends and family, and explore their identities. These practices do not always sit comfortably alongside one another, particularly when private moments unintentionally become part of a public image. The online reputation management industry offers strategies to help clients exert control in instances when the balance that enables ideal privacy levels has been upset. Although much of the content posted online languishes in obscurity, noticed and engaged with by a limited audience, the ease with which digital content is replicated and disseminated means it can quickly take on a life of its own. The power that comes with being able to build one's own web presence is complicated when doing so occurs within an environment where information can stick to an individual long after its original context has faded.

Reconstructing Boundaries: Learning to Ignore and Working to Forget

In 2006, Michael Fertik founded the leading online reputation management company Reputation.com (originally ReputationDefender) in response to what he saw as the continuing and compounding negative effects of persistent and searchable digital information. "It felt un-American that when the conduct was online, it could have permanent effects on the speaker and the victim," Fertik told Jeffrey Rosen in a 2010 interview. "The right to new beginnings and the right to self-definition," he continued, "have always been among the most beautiful American ideals."[20] Fertik was particularly troubled by the ways online actions could follow children and teenagers beyond youth and into adulthood.

This perspective on the enduring consequences of digital information recalls a parable that often pops up in discussions about reputation.[21] The story begins with a man, who is sometimes a priest and sometimes a rabbi, asking a child to tear open a sack or pillow that is filled with feathers. Once the feathers have blown away, the man asks the child to gather them all up and return them to the sack. When the child announces the impossibility of the task, the man responds with some version of the following: "Such as it is with gossip. It's easy to spread, but much harder to get back." And so it is with digital information: once something is published online, where it can be duplicated and shared, deleting it is a task that can feel on par with gathering errant feathers. Since this parable predates the advent of the web, however, it is vital to consider what makes online reputations unique.

Over time, societies develop structures—physical, legislative, technological, and normative—that, although imperfect guarantors of privacy, support collective understandings about the information, spaces, and behaviors that are generally considered to be public. Although Western modernity is identified as having public-private boundaries that are more clearly defined than those in the premodern period,[22] these, too, are the result of negotiations regarding society's structural and cultural organization. Even in spaces where these borders appear well defined, the introduction of a new technology often necessitates a reassertion or reconsideration of those boundaries. Take, for example, the case of photography in semipublic spaces such as gym changing rooms or public bathrooms. There is an expectation, perhaps supported by institutional rules, that people do not bring cameras into these facilities. This accepted practice, however, required explicit renegotiation and enforcement when the widespread adoption of camera phones introduced recording devices in these areas.[23]

Just as the introduction of a new technology can disturb the physical boundaries created to ensure the preservation of privacy in offline spaces, the unwritten social rules or norms that allow for some measure of anonymity in public spaces often translate poorly into mediated environments. Although we are not technically invisible in most offline public spaces, the feeling of anonymity we often experience in public comes from social conventions that mean we are generally ignored by others who are too polite, busy, or uninterested to pay attention to our actions or conversations. Sociologist Erving Goffman referred to this phenomenon of mutual disregard in public space as "civil inattention."[24] When riding the subway, for example, we understand that the conversation occurring between two people seated beside us is not intended for our ears. Even though we can hear the words being exchanged, Goffman observed most people will do their best to ignore them. When information is posted online, however, the boundaries that define an intended audience can be less apparent. Certainly, an email, text, or a private message has a clearly intended addressee, but what happens when those conversations are forwarded to others? How do we interpret exchanges occurring in semipublic spaces such as a Twitter feed, Facebook wall, or Instagram stream? Exactly how public are those conversations?

Transferring the logic of civil inattention online is further complicated by the proliferation of digital technologies, often in our pockets, that are constantly paying attention. In spaces populated with connected devices, our actions are no longer quite as discrete and information about our behaviors is no longer quite as ephemeral. Philosopher of technology Helen Nissenbaum writes that "with digital technologies, the observers might be coordinated: networked systems of video cameras, footage stored and analyzed at a central point, able to be recorded and conjoined with past records."[25] This ability to track actions across time and space facilitates a blurring of contexts in which the narrative of daily life is not segmented or interrupted by physical boundaries such as time and space. The persistence of information across these borders further reduces the power of civil inattention to act as an effective barrier against unwanted visibility.

In his book *Delete: The Virtue of Forgetting in the Digital Age*, internet policy scholar Viktor Mayer-Schönberger argues that the ability to forget is an essential aspect of society.[26] Forgetting, he argues, is what allows us to forgive as a community and evolve as individuals. Technological forgetting, on the other hand, is often viewed as the result of a bug or glitch. It's what happens when a hard drive crashes or a latté is accidentally spilled on a laptop. The plummeting cost of digital storage has made it less expensive to save by default rather than deliberating over the value of each individual piece of content.[27] In the digital era, it is easier—and often less costly—to store information than it is to delete it. When the functionally unlimited storage capacity of digital media is combined with search capabilities, the consequences for personal evolution can be profound. The persistence of digital content, which adds additional complexity to attempts at online identity management, have made it increasingly difficult, as Michael Fertik observed, to dissociate oneself from past actions.

Just as the introduction of social network sites shifted the practices and consequences of disclosure, the ubiquity of search engines has transformed the way we organize and access information. Media scholar Siva Vaidhyanathan, for example, has described the powerful role Google plays in shaping the contemporary information landscape. "If Google is the dominant way we navigate the Internet, and thus the primary lens through which we experience both the local and the global," Vaidhyanathan writes, "then it has remarkable power to set agendas and alter perceptions."[28] Search engines not only have tremendous power in determining the visibility of digital content, they also allow information to be "discovered" with limited effort.[29] The availability of digital search means people are no longer required to know exactly what they are looking for when they research another person. Instead, an online search for an individual's name can lead to serendipitous or unexpected results, including publicly available information about marriages, home purchases, gun ownership, arrests, and bankruptcies. Although this information is part of the public record, its searchability in digital databases makes it imminently more findable than when access requires purposeful engagement with a public records office.

The ease with which this information can be found once it is digitized challenges the legal principle of "practical obscurity," which recognizes the type of privacy afforded to information that is publicly available but not easily accessed without burdensome effort.[30] Like civil inattention, practical obscurity does not make actions or information invisible; rather, it facilitates privacy by raising the barriers to information discovery. The near-perfect memory of digital media coupled with the ease of recall facilitated by search not only challenges social norms that encourage us to forget or ignore information unintended for wide public consumption, it also challenges existing laws that aim to balance rights to free speech with the value of a personal reputation.

Having completed a law degree at Harvard University before starting Reputation.com, Michael Fertik was particularly bothered by what he saw as the inadequacy of existing laws to address the realities of the online environment. "Right now," he told me during a 2013 conversation at the company's Redwood City offices, "the law is such that if there is something actually found to be libelous in a court, it will not be removed from the internet." In the United States, the difficulty with mandating content removal is due in part to Section 230 of the Communications Decency Act of 1996, which states, "No provider or user of an interactive computer service shall be treated as the publisher or speaker of any information provided by another information content provider."[31] Interpretations of this statute have effectively insulated websites from responsibility for content posted on their platforms. By positioning these online publishers as neutral information hosts, this approach has made it possible to assign responsibility for content to individual contributors rather than to those hosting the site itself.[32] The law, which is designed to promote free speech online, has made it difficult to compel websites to remove content, including that which shames, harasses, or demeans.

Efforts to fight a negative digital image through more traditional channels can be slow and ineffective. Legal maneuvers to get unwanted content removed can generate more visibility for that material—a version of what is sometimes referred to as the Streisand effect.[33] This term refers to singer Barbra Streisand's efforts to have a picture of her home, which had been posted online as part of an environmental survey, removed from the web. The response from those concerned about the consequences of these actions for freedom of information and speech was to spread the digital image, thereby increasing its visibility. The Streisand effect describes any incident where the use of legal tactics to remove information from the internet functions instead to increase its visibility.[34] Because of these challenges for dealing with unwanted content through legal channels, online reputation management firms have developed strategies that operate outside the court system for addressing such cases.

As courts grapple with how to apply legal precedent in a digital environment or draft new laws that fit the current technical context, online reputation management companies have intervened.[35] Much as the companies behind the first-generation consumer privacy tools argued they were addressing the gap created by insufficient attempts at industry self-regulation coupled with government efforts that were too slow to keep pace with technological change, the online reputation management industry emerged to respond to a perceived lack of opportunities for redress when individuals found themselves to be the targets of negative online content. Reputation.com and other companies in this industry present their solutions as practical and expedient remedies for victims of unwanted online visibility who have found existing solutions inadequate for addressing their problems. These companies aim to offer control in a digital environment where the ability to manage the flow of information and impressions often seems impossible.

Managing the Google-Sphere: Claiming Your Space and Telling Your Story

When he was a college senior Patrick Ambron, along with a few friends, began developing a tool that would address negative search results to help people repair or improve their online image. These efforts eventually resulted in the decision to found the online reputation management company BrandYourself. When I visited the BrandYourself offices in 2013, I asked Ambron about the motivation behind his decision to start the company. In response, Ambron evoked a popular industry metaphor: the digital doppelgänger. Before he co-founded BrandYourself in 2009, Ambron had a friend who was having difficulty getting an internship position. Pete Kistler had been turned down for several jobs for which he seemed to be a good candidate. Kistler, who went on to co-found BrandYourself with Ambron, was encouraged by a friend to look himself up online. When he Googled himself to see if there might be something in the search results that was throwing up a red flag for employers, Kistler found that the stories occupying the top results were about a drug dealer in Florida who shared his name. "Lots of people [are] like my co-founder Pete," Ambron told me. "He couldn't get an internship because he was being mistaken for a criminal with the same name." Kistler had found his digital doppelgänger: someone who was disrupting his reputation because of his prominence in search results for the name they shared.[36]

In interviews, public talks, and editorials, members of the online reputation management industry warn about the negative consequences of failing to control one's "name space." This term refers to the virtual real estate connected to an individual's name, including search results, web addresses, and social media profiles. In addition to "digital doppelgänger" and "name space," industry representatives use terms such as "digital DNA," "digital footprint," "digital shadow," and "digital tattoo" to stress the potential dangers posed by the perpetual availability of information. Digital cultures scholar Sally Wyatt writes that metaphors are powerful tools in shaping how we understand digital media. Policy makers, industry spokespeople, and journalists, Wyatt argues, use metaphors to help anchor expectations of unstable, uncertain, and unfamiliar technologies. The metaphors used by the reputation management professionals as their industry was emerging perform a similar function: they help make the abstract risk of a negative online image concrete and recognizable.

Metaphors, however, do more than simply describe conceptual ideas in concrete terms. The normative assumptions of metaphors, Wyatt writes, can guide science and policy in ways that reconstruct the imaginary as reality.[37] The pervasiveness of terms such as "doppelgänger," "footprint," and "shadow" in the industry reveal how online reputation management companies articulate the unique threats to privacy and identity posed by digital technologies. Moreover, they play a central role in how the industry constructs and markets its solutions. By evoking images of shadows and footprints, the reputation management industry warns that everyone has a digital identity and, perhaps more important, that those identities can be hard to shake. Even for people who are careful about the information they provide online or who opt out of the social web altogether, there are reputational risks: failure to occupy your name space, the industry warns, opens the possibility that someone else will occupy it for you. These metaphors help cultivate a pervasive sense of reputational insecurity—a persistent vulnerability to online image crises.

The Reputation.com and BrandYourself offices are similar to those depicted in movies and televisions shows about Silicon Valley. In Reputation.com's Redwood City headquarters, desks are clustered, separated by low partitions, and surrounded by meeting rooms where walls are either windows or white boards. Interior walls are painted in vibrant colors, and there are common workspaces scattered throughout the office. On the East Coast, the BrandYourself office I visited in 2013 was housed in loft-style building in New York City's NoHo district and had the feel of a conventional tech start-up. Wood floors and brick walls surrounded tables where employees worked on laptops. There was a seating area equipped with comfortable couches and a large flat screen TV. The space was open, and only the offices and meeting rooms along the back wall had doors. Like many contemporary tech companies, Reputation.com and BrandYourself are not in the business of creating material products (i.e., those requiring factory production and assembly). Instead, these companies produce digital reputations.

Across the ORM industry, people describe an online reputation as comprising any information found through a digital search. Although this characterization has overlaps with academic definitions that refer to reputations as the collective opinions others share about a person,[38] the industry definition focuses on information that is easily accessible using digital tools. Members of this industry argue that the power of search engines to collect and aggregate information from all corners of the web has changed how we relate to others. "A résumé is no longer the piece of paper you send," Michael Fertik observed in 2008. "It's your top 10 results when [prospective employers] Google search your name."[39] Noting the ubiquitous practice of conducting an online search for those we have just met or are about to meet—a custom sometimes called the "Google handshake"—the industry encourages individuals to approach their online image with the same purposefulness and precision used to manage their professional image.[40]

Just as the goal of public relations is to influence the *media* environment, online reputation management focuses on shaping the *digital media* environment to promote a positive client image. There are three related activities in this process. The first is identifying and assessing one's online image. This step is followed by the careful construction of a preferred personal narrative that is embedded in digital content. The final step involves the promotion of that content disseminated via various digital channels. Together, the industry proposes, these strategies allow individuals to exercise some control over how they are presented online and to respond to and defend themselves against an assault on their digital image. The services of a reputation management professional can be retained either in response to the presence of negative content or as a proactive measure to defend against the possible emergence of unwanted information. When we spoke in 2013, Stephen Hess, a product manager at Reputation.com, described how the company's ReputationDefender product supports clients' online image: "ReputationDefender is focused on the information that shows up in search. So when you Google someone's name," Hess asked, "what shows up? . . . [ReputationDefender] seeks to help you monitor how that information is shifting and understand the significance of people searching for you and how that could affect your personal life and commerce and how to get jobs. And then we have tools to help you put your best foot forward by creating professional biographies and helping you groom your social networking profiles."

Other ORM companies offer similar products and services. When first registering an account with BrandYourself, for example, clients are invited to review the top results in a Google search for their name. They indicate whether each result returned through the search is positive, negative, or "not me." The "not me" category is treated as equally important to the other two categories since the company argues that irrelevant content which confuses searchers or dilutes the continuity of one's narrative—perhaps introduced by a digital doppelgänger—can be as harmful to one's digital reputation as negative content. After the client has evaluated their search results, BrandYourself provides a reputation score—that is very similar in appearance to a credit score—to indicate the strength of the client's online visibility. Accompanying this metric are tips, strategies, and tools to improve that score.

The strategies used by online reputation management companies to protect clients' identities borrow heavily from the field of public relations, where a strong brand identity is presented as essential for weathering a crisis. Many online reputation management companies have both individual and corporate clients. The techniques used to create, monitor, repair, and defend the online reputations of individuals overlap with the strategies employed for commercial clients. During my interview in 2014 with Chris Martin, CEO of the company Reputation Hawk, he noted that while the interests of individuals and companies may differ slightly—businesses, for example, tend to be more concerned with online product and service reviews—the approach his company takes to support a business does not differ dramatically from that used to help an individual. In both cases, the goal is to create positive content along a defined narrative and disseminate that content through carefully selected media channels.

Within the ORM industry, a damaged reputation is viewed as the result of content that draws unwanted attention and is out of line with an individual's preferred personal narrative. Whether responding to a crisis or preparing for an impending threat, these companies suggest that strengthening one's reputation includes the cultivation of a narrative that defines who that person is. Online reputation management firms encourage the creation and publication of content that supports this effort. Many firms offer services that will produce content such as websites, press releases, or social media profiles on their clients' behalf. BrandYourself, one of the few companies to offer a do-it-yourself platform, provides templates that individuals can use to create personalized content for use in their own profiles, but will take on some of these tasks if clients sign up for a paid membership.

Reputation management firms' efforts to help clients distinguish and articulate their so-called authentic narrative self represents the industrialization of a practice recognized by sociologists as central to the project of modern identity construction. In *Modernity and Self-Identity: Self and Society in the Late Modern Age*, sociologist Anthony Giddens describes identity as a *reflexive project* whereby individuals engage in an ongoing process of creating and revising a coherent personal narrative.[41] Giddens argues that the late modern period differs from previous eras in that it offers people the freedom to select from among a plurality of narrative possibilities through which to construct their biography.

As discussed in chapter 1, a defining characteristic of the late modern period is the proliferation of what Giddens calls lifestyles—the cohesive sets of practices that provide materiality to the narratives that make up a person's identity.[42] Here the strategies offered by the reputation management industry and Giddens's articulation of the process of modern identity formation converge: just as reputation management firms encourage clients to strengthen their online image to defend against the risks of undesirable content, Giddens observes the importance of lifestyle cohesion for avoiding the risks implicit in an environment where identities are constructed rather than given.[43] Together, these theoretical and practical approaches stress the benefits of adopting prefabricated scripts to facilitate the construction of a coherent identity that will be recognizable and compelling to others.

Machine Readable: Ensuring Algorithmic Authenticity

In addition to creating an appealing image for consumption by others, the online reputation management industry argues that the materials associated with an online identity must also be attractive to search engines. More specifically, narratives must be visible to the algorithms that inform search results, a process media scholar Tarleton Gillespie describes as becoming "algorithmically recognizable."[44] Given the tremendous power search engines possess to shape the way individuals experience the web,[45] ORM companies work to ensure that content, carefully crafted to reflect the individual's preferred image, rises to the top of relevant searches. Most of these companies do not spend the bulk of their energies trying to have content removed, which can be challenging and time-consuming.[46] Instead, they flood the web with positive content that will obscure negative material by burying it in the deep pages of search results. Using a strategy called search engine optimization (SEO), they aim to produce content that will be visible to and highly ranked by search algorithms. In doing so, online reputation management firms help clients influence the information environment surrounding their name space.

In the late 1990s, researchers identified the "law of surfing" based on observations that "an individual will continue to surf until the expected cost of continuing is perceived to be larger than the discounted expected value of the information to be found in the future."[47] This general idea, originally published in *Science*, has been extrapolated into what might usefully be referred to as the "law of search"—the perception that people focus their time and attention on content appearing on the first or second page of search results. Commonly referred to as the "Google truth," this observation recognizes a pervasive belief that search engines list the most relevant, useful, and authoritative content early in the results. Moreover, it validates approaches to image management that encourage burying unfavorable content and promoting positive information so that it appears at the top of search results.[48] Since SEO operates on the logic that people tend not to dig deeply into results, particularly if they find relevant content near the start of their search, if negative content can be "buried" on the later pages of results it is far less likely to be discovered during an online investigation.

The strategy of shaping search results so that they conform to a client's preferred version of reality mimics long-established public relations strategies. Ivy Lee, a pioneer in the field of public relations, described what he saw as the fallacy of objective reality: the impossibility of presenting all possible facts coupled with individuals' propensity to interpret available information in terms of their own interests. "To present a complete and candid survey of all the facts concerning any subject," Lee wrote in *Publicity: Some of the Things It Is and Is Not,* "is a human impossibility."[49] He continued, "All I can do is to give you my interpretation of the facts."[50] Search engine optimization applies a similar logic to the digital information landscape. Search engines were developed to help index, sort, and display the vast quantity of information available online. Using tactics associated with search engine optimization, the online reputation management industry works to influence this process on behalf of its clients. Through the promotion of client favored content, ORM companies adopt Lee's strategy of using the media to present a preferred version of reality.

While the theory behind the creation of content that will be attractive to search engines may sound straightforward, achieving desired results is far more complicated. Proprietary algorithms weigh many factors to determine the results that will be returned in response to a query and the order in which they will appear. The algorithms of dominant search engines are not publicly disclosed and are adjusted frequently to discourage manipulation.[51] SEO strategies, then, aim to create content that appeals to the stable or predictable features of search algorithms. To capitalize on search engines' favorable treatment of recognized media outlets, for example, the ORM industry suggests creating profiles on established websites, including popular social media platforms such as LinkedIn, Twitter, and Facebook. These sites, which are recognized by search engines as trustworthy and authoritative, tend to be returned high in search results.[52] Search algorithms also tend to privilege sites with high visibility, a feature that is operationalized in part by the number of external websites that link to the content. While individuals can achieve this by linking their online profiles to one another, online reputation management companies have more systematic and sophisticated methods for establishing the popularity of a site. For example, Chris Martin told me about a team of employees at Reputation Hawk that build links between sites across the web. The result, he said, is that as "search engines view these links to this new content, the search engines index that content, and then you basically start to see [that content] move higher in that person's search results."

By taking advantage of existing platforms that allow users to create profiles, highly curated content can become part of a seemingly organic online image. To exert further control over the media environment, some ORM companies have partnerships with online publishers through which they can disseminate content. Brand.com, the now-closed "full service" ORM company that opened shop in 2009 as Reputation Changer, reported in its promotional materials that it had connections with influential bloggers who helped distribute its content. The company also advertised its ownership of news sites, which supplied "independent editorial content" alongside "sponsored posts."[53] According to a press release, the company's "philosophy is that the only way to *control* the media is to *become* the media."[54] Chris Martin described his programmers as publishing content through the company's "networks of business-oriented sites." Reputation Hawk would "also create new domains, new hosts, for clients and basically take the articles and place them on these sites." Similarly, Reputation.com reportedly has ties to hundreds of websites, which the company uses to "cross-pollinate links" and raise the position of the content in search results.[55]

Since search engines promote themselves as impartial conveyers of relevant information, they tend to be sensitive to promotional or empty content that pollutes the so-called organic search results with inauthentic material that takes space away from more meaningful results. Search engine algorithms are designed to ignore content that seems to be a carbon copy of material that appears elsewhere on the web. They also actively discourage link building, a practice that tricks algorithms and users into overestimating the importance or relevance of content. Google is known to be vigilant in punishing websites that attempt to manipulate the algorithm through the creation of spurious content by reducing their visibility in search results.[56] Strategies that use link-based optimization, therefore, must consider the relevance and quality of the material they are linking to in order avoid being disciplined by search engines.

The advice provided by ORM companies on identity construction encourages vigilance around what could be called "algorithmic authenticity." Chris Martin described the content creation strategies at Reputation Hawk as attentive to the efforts of search engines to remove promotional content from their organic results. The process of generating "client approved" content, which begins with a careful evaluation of the client's image, relies on the labor-intensive process of unique content creation:

> It starts with writers who are typically based usually in the U.S., U.K., Canada . . . and the writer takes a look at the client's website and they have to create new content. The reason they have to create new content is we can't take an article authored by a client's website and replicate it on twenty or thirty sites and just fill the client search results up with that. Google has content algorithms so all of that just gets washed out of Google. So basically what we have to do is start with the writer. The writer has to take a look at the company, learn about the company, learn about the person, and then write articles, blog posts, you know things about the person, you know each article has to be different. It can be the same, say generally the same things, but it just can't be a copy of the article—the sentence structure, everything has to really vary.

Rather than simply flooding the web with vacuous content intended to drive down negative search results, most online reputation management firms stress the importance of creating "quality content" that paints a consistent and appealing image of the individual or company. Consequently, narrative material must appear organic and authentic *both* to the search algorithms that catalog it and discard irrelevant or duplicate content and to the human audiences that evaluate its legitimacy.

In a 2013 story for the NPR program *All Things Considered* about the online reputation industry, reporter Steve Henn spoke with the founders of BrandYourself. Like me, Henn was told how Pete Kistler's failed job search crystallized the need for a company that would help clients' repair their online reputations. Henn listed several media outlets where this story had been repeated, but revealed that he had not been able to find evidence of Pete Kistler the drug dealer. "Still," Henn reported, "this tale of the two Pete Kistlers has become the Internet's approximation of truth."[57] The *ubiquity* of this narrative, in other words, had become more important than its *veracity*. Henn's inability to verify the story is beside the point. In fact, as Henn astutely noted, the illusive Pete Kistler provides a perfect allegory for the strategies employed across the online reputation management industry. "You take the story about yourself that you want to tell," Henn observed, "then repeat it—until that's the only story about you anyone sees."[58] For the online reputation management industry, the creation of an authentic digital image similarly relies on reshaping the online reality until it conforms to the client's preferred narrative.

Controlling the Narrative: Privacy through Strategic Transparency

Unlike the approach taken by the anonymizers and infomediaries, which promised privacy based on a choice of when to be visible, the online reputation management industry aims to provide clients with control over information that is already public. One representative, for example, described his company's approach to me as a strategy for maximizing individual control: "We believe that everyone has the right to [protect their reputation] online. We believe if people write things about you, you have the right to confront that and to manage it and control it, because if you don't do that then you are exactly who Google says you are. And that could be anything, which is not necessarily an accurate portrayal. So, our mission is to allow people to control and manage their own reputation." Framing privacy as a function of personal control is a common strategy across the industry. When I asked about BrandYourself's mission, Patrick Ambron replied, "Simply put, we just want to make sure everybody can kind of take control over what happens when someone looks them up online." The premise—one that echoes those put forward by the anonymizers and infomediaries—is empowerment through the ability to manage the circulation of one's digital image.

In his seminal work *The Future of Reputation: Gossip, Rumor, and Privacy on the Internet*, legal scholar Daniel Solove describes online reputation management services as having the potential to provide informal and efficient tools that can work alongside legal reforms to help people address the presence of unwanted digital information.[59] By burying this information in the rarely accessed recesses of search results, companies hope to recreate online the experiences of civil inattention and practical obscurity that occur offline. It is a version of control that acknowledges that some content will be beyond an individual's capacity to manage. By hiding information deep in search results, however, companies aim to do two things: make it less findable and signal its lack of importance.

This practice replicates efforts to achieve privacy in public and thereby parallels strategies of self-presentation common in the offline world.

By proactively managing the creation, publication, and promotion of positive online content, ORM professionals argue that it may be possible to drown out unwanted information about past transgressions even if that information cannot technically be removed or erased. This strategy is a version of obfuscation—hiding information within an overwhelming amount of unrelated or irrelevant content. In their handbook *Obfuscation: A User's Guide for Privacy and Protest,* Finn Brunton and Helen Nissenbaum define obfuscation as "the deliberate addition of ambiguous, confusing, or misleading information to interfere with surveillance and data collection."[60] They describe efforts for maintaining privacy by overwhelming the observer with irrelevant material as a well-worn strategy for counteracting information asymmetries—not by becoming invisible, but by creating confusion around one's visibility. Strategies identified by the online reputation management industry for achieving some semblance of control over one's digital image echo many of the approaches offered in Brunton and Nissenbaum's handbook. Instead of offering irrelevant or confusing material to obscure the visibility of unwanted information, however, ORM strategies distribute positive or neutral content designed to minimize the prominence of negative material.

This form of obfuscation is a suitable strategy for an industry that sees visibility and sharing as inescapable cornerstones of the contemporary digital landscape. The entrepreneurs in this industry are not alone in such an assessment. Media commentator Jeff Jarvis identifies offering ourselves up for public consumption as a growing obligation. "We'll get to a point in society," he has reportedly said, "where a decision not to share will be seen as antisocial."[61] ORM companies agree that, given the pleasures and obligations of being visible online, we've reached a point where, for most people, some degree of online exposure is inevitable. Therefore, they promote the power of a well-crafted online presence to obscure unwanted information that cannot be erased and limit its circulation. One company representative told me that "being known online is not necessarily a bad thing as long as you do your best to protect your image, control it, manage it, and ensure the best information is out there."

Although industry accounts focus on strategies to tackle the circulation of information that is already moving through the digital environment, they pay less attention to efforts that might reduce one's digital footprint. In her work on digital media abstention, media scholar Laura Portwood-Stacer presents the decision to avoid social media platforms as a performative act of consumer resistance. This choice, which Portwood-Stacer calls media refusal, is "a kind of conscious disavowal that involves the recognition that non-use signifies something socially or politically meaningful about the non-user."[62] The decision not to engage in practices of disclosure and information sharing is, as Portwood-Stacer describes it, a political act. For those who promote online reputation management, however, strategies of opting out are treated as both ineffective and dangerous. These parties stress the negative consequences that can result from a person's failure to occupy their "digital real estate." Referring to the dangers of invisibility, Patrick Ambron argues, "Good results help as much as bad results hurt you. . . . Not existing or being completely irrelevant is also harmful."[63] Not only does industry logic assert that abstaining from digital life introduces the opportunity for someone else, perhaps a doppelgänger, to occupy a person's name space, these companies also cite the social skepticism that confronts those without an online presence. Opting out of information sharing, which was considered by those behind the first-generation privacy-enhancing technologies as a viable strategy for maintaining control in an overexposed online world, has been recast in this environment as a threat to effective self-presentation. This view, which I consider further in the following chapter, positions visibility as a requirement of contemporary life—a perspective consistent with the logics of an attention economy in which value is derived from the ability to commend audience attention.[64]

By allowing for carefully selected parts of our lives to be publicized, the industry logic goes, we create space for the information we wish to keep private. This strategy parallels a public relations approach known as "radical transparency" in which companies attempt to mediate crises by getting out in front of negative stories through the disclosure of information that appears genuine, but ultimately allows them to define the narrative.[65] The underlying rationale is that the strategic disclosure of information allows for the promotion of an authentic, but highly controlled, narrative. When applied to individuals, rather than companies, this tactic may more appropriately be titled "strategic transparency." People are encouraged to bury content that does not support their desired image by producing and sharing carefully selected information to create an identity that is consistent, legible, and palatable for a broad audience, but one that does not violate norms about the types of information deemed appropriate to share. These strategies represent a digital version of space-making behaviors, or what Irwin Altman called boundary regulation, that aim to foster a preferred degree of visibility.[66] The underlying principle is that by revealing enough of ourselves to satisfy the curiosity of others, we can divert attention away from the elements of our lives we wish to keep private. This strategy of privacy through publicity suggests, following the philosopher Michael Warner, that engagement within publics is necessary to "enable privacy."[67]

The online reputation management industry's strategies for balancing the social rewards of visibility with the associated risks of overexposure by carving out space for privacy in public, represent industrialized versions of strategies practiced in everyday life. Digital media researcher Alice Marwick identifies an approach to visibility, common among the technorati of Silicon Valley, which differentiates between making information public and publicizing that information.[68] While public information is anything that is viewable, publicized information is that which is purposefully promoted with the aim of achieving wide visibility. Marwick describes efforts among members of this tech-savvy community to share—or publicize—some details of their lives as a strategy for shielding other elements from public view. While Marwick's respondents are part of a culture that often demands digital visibility as an informal condition of employment, danah boyd has observed similar practices in young people's use of social media.[69] boyd notes that teens share certain content publicly so that it is visible to parents and other authority figures. In doing so, they obscure private profiles intended to be found and seen only by their friends. boyd and Marwick refer to this strategy of hiding information in plain sight as "social steganography."[70]

Writing in the *New York Times*, Valeriya Safronova identifies the use of finstas—or fake Instagram accounts—for a generation of young people seeking opportunities for authentic self-expression online.[71] Safronova describes these accounts—which are private and tend to have fewer followers than users' primary profiles—as revealing a truer, less performative version of reality.[72] Strategies of hiding private information behind a veneer of publicity are not, however, always effective, nor are they universally accessible. While some of the challenges are unique to the digital world, others highlight persistent challenges faced by those who find themselves more subject to observation and less able to hide in public.

The Technological and Social Limits of Strategic Transparency

The strategies offered by the online reputation management industry provide a practical method for addressing unwanted digital content—at least temporarily. Those in the industry acknowledge that strategies to bury, rather than remove, undesirable online content do not provide comprehensive protection. There is always a chance that the information will be uncovered through more effective or persistent research strategies. Additionally, changes in search algorithms or website settings can cause previously buried content to appear at the top of search results. This was the case for a British solicitor who was suspended for six months because of "accounting irregularities." After he was deemed "fully rehabilitated" by the Law Society, he was permitted to return to work. When a popular law journal digitized its collection, however, reports of the solicitor's suspension, which had effectively been erased from his professional record, appeared at the top of online search results for his name, making the story a part of his digital record.[73] Some of Brand.com's clients reportedly had a similar experience when Google changed its algorithm, thereby undermining the strategies used by the online reputation management company to bury unwanted content.[74]

When I asked about the limitations of their services, industry representatives acknowledged the technological barriers that impede efforts to influence the digital landscape. Some of those I spoke with described the strategies their companies offer as a partial but immediate remedy to deal with a problem that currently lacks other viable solutions. Chris Martin described online reputation management, including the work done by his company Reputation Hawk, as more of a "Band-Aid" than a permanent fix: "You can get something where the client is satisfied, where whatever this was that was at the top of the search results is now out of the top twenty, so she knows only one percent of people who search for her will come across that content and then all of a sudden it can pop back up. So it's not like a permanent solution. I mean that's definitely an imperfect situation." Michael Fertik offered a different metaphor to make a similar point regarding the limits of strategies that simply bury digital content deeper on webpages. "Technology cannot, at scale, remove content that is unlawful from the Internet," he noted. "Technology cannot compel the removal of content that is unlawful from the Internet. It doesn't mean it's perfect. . . . It's never a blanket; it's a net, but it's a pretty good net." While using search engine optimization strategies to bury unwanted content might not allow for the comprehensive or permanent removal of information, industry advocates argue that these approaches offer a timely remedy for a problem that is likely to compound the longer it goes unaddressed.

While the representatives I talked to spoke about challenges introduced by digital tools, there are additional social considerations that may limit the effectiveness of efforts to shape the digital environment. The responsibility to make one's image available for public consumption, for example, raises an important set of issues regarding the ways people experience visibility. There are those for whom being in public introduces forms of personal risk; for these individuals, presence in public spaces—whether online or offline—can be deeply threatening. Consider legal scholar Deirdre Davis's argument that street harassment causes harm by "genderizing" public spaces.[75] By marking these areas as masculine, practices such as catcalling and other forms of harassment introduce a sense of belonging and ownership that is denied to some populations including, most notably for Davis, African American women.[76] Consider further the ways discourses of safety have been appropriated and employed in debates about access to public restrooms to obscure the dangers transgender people experience in these spaces.[77] The differential experience of public domains in the offline world is replicated online, where many of these same populations are more likely to be the targets of digital harassment, cyber assaults, and trolling.[78] Approaches that point to the occupation of space as a strategy for self-protection risk overlooking the dangers some people experience when navigating digital spaces.

Nevertheless, industrial logics that inform efforts to save a tarnished online image insist on the dangers of choosing not to be public. There is, as one commentator noted, "a terrible irony that people who'd probably wish to remain more private should have to make themselves more public in order to save their damaged reputation."[79] This irony is evident in the story of an American college student whose "mock thesis" about her sexual exploits, in which she detailed and ranked her sexual encounters with a number of student athletes, went viral.[80] Despite the student's explanations that the PowerPoint presentation was a joke intended for the amusement of a few close friends, the document was forwarded beyond its intended audience, eventually being picked up and published by online media outlets such as *Deadspin* and *Jezebel*. The second photo, which might depict drug or alcohol use, reference guns or violence, or display a mug shot, showed the image [that] the poster felt the media would select should he or she be involved in an altercation with authorities.

Technology journalist Kashmir Hill, writing in *Forbes*, describes this impulse to hide as unwise. By eliminating other parts of her online presence, the college student allowed the story to dominate search results for her name. "If this ever happens to you," advises Hill, "it's best to keep your LinkedIn profile and Facebook page up, just make sure to lock down the privacy settings so that nosy journalists like me can't come looking."[81] And yet, strategies of going dark and withdrawing from digital life are often the only viable option for those who have become the target of online mobs. In her research on cyber harassment, legal scholar Danielle Citron observes that victims of unwanted or aggressive attention may forgo the productive benefits of connectivity by withdrawing from online discussion groups or limiting others' ability to find or comment on their websites or profiles.[82] Individuals facing coordinated harassment campaigns, therefore, may not see visibility and exposure as a feasible solution to unwanted publicity.

Approaches to privacy that rely on strategic visibility either assume the experience of being in public is universal or ignore the ways in which it is not. Strategies that employ managed visibility, which is considered by the ORM industry as being generally desirable, do not provide solace for everyone. Certainly, individuals with a celebrity doppelgänger—a famous person with whom they share a name—will find it difficult to occupy the top results in online searches for their name. I myself share my Google results with an atelier in the United Kingdom. For these individuals, "hiding" in the recesses of search pages is far easier than breaking through to occupy the top spots. While those with a common name may be spared the unwanted visibility that comes with "owning their search results," they also face the problem of persistent identity scarcity—the inability to break through the curtain of online obscurity.[83] These people may lose out on what Warner calls "the privilege of being visible."[84]

This somewhat benign example of sharing a name with a celebrity doppelgänger points to more pernicious examples of what happens when people lack the option to choose how their image circulates in digital spaces. For some, the impossibility of managed visibility—the choice of which parts of our identity to make public and which to keep private—is not a functional problem that results from having a common or obscure name. Discussions about privacy tend to focus on the problems of unwanted publicity—on the risks that occur when a person is too recognizable or becomes visible in ways they don't expect or welcome. There is, however, a parallel problem: that of being unseen in a digital world. Attorney Jonas Lerman describes this issue of unwanted invisibility as it relates to the data economy. He argues that legal debates about information collection in the digital era fall into this common privacy trap: they "tend to focus on the privacy and civil liberties concerns of those people swept up in its net, and on whether existing safeguards such as data minimization, consent, and anonymization provide sufficient protection."[85] These, Lerman says, are problems of inclusion.

While important, a preoccupation with the consequences of being seen ignores the challenges of those who experience systemic exclusion from digital surveillance efforts—those individuals and groups contemporary technological systems tend to ignore. Those not recognized by surveillance systems may suffer political and economic harms when politicians and businesspeople fail to notice their needs because they are not captured by analytic systems that track behavioral patterns. These unseen populations, Lerman warns, are often minority groups who are already marginalized in the economic and political spheres.[86] While Lerman is talking about being visible to big data tools and technologies, there is a similar lesson for the types of visibly that concern online reputation management companies. There are consequences for those who are unable, not by choice but by circumstance, to make themselves visible in digital spaces.

The complicated realities of setting the terms for one's own publicness is epitomized in the social media campaign that coalesced around the hashtag #IfTheyGunnedMeDown.[87] In the wake of the 2014 shooting of Michael Brown, an unarmed African American man, by a police officer in Ferguson, Missouri, this hashtag was used to bring attention to the persistent problems of self-narration for ethnic and racial minorities. Using this hashtag on Twitter and Tumblr, young people of color posted two pictures of themselves, side by side, with the question "if they gunned me down, which picture would they choose?" The posters shared these images as representative of two of the possible narratives that could be used to tell their story. The first picture, selected as an image that would be generally inoffensive, often featured the poster in a cap and gown, military uniform, or standing with family. The second photo, which might depict drug or alcohol use, reference guns or violence, or display a mug shot, showed the image [that] the poster felt the media would select should he or she be involved in an altercation with authorities.

This hashtag makes several claims regarding the nature of visibility in the digital era. On the one hand, it pushes against what film, television, and new media scholar Anna Everett observes as the damaging elision of technical skill with white masculinity.[88] In response to conclusions about the consequences of a digital divide, Everett describes the reproduction of black public spheres online as these communities bring their experiences navigating the structural and systematic challenges encountered in the offline world into these mediated spaces. As media studies scholar Catherine Knight Steele similarly observes, black feminist digital spaces experience a conflation between public and private that is familiar across social media environments; however, Steele argues, black women living in the United States bring with them a history of and experience with navigating environments where a separation between public and private spaces is not recognized.[89] For Steele, the skills established within these communities to engage in multiple and concurrent acts of self-presentation and to recognize that spaces marked as private may not be experienced in that way, transfer to digital spaces where these boundaries are being continuously negotiated. Those speaking through the hashtag #IfTheyGunnedMeDown are making claims about the importance of self-authorship while at the same time calling attention to the ways cultural and industrial systems privilege some versions of a narrative over others. Although the power of this hashtag underscores the use of digital tools to tell stories often ignored in mainstream media outlets, its subject matter points to the persistent dominance of these systems.

In her work on search engine algorithms, digital media scholar Safiya Umoja Noble considers how underlying classification logics, those that guide results but remain unseen by the user, shape opportunities for visibility in digital spaces.[90] Through the application of critical race theory to understand the ways in which maleness and whiteness are prioritized in digital systems, Noble stresses the role search algorithms play in informing cultural understandings of race. Based on an analysis of search results for the term "Black girls," Noble identifies the visibility of highly sexualized images, which favor depictions that cater to commercial interests over those of Black women and girls. Whereas African American women and girls may be highly *visible* in these spaces, their persistent characterization as objects of desire renders their own interests *invisible*. Within a context where search is naturalized as objective, results have immense power to shape perceptions of constructed cultural categories, including race.

Noble's work stresses the way algorithms can work to undermine efforts at self-presentation and controlled visibility. These instances force an awareness of the invisible labor of algorithms by highlighting the technological and cultural intersection of computational design—what media researcher Taina Bucher has called the algorithmic imaginary.[91] Technology scholar Latanya Sweeney's research regarding online contextual advertising and racial bias provides a further example of how technological, cultural, and industrial forces work together to undermine the autonomy sought through efforts at digital self-narration. When entering a name in an online search engine—as a college admissions office or potential employer might do—the searcher is often confronted with tailored advertisements that promise public records information for the name being searched. In her work, Sweeney found that searches for black-identifying names were more likely to yield personalized ads that offered arrest records while searches for white-associated names were more likely to yield neutral content.[92] Sweeney asks about the consequences for people applying for jobs, loans, or apartments, or for those who are joining social groups, dating, or simply seeking to make friends.

"Appearing alongside your list of accomplishments is an advertisement implying you may have a criminal record, whether you actually have one or not," Sweeney writes. "Worse, the ads may not appear for your competitors."[93] As Noble and Sweeney's research point out, the structural biases of search engines can frame results in ways that simultaneously reflect and reinforce existing social prejudice, fostering an environment in which efforts at self-presentation are routinely undermined.

Celebratory rhetoric about the democratic potential of digital media points to opportunities to work outside established systems where access has been routinely denied to some cultural groups. Nonetheless, as Citron writes, the power of the internet to amplify voices is a double-edged sword. "While it can facilitate the empowerment of people who often face discrimination," she writes, "it can also be employed to disenfranchise those very same individuals."[94] While digital tools can be helpful in identifying and building community, and providing those communities with a platform, these same technologies rarely attend to structural inequities related to autonomy and, at times, they even exacerbate them.[95] Critiques regarding solutions to privacy grounded in arguments that individuals should "own" and "control" their personal story are not about the absence or presence of a narrative voice. Rather, they point to the different structural and cultural barriers people face when they tell those stories. When considering the efficacy of identity management solutions that prioritize visibility, it is therefore essential to recognize the social contexts that shape the choices made by technological systems.

Invisibility Is Not an Option: The Responsibility of Self-Presentation

Strategic transparency is meant to provide individuals with some sense of agency in a situation where it is easy to feel powerless. And while the opportunity to craft, monitor, and promote a preferred digital image is positioned by the ORM industry as a right, when these same companies describe such practices as a necessary part of modern life those rights quickly become responsibilities. Ryan Erskine, a brand strategist at BrandYourself, describes the dangers of failing to cultivate an online identity. "Without any positive content out there to defend against digital attacks," he writes, "you have no chance of keeping your online rep clean. While you're hiding behind privacy settings and unidentifiable usernames, your real name suffers. Anything negative goes undefended, immediately rising to the top of your search results for the whole world to see."[96] It is not enough, these companies argue, to clean up after a reputation crisis; an effective defense against an unwanted online image involves proactively creating and managing a positive online presence. This is not only based on the assumption that a good online reputation is the best defense against negative content, but because of the social expectation that we are findable online. When strategic online self-presentation through practices of personal disclosure becomes a necessity of digital life, strategies that support a right to privacy can quickly lead to obligations of visibility. Even if privacy is not dead, the option not to be public may be rapidly diminishing.

Anthony Giddens's description of the continual and reflexive construction of identity as a requirement of the late modern era is consistent with arguments that the monitoring and management of one's online image has become a requirement of digital life. The burden and freedom tied to the set of obligations attached to continual self-development[97] is noted by Giddens, who writes, "We have no choice but to choose how to be and how to act."[98] In other words, the assumed necessity of this enduring project of the self introduces an explicit responsibility for image management. The problems of "responsibilization"—a term used by sociologist Ulrich Beck to describe the neoliberal impulse to make individuals accountable for tasks traditionally attended to by institutions—will be discussed further in the next chapter. It is worth noting here, however, that the expectations that individuals will take the necessary steps to protect their own privacy mean they often shoulder the blame when violations occur. The result of responsibilization around privacy is that we are expected to regulate our behaviors and build publicly available images that help guard against the emergence of unwanted content. Online, this includes the publication of an audience-ready identity and the proper concealment of information commonly expected to be kept private. When people are unsuccessful in these efforts, the implication is one of failed personal responsibility. Comments that individuals "should have known better" or "should have set their privacy settings with more care," which have the distinct tenor of victim blaming, can follow the public release of private information.

Faulting those whose reputations have been tarnished by the unwanted circulation of information tends to ignore the reality that, as with strategic visibility, opportunities for self-narration are shaped by social realities in which some stories are given preference over others. Cultural constructs such as gender, class, ethnicity, sexuality, and race can challenge efforts to, as the industry suggests, control the narrative. The continued dominance of traditional media organizations and powerful digital platforms mean that certain content is favored over others. Communication scholar Sarah Banet-Weiser observes that the availability of narratives or "scripts" for those looking to present themselves online are not as radically open as celebrations of digital self-narration may suggest.[99] As Matthew Adams observes in his critique of Giddens's reflexivity theory, "The individual cannot stand aside from her social and cultural origins and use them, transparently, as a variety of options with which to resource an individualized reflexive self-identity."[100] Self-presentation that takes place online is not free of those cultural forces that shape the boundaries of self-narration. Although largely absent from industry discussions, cultural artifacts and assumptions that privilege certain narratives over others restrict the possibility of certain performances.

In *Hiding from Humanity: Disgust, Shame, and the Law*, philosopher Martha Nussbaum introduces the concept "primitive shame."[101] Stemming from an inability to exert complete control, Nussbaum describes primitive shame as "shame at the very fact of helplessness."[102] The view of privacy violations as a consequence of a personal failure to properly guard one's information underscores this emotional experience. Not only might an individual be embarrassed by the unwanted display of personal information, but the notion that its visibility is the result of a failure to exert adequate control may compound these sentiments. Nussbaum observes, in the case of privacy, that access to control is further complicated. "The public-private boundary," she writes, "does not function symmetrically on both sides because it protects 'normals' both in their choice to conceal and in their choice to make public, whereas 'abnormals' are required to conceal."[103] Those, therefore, who are either willing or able to conform to social expectations around personal disclosure, are less likely to be implicated by the shame associated with a lack of personal autonomy. And, Nussbaum notes, for those who buy into the myth that control is possible, the shame experienced when control is not achieved is likely to be more severe.[104] It is possible, therefore, that efforts to equate privacy with successful mastery over one's personal narrative heighten feelings of shame when failure occurs.

Reframing Practical Obscurity: The Search for Privacy in Digital Publics

In February 2014, actor Alec Baldwin wrote a farewell address in the pages of *New York* magazine. Reflecting on 2013, a particularly bad year in which he was ridiculed in the media for allegedly making homophobic remarks and his failed forays on Broadway and television, Baldwin lamented the changing nature of celebrity. "I haven't changed" he wrote, "but public life has. It used to be you'd go into a restaurant and the owner would say, 'Do you mind if I take a picture of you and put it on my wall?' Sweet and simple. Now, everyone has a camera in their pocket. . . . You're out there in a world where if you do make a mistake, it echoes in a digital canyon forever."[105] Baldwin's complaints reveal the challenges for celebrities who have to learn new strategies for cultivating a private life separate from their public persona in a culture saturated by digital media.

Developing strategies for maintaining privacy is an enduring feature of celebrity life. As we will see in the next chapter, ordinary people are increasingly being told they face similar challenges and, consequently, need to adopt similar strategies to protect themselves. Warnings about being burned by a negative review or unflattering news story are no longer limited to businesses, celebrities, and politicians. In the contemporary moment, a digital image operates simultaneously as a site of opportunity and a source of risk. This risk is amplified in a media environment in which the ability to publish content that is searchable and enduring has been dramatically expanded. For those with the capital— social, cultural, and economic—to invest in strategic identity construction, perhaps aided by the services of an online reputation management company, digital images can become an important strategy for mitigating the risks of a precarious virtual environment. For others, however, who lack access to the resources or cultural position necessary to cultivate an online image that will be plausible to family, attractive to employers, and endearing to friends, online reputation can be fraught with challenges.

In his farewell to public life, Baldwin mourned what he perceived as a loss of anonymity. He wrote "I've lived in New York since 1979. It was a place that they gave you your anonymity. And not just if you were famous. . . . We allowed people privacy, we left them alone. And now we don't leave each other alone. Now we live in a digital arena, like some Roman Coliseum, with our thumbs up or thumbs down."[106] Baldwin's lament reflects the loss of practical obscurity and civil inattention at the hands of new media technologies. His assertion regarding the disappearance of access to private spaces is pervasive in contemporary discourses about digital media and demands new strategies for those wishing to carve out opportunities to be unobserved. The ORM industry offers a practical strategy for achieving privacy through exposure: the crafting of a compelling image that will redirect attention from the information one wishes to keep private. In creating this identity for public consumption, the industry argues, we can deflect attention and create private spaces. Much like the Wizard in *The Wizard of Oz*, the industry encourages the use of technology to obscure the figure behind the curtain in favor of a carefully crafted public image.

There is a tension in the central logic of the online reputation management industry's commitment to privacy through publicity: in order protect some elements of one's life from exposure, one must disclose enough information to simultaneously obscure undesirable content and ward off the suspicion associated with those who appear to be completely off the grid. To avoid the dangers of a negative reputation, one needs to labor to fill the digital media landscape with content that will yield a positive (or at least unassuming) image. Baldwin, seeming to pick up on this contradiction, writes, "I'm aware that it's ironic that I'm making this case in the media—but this is the last time I'm going to talk about my personal life in an American publication ever again."[107] But of course it wasn't. Celebrities require the media spotlight to sustain their fame. Similarly, we are told that ordinary people risk irrelevancy (or suspicion) when we withdraw too far from the glare of digital life in the hopes of managing the risks of unwanted exposure.

The rationale driving the ORM industry is that by occupying enough of the existing media environment with strategically crafted content, one can carve out some semblance of privacy. These companies have supported the development and promotion of a culture that understands a well-crafted online image as an essential tool for mitigating risk and creating opportunities for privacy. As we will see in the next chapter, this ideology of managed visibility as a risk-management strategy is now repeated in self-help books, do-it-yourself guides, and college courses. Technological changes and shifting cultural expectations mean the construction of privacy offered by online reputation management companies is qualitatively different from those provided by anonymizers and infomediaries. Rather than accessing privacy primarily through opportunities for anonymity and pseudonymity, online reputation management companies describe an environment in which identity is protected and defended through strategic deflection. Using these strategies, this collection of companies has helped normalize online visibility as a requirement of contemporary life.

The early days of this industry focused on strategies to address and repair a negative online image. It has not taken long, however, for the focus to turn from protection to promotion. This industry has helped instill strategic self-promotion as a contemporary necessity for the masses. Strategies for burying negative digital content as a crisis response to unfavorable information are now positioned as a proactive requirement for participants in the digital environment. The next chapter examines how industrial strategies of digital self-preservation have morphed into opportunities for digital self-promotion.

5

Reputation Promoters

Building Identity Capital Online

As the online reputation management industry has matured, the companies that make up this field have altered their approach to digital reputation. While the early focus was on the protection and repair of damaged online identities, companies have more recently broadened the scope of their services. As employers turn to online search to screen potential employees and as online platforms develop reputation-scoring metrics to evaluate users, online reputation management companies have begun to consider the social and economic advantages that accrue to those with a positive digital image. This departure from online reputation management services as primarily ad hoc crisis response includes the addition of services to support strategic self-promotion. In response to mounting cultural expectations that experiences are lived, documented, and shared online, these companies promote strategies of image management as optimizing the benefits of online visibility while doubling as a proactive defense against possible attacks.

In their 2010 book *Wild West 2.0: How to Protect and Restore Your Online Reputation on the Untamed Social Frontier*, Michael Fertik and David Thompson wrote about the changing rules for reputation online. "Today," they wrote, "your reputation can be created or destroyed in just a few clicks."[1] Who might want to destroy your reputation? they asked: "Bullies, people jealous of your success, competitors for jobs or customers (or even lovers), and gangs of disaffected teenagers."[2] Only five years later, in *The Reputation Economy: How to Optimize Your Digital Footprint in a World Where Your Reputation Is Your Most Valuable Asset*, Fertik and Thompson defined the digital landscape in somewhat different terms. As veterans of the online reputation management world through their work with Reputation.com, Fertik and Thompson remained concerned about a world where "other people will be able to instantly access information about your reputation—with or without your knowledge or consent."[3] But rather than being focused exclusively on the threats to one's online image, *The Reputation Economy* is a guide to leveraging the potential of a new economic system in which a strong reputation is an asset. The book, Fertik and Thompson wrote, will "show you how to become 'reputation rich' in a world where your digital reputation is as valuable as the cash in your wallet."[4]

This chapter explores industry efforts, through promotional materials and community engagement, to educate the public about the importance of protecting and promoting their online reputation. The industry's strategies for digital image construction and protection, originally introduced as tools for those experiencing a reputational crisis or severe breach of privacy, have been repositioned as mandatory proactive practices for everyone living in the digital age. This pivot from thinking about the threat of a negative digital reputation to the positioning of an online image as an asset has created new opportunities for companies in the consumer privacy industry. Instead of limiting their clientele to those whose reputations are particularly vulnerable or in need of repair, the rebranding of online reputation management as a tool anyone can use to create a visible and valuable digital image broadens the industry's purpose and scope.

On its website, BrandYourself makes an explicit argument for the power derived from the ability to control one's image. "BrandYourself," the site reads, "is the only free do-it-yourself product that empowers you to control what people find when they Google you." Rather than positioning the company as engaged in efforts at reputation defense or repair, the site offers a more universal approach that takes online visibility as a given. Borrowing from strategies honed in advertising and public relations, the online reputation management industry applies the logic of promotional culture to the creation of online images that promote at the same time as they protect. These strategies, referred to as self-branding or personal branding, encourage individuals to think of themselves as commodities and, in doing so, to identify the unique features and qualities that set them apart. It is an approach that demonstrates the industry's investments in a political economy that sells privacy through strategies of self-promotion.

The previous chapters considered how arguments that everyone has the right to control their online image ignore differential experiences of privacy and visibility and minimize the difficulties encountered by those who face structural challenges in the construction and management of their personal narrative. This chapter further examines industry challenges through an exploration of the unique ethical questions facing companies that support the commodification of self-presentation. Moreover, it considers the complicated ethical position of an industry that profits from the distress that follows privacy violations and digital shaming. The problematic actions of companies that are industry adjacent and occasionally confused with more reputable firms raise issues for those trying to establish themselves as essential and legitimate players in the digital economy. Although keenly aware of these ethical issues, the loosely connected set of companies that constitutes an industry with little oversight or regulation, has struggled to respond to these challenges in a systematic or holistic way.

By introducing another moment in the evolution of efforts to sell privacy online, this chapter explores how investments in online reputation management and promotion have shifted industry definitions of privacy by supporting a formula that equates visibility with empowerment and identity with capital. By downplaying anonymity as a viable strategy for privacy protections online and promoting image management as a required part of contemporary life, the industry supports an ideology that fits firmly within the neoliberal logic of an attention economy where self-production and promotion are identified as parts of a successful professional and personal identity, and self-presentation becomes an important component of social and economic achievement. Through its insistence that reputation management can only occur when there is an image to control, the industry rejects strategies of resistance that rely on media refusal. Instead, these companies promote a logic that encourages participation that can be recognized and evaluated. The online reputation management industry's shift from crisis management to personal brand advocacy deepens responsibilities around digital self-presentation that privilege visibility. Before considering these responsibilities and their consequences, it is important to examine the function of reputations and reputation systems online.

The Role of Reputation Online

In digital spaces, as in offline contexts, we do not produce our own reputations. Rather, reputations are assigned based on the collective judgments of others.[5] The power of communities to define and circulate information that determines the social and economic position of its members gives individuals an incentive to control what others think of them. Through strategic interactions, people can attempt to influence the perceptions of others, but as legal scholar Daniel Solove notes, the disconnect between the desire and ability to control one's reputation presents an enduring and often frustrating tension.[6] Fears about the power of reputations intensify when established strategies for controlling the spread of information are threatened. Writing in the late nineteenth century, E. L. Godkin described novel threats to individual reputation introduced by changing journalistic practices.[7] A journalist and newspaper editor himself, Godkin worried that a turn toward sensationalist stories featuring details about the personal lives of public and semipublic figures would challenge established legal structures that protected reputations. Godkin feared that the repercussions of stories, previously the province of gossipy neighbors, would gain portability and permanence once they were enshrined in print. By printing damning information in newspapers, Godkin wrote in an 1890 issue of *Scribner's Magazine*, the journalist would make "its victim, with all his imperfections on his head, known hundreds of thousands of miles away from his place of abode."[8]

The stigma associated with a negative reputation operates as a powerful extralegal tool for disciplining individuals who fail to conform to social norms. In *The Costs of Privacy: Surveillance and Reputation in America*, sociologist Steven Nock writes that the threat of shame acts as a form of societal control.[9] The consequences of a bad reputation, including expulsion from communities, can be so severe the mere anticipation of its penalties provides an incentive to conform to social norms. This social power of reputations to encourage acceptable behaviors is often applied in face-to-face groups where community members are known to one another. "In a shame culture," Nock writes, "whoever fails to meet the demands of the code of honor loses his good reputation."[10] In larger societies, those in which people enjoy greater anonymity, Nock argues that shame plays a reduced role. Mechanisms for producing and reporting information about past behaviors have, however, allowed for the continued role of reputations in communities where the participants are largely unknown to one another. The development of portable reputations mechanisms,[11] such as credit cards or driver's licenses, are examples of how reputations have been institutionalized to evaluate trust without the benefits of shared histories or social networks.

The use of reputation mechanisms to demonstrate trustworthiness to strangers has been essential in the development and management of online communities. Cultural critic Howard Rheingold describes the power of reputation systems in early digital networks. The ability to track and evaluate the character of community members, he observes, helped establish order in these nascent networks by amplifying the power derived from the unassailable human desire to avoid public shame.[12] Although early online communities are often associated with anonymity, unfettered identity experimentation, and the ability to investigate the fractured and often discordant elements of the self,[13] there were networks that encouraged and even insisted on participation under a single identity. A virtual gathering site called the WELL (short for the Whole Earth 'Lectronic Link), which originally launched in 1985, stressed the importance of authentic community engagement under a consistent persona. To encourage responsible and respectful discourse, the WELL did not offer anonymous accounts. The phrase YOYOW, which stood for "you own your own words," guided participation in this community.[14]

Because reputations are allocated and evaluated by members of a community, they often reveal as much about the cultures that create them as they do about the individuals to whom they are attached. By looking at the practices that constitute good and bad reputations, we can uncover details about a community's norms and expectations.[15] According to an updated version of the WELL website, the YOYOW mantra "reminded you that your words determine your reputation." This acronym, the website continues, "didn't eliminate personality clashes or conflicts, of course, but this shared value of owning up to your actions tended to lead to a desirable level of authentic discourse—improving the signal-to-noise ratio, if you will."[16] Grounded in the community values of responsibility and civility, the YOYOW ideal promoted community members' reputations as mechanisms through which to maintain order and respect.[17]

In the years since the introduction of the WELL, many online platforms have formalized online reputation systems so that information about past actions is easily accessible and clearly visible. eBay uses perhaps the most well-known online reputation system. The auction site relies on reciprocal rating between buyers and sellers to generate trust and accountability in a market where sales are often one-off interactions among strangers.[18] "In such a system," digital sociologist Alessandro Gandini writes in *The Reputation Economy*, "reputation functions as a networked asset that intermediates unequal transactions in the allocations of resources, information, and goods."[19] As more and more platforms incorporate reputation metrics as part of their infrastructure, there has been a proliferation in opportunities to rate and rank others. The resulting reputation scores act as proxy measures for a person's social or economic worth. For example, platforms that support the informal or sharing economy—the companies that facilitate connections between those looking to sell or loan and those looking to buy or rent—rely on reputation systems to help generate trust between sellers and buyers in the absence of previous interactions. Other metrics, such as the use of karma points by social news sites like Slashdot and Reddit, indicate the aggregate popularity of an individual's contributions and provide a measure of social value. Computer scientist Paul Resnick describes the importance of reputation systems for facilitating "sociotechnical capital," a measure of trust based on persistent interactions within a technologically mediated social or economic network.[20]

The use of rating schemes helps to socialize new members into the norms of an online community and to sanction behaviors that breach those expectations.[21] The reputations that result from these ongoing feedback practices, however, do more than simply police behavior within specific communities. In fact, digital reputations have become an organizing principle for the virtual world. Thanks to an expanding interest in portable reputation metrics, these scores have taken on relevance beyond the communities in which they are constructed and assigned. Some digital reputation scores are publicly available, accessible to others regardless of their membership in a community or their understanding of its norms. The visibility of these reputations, combined with the easy legibility that results from quantification and display, provides an added incentive for individuals to strive for a positive score. After all, this information might be an influential factor when someone is deciding whether they want to interact with us, whether as a potential employer, client, business associate, or romantic partner.

The potential consequences of a negative online rating, ranking, or review introduce additional incentives to manage the circulation of reputation scores. As online reputation management companies insist, however, these metrics also produce opportunities. Just as a negative online image can signal exclusion from a digital community, positive reputations can be leveraged as evidence of competency in an area and exploited as a form of social capital.[22] To complement their investment in repairing damaged images and guarding against possible future attacks, companies in this industry have introduced services that inspire the creation and promotion of a positive online image. Not only do these companies argue that strong reputations are valuable, but also that maintaining a powerful public image helps to mitigate the consequences of an attack, acting as a form of "reputation insurance."[23]

As the proliferation of reputation systems encourage an acceptance of the idea of being ranked and rated, the ubiquity of these metrics also heightens their significance. By framing a good online reputation as essential for economic and social success, the online reputation management industry has helped to promote the value of managing, improving, and optimizing one's online image. Although they share several similarities with offline reputations, digital reputations are both more visible and more concerned with visibility than are their analog counterparts.[24] Just as the values informing the WELL community were visible through the mandated use of real names to maintain a collegial and supportive environment, the cultures of more contemporary platforms are revealed through their use of reputation scores. Digital media scholar Alice Marwick, for example, describes the work of tech entrepreneurs to build cultural preferences for visibility and attention into digital platforms through the inclusion of status metrics that reward publicity.[25] The digital reputations comprising these metrics—which incorporate information such as the number of likes, followers, or friends a person has—offer a measure of socio-technical capital, assigned based on the structure of social relationships rather than on any particular skill.[26] In other words, contemporary digital reputations tend to be based on measures that privilege one's popularity or visibility in a specific network.

The online reputation management industry stresses the importance of status metrics for informing one's online image. Much as a company needs to be concerned with their ratings on sites such as Yelp, Google, and Amazon, reputation management professionals encourage individuals to monitor and invest in the strength of their own virtual ratings. During a casual conversation with a representative from an online reputation management company in 2012, I was encouraged to enhance my own digital image. By tweeting a couple of times a week and developing a blog about my research, this reputation management professional counseled, I could increase my profile as an expert on digital privacy and online identity. The suggestion that greater investment in my digital presence could have positive repercussions for my professional life is likely familiar to academics and other professionals who have been encouraged to use social media, blogs, podcasts, and research-sharing platforms to enhance their professional visibility;[27] however, through the industrialization and professionalization of these activities, online reputation management companies have helped institutionalize these practices and normalize them as a necessity. Much like showering and brushing one's teeth, for those in the industry, "digital hygiene" should be a part of one's daily routine.

The encouragement to invest in my digital presence as a path to enhancing my career reflects what communication scholar Alison Hearn describes as a system of cultural production in which reputations generate cultural meaning and social importance.[28] The quantification of relationships through status metrics that allow social practices and interactions to become visible and traceable turns personal connections into sources of economic value. Importantly, however, Hearn observes that the power to define the value created from this unique form of cultural production resides with those who build the mechanisms that extract, measure, display, and assign worth. Consequently, the qualities valued in contemporary tech culture—characteristics that include visibility, popularity, centrality, and attention—get reproduced and prioritized in status metrics.[29] The construction of digital reputations based on these metrics, therefore, functions as a form of market disciplining to privilege efforts at self-presentation that are profitable and intentional.[30] When reputation management professionals stress the importance of a carefully crafted public image—one that takes into consideration visible and routine actions with social media environments—they are embracing a media system that assigns importance and value based on engagement within that system.

Personal Branding: Building the Brand Called You

In 1997, the business and innovation magazine *Fast Company* ran a cover story titled "A Brand Called You." In the article, Tom Peters introduced personal branding as a strategy for standing out in "The Age of the Individual." In an unpredictable labor market, fueled by rapid technological advances, he wrote, "we are CEOs of our own companies: Me Inc. To be in business today, our most important job is to be head marketer for the brand called You."[31] The need to think about oneself the same way a company thinks about its brand, Peters wrote, is inescapable. He urged readers to identify the characteristics and qualities they possess that add remarkable, measureable, and distinct value. But thinking about oneself as a brand, Peters warned, is only half the battle. We also have a responsibility to sell ourselves. Just like any major brand, Peters noted, the brand called You requires visibility to be successful. "When you're promoting brand You," he wrote, "everything you do—and everything you choose not to do—communicates the value and character of the brand."[32] Ending his article with a call to readers to get started building their own brand today (or else!), Peters's description of self-branding suggested a form of reflexive self-presentation so deeply tied to promotional logics that the distinction between person and product disappeared.

The application of language common in advertising to individual self-presentation was relatively novel when it first appeared on the cover of *Fast Company*.[33] The notion of packaging and selling oneself, however, has parallels in academic discussions of "enterprise culture" and the construction of the "entrepreneurial self."[34] In his book *Consumption and Identity at Work*, Paul du Gay defines an enterprise culture as "one in which certain enterprising qualities—such as self-reliance, personal responsibility, boldness and a willingness to take risks in the pursuit of goals—are regarded as human virtues and promoted as such."[35] The corresponding entrepreneurial self is a worker who, in the competitive and flexible work environment Peters described, views labor as a path toward self-improvement.[36] Critical academics, including Hearn, argue that this slippage between the self as commodity worker and the actualized self described by du Gay, is the consequence of a neoliberal environment that prizes achievement through personal choice, initiative, and risk.[37] For the entrepreneurial self, the ability to package strengths and promote achievements is not only an economic requirement but also the path to self-fulfillment.

In previous chapters, I describe the use of promotional language to emphasize the importance of privacy-enhancing technologies. To explain how the sale of personal information by individuals through data intermediaries could minimize inequalities in the emerging data economy, entrepreneurs in the 1990s were already using terms such as "personal datamart," "meBay," and "identity commerce." By 2010, however, the application of promotional language to discussions about self-presentation and privacy protections had become commonplace. At this point, the commodification of self-reflection was big business for image consultants, and narratives of personal branding could be found in numerous books, workshops, and seminars.[38] The how-to book *Personal Branding for Dummies*, for example, describes a personal brand as an authentic expression of self—the story of *you*—that allows individuals to identify and communicate their strengths.[39] This guide, and the many others like it, describes an opportunity for self-making that sociologists Anthony Giddens, Ulrich Beck, and Zygmunt Bauman have identified as a distinct feature of modern society.[40] Each writes about the opportunities and responsibilities of engaging in identity work outside the traditional structures that once defined lived experiences. For Bauman, the labors of self-construction prescribed by late modernity, or what he calls liquid modernity, have refigured identity from a given to a task.[41] Giddens's description of late modern identities as reflexive projects, ventures in which identity construction is a continuous process, is reflected in the definition of personal branding as "an ongoing, conscientious effort to show the world your best authentic self . . . the process of bringing every aspect of your life into alignment with your characteristic strengths, values, and goals so that you can make an instant and lasting impression."[42] The logic of creating a personal brand through the routine promotion of a consistent self-narrative closely mirrors this perspective.

This logic of the commodified self is apparent in promotional materials and services offered by companies across the online reputation industry. Reputation.com's Michael Fertik warns that like it or not, you have a "personal brand."[43] Others describe the need to build a "virtual store-front" that will break through the clutter and demand attention.[44] Like the metaphors identified in the previous chapter—those that referred to digital tattoos and footprints to signal the dangers posed by persistent digital content—terms like "personal brand" and "virtual storefront" demonstrate the necessity of cultivating a positive online image. These phrases, which emphasize the collapsed boundaries between people and products, evoke carefully and intentionally curated versions of self. Much as a store might create an attractive display to entice shoppers to step in off the streets, this industry stresses the value of producing an online identity that will garner the attention of those browsing online. Notably, Fertik's assertion about the inevitability of a personal brand implicates *everyone* in the practice of self-commodification. This approach suggests that those who fail to cultivate their digital image—like stores that put little effort into their outward appearance or generic products that do not rely on advertising—are not "unbranded"; rather, their lack of brand awareness or promotional efforts is itself a signal.

The architecture of the social web operates within an attention economy in which capital comes from the ability to capture and engage with an audience.[45] In the attention economy, practices of self-presentation are infused with economic logics that demand visibility, narrative consistency, and performed authenticity. Informed by the commercial logics of self-branding, identity projects become contentious as deeply personal practices of self-discovery are constructed and performed through the framework of commodity culture. Hearn notes that the forms of flexible production made necessary in a neoliberal economy require us to make and remake ourselves with respect to the ever-changing economic environment. She argues that in this atmosphere we see "the self *as* work in the form of a self-brand with reputation as its currency."[46] The result is that individuals are encouraged to invest in the promise of visibility both as a defensive strategy and as a proactive tactic of self-promotion.

Personal branding demands the publication of content that supports a carefully crafted image. The personal narrative, which is positioned as the core component of a self-brand, is described in reputation management materials as a statement of one's true self that is replicated via digital outlets. Through the reproduction of this content across online platforms, companies help create a consistent narrative in support of a client's preferred brand. The industry emphasizes that, in addition to being compelling, the personal narrative serves as the foundation for one's online image and, as such, should reflect one's "true" and "authentic" self.[47] This emphasis on the production and display of a "genuine" persona demonstrates a commitment within this field to the construction of images that are validated based on their connection to some fixed version of identity. In the absence of this single, static self, however, self-branding's commitment to authenticity is best understood as a commitment to consistency and believability.

Although the disclosure of personal information is offered as a key strategy for those seeking to cultivate intimacy and present an authentic and compelling image, too much disclosure can be damaging. The dangers of revealing too many of the wrong kinds of details are signaled by colloquialisms such as "oversharing" or "too much information."[48] There is cultural pressure to engage in enough self-disclosure to seem compelling and authentic, but without engaging in revelations likely to be perceived as tacky. And despite social expectations that anticipate and even demand visibility, there is a commensurate condemnation of cultural practices read as overly exhibitionist or self-promotional. Those promising empowerment through the performance of interiority that supports "real" or "true" identities rarely consider the ways in which the performance of authenticity is socially bounded and culturally constructed.[49] Communication scholar Sarah Banet-Weiser's work illustrates that while digital platforms deliver opportunities for empowering and reflexive performances, particularly for young women, contemporary culture restricts access to authenticity, thereby limiting the types of bodies considered brandable.[50] In what Banet-Weiser calls the "current economy of visibility," women of color and working-class women face different expectations regarding their self-presentation.[51] The result, she argues, is that those who do not fall into normative standards of white femininity are left with a very narrow course in which to chart performances that are both culturally acceptable and authentic—those that walk the line between disclosures that cultivate intimacy and those read as overly exposing. Industrial approaches that espouse the freedom and choice stimulated by chances to craft one's online image largely fail to acknowledge the ways these opportunities are inscribed within a set of cultural logics that label some narratives as more authentic, brandable, or readable than others.

Digital Hygiene: The Unavoidable Work of Reputation Management

Public discourse about the importance of protecting and promoting one's online image is so pervasive that this practice has come to feel like a routine part of contemporary life. An Amazon search, for example, yields over six hundred titles related to personal branding. Although the online reputation management industry did not invent anxieties about a negative digital image, these companies have played a central role in defining what those risks are, identifying the consequences, and promoting a set of approaches for mitigating these threats. Efforts to define both the problem and the range of solutions have included education initiatives that strive to normalize reflexive self-promotion as a requirement of the digital era. Media scholar Mark Andrejevic describes how this process of normalization has occurred in a related field: digital advertising. Practices that once seemed invasive or creepy—for example, Google's scanning of emails to inform contextual marketing strategies or Amazon's customized recommendations based on the buying habits of millions of customers—have become so ubiquitous that they are now a routinized and largely overlooked part of digital life.[52] By reframing digital image management as an obligatory and even mundane part of everyday life, the online reputation management industry has similarly normalized self-protection and promotion as part of a commonsense strategy of digital self-presentation.

Just as those behind the anonymizers and infomediaries viewed one part of their mission as educating the public about the possible privacy issues introduced by digital media technologies, those in the online reputation management community view public awareness as a core component of their business strategy. Michael Fertik described the early efforts behind Reputation.com as building a public consciousness about the possible dangers of unwanted visibility online. Fertik told me he had spent the better part of a decade educating the world about the importance of reputation management through speeches at conferences and media appearances. The result is that Fertik and others in this industry see themselves as playing an important role in shaping public understanding about privacy and reputation online.

When he started Reputation.com in 2006, Fertik observed, the public had a limited understanding about the importance of digital reputation, privacy, or the security of personal data online. Now, he told me, "everybody in North America believes there is something called privacy on the internet; believes there's something called reputation on the internet." Moreover, Fertik proposed that "probably more than any other civil entity, Reputation.com has been responsible for educating the world on this topic." The company founder has a prominent public image and is routinely sought as an expert in news stories about online reputation and digital image management. This has given Fertik and Reputation.com a platform from which to warn the public about the dangers of a negative online image and to advocate for the importance of active reputation defense strategies.

Reputation.com's efforts at public pedagogy—and its change in name from ReputationDefender to Reputation.com in 2011—reveal a broadening focus, beyond image protection and repair, to include promotion. The company's more recent education efforts include a focus on the importance of leveraging personal information that goes beyond image defense. The dual mandate of protection and promotion is evident in the description provided by Stephen Hess, a product manager at Reputation.com, of the educational tools that are built into the company's suite of products:

> I think we do educate people about the type of information that exists about them online and the impression that that information has, or as we talked about earlier, the insight that can be derived from that data. And so, part of our product thesis is that, for free, we will tell you about your online reputation; we will explain to you the information that exists about you online, that [is] being collected as you surf the internet, and the impact that information may have on your life. And then our paid services are targeted at helping people control or mediate issues that they may have with that digital footprint.

Through public statements and product promotion, Fertik and the company he built have helped to normalize the idea that every individual has a digital reputation that requires continuous monitoring and attention for its potential to be fully realized.

Perhaps due to these early pedagogical efforts combined with the media's sustained attention over the past decade to incidents in which an individual's reputation was ruined over information shared online, others in the industry describe a pervasive public awareness around the risks of unwanted online visibility and the importance of maintaining a positive online presence. For these companies, a consumer population that is already convinced of the need to maintain a strong digital image has meant less time spent explaining the need for their products and services. BrandYourself's Patrick Ambron told me his company has achieved publicity entirely through "word of mouth with bouts of good press." A representative at a different online reputation management firm told me most of his company's business comes through a combination of referrals and "people just becoming more exposed to the industry and realizing the importance of it."

During our conversation in 2013, Ambron described the existing climate as one where people had an inherent understanding of the need to manage one's online presence. "You know," he told me, "it's at a time now where I think that most people understand this." Whether from personal experience or from a story of a friend or a friend-of-a-friend, Ambron said, everyone is aware of the consequences of having negative search results or a poor digital reputation. Due to this seemingly instinctive appreciation for the importance of their services, many reputation management companies forgo mass advertising campaigns. These companies do, however, engage in efforts to remind potential customers about services that will assist them in efforts to monitor, protect, and promote their online image. In addition to relying on positive buzz, companies tend to use promotional strategies that allow them to find clients when they are most in need of the company's services—moments Reputation.com's Stephen Hess refers to as "acute pain points." Examples of these strategies might include displaying an online ad to a person who had entered "fix a negative online reputation" into an online search, or paying for ad space promoting the company's information removal services on a "people finder" website. These strategies of "showing up" when people are looking for solutions help contribute to the perception that online reputation management is the commonsense response to an unwanted digital image.

In her 2014 article "Toning Down the Tweets Just in Case Colleges Pry," *New York Times* reporter Natasha Singer describes increased student attention to their online images even before they enter college. Although not all college admissions departments use social media searches to evaluate applicants, some students are not willing to take the chance. Singer writes that "in their junior year or earlier, many high school students have started sanitizing their online profiles—making them private, deleting certain posts, removing name tags in photos, using pseudonyms."[53] Students—many of whom have grown up with social media accounts—represent a particularly important market for the online reputation management industry. BrandYourself, for example, has pursued a strategic relationship with college students, whom the company believes have a particular interest in their digital reputations. The company's co-founders have partnered with their alma mater, Syracuse University, to offer reputation repair and self-promotion services to students and recent graduates who are looking for a leg up in the job market.

Ambron told me they sought these partnerships because the current generation of college kids grew up online and are about to go on the job market. He observed that while college students have concerns about their online presence, they tend to put off managing it until they are about to enter the professional world. Partnerships with universities allow the company to get in front of students early and introduce the value of their services. "Once they leave their bubble and they're in the real world," Ambron hoped, "they really start remembering, 'Oh, I've got to go and use that tool.'" Syracuse is not the only university encouraging students to think about their online image. Johns Hopkins University has pursued an arrangement with BrandYourself like Syracuse's that provides students with access to a paid version of the service free of charge.[54] The University of California, Santa Barbara has offered workshops on the topic and Villanova University has provided a course on managing one's online identity. Similarly, Northwestern University has offered a ten-week course called "Manage Your Online Reputation," which blends stories about the risks of negative reputations with strategies to help construct a strong online image that is socially and economically valuable.[55] Thanks in part to these services, online reputation management has become part of the curriculum for college students at campuses across the United States.

More recently, BrandYourself has launched a new product aimed directly at helping high school and college students detect and remove problematic content before admissions officers or employers see it. Branded as a "student makeover" tool, the product is geared toward parents as a graduation gift to help their child clean and build their online presence. Once purchased and launched, the product uses an algorithm to search for "unprofessional" social media posts, images, and search results. Using what the company calls cutting-edge machine learning and "CleanImage" technology, the program "automatically finds any images that could be considered unprofessional, including photos involving drinking, drugs, partying, and lewd behavior."[56] Consistent with its broader educational mission, BrandYourself does not simply remove the content it finds. "Your child," the promotional material explains, "has the choice to delete or ignore their flagged images, learning what hiring managers consider unprofessional behavior along the way."[57] The confluence of technical tools and normative assertions about what constitutes "unprofessional behavior" is essential to understanding the pedagogical efforts motivating BrandYourself and other digital image management companies. Through their tools and services, these companies do more than simply help to "clean up" online reputations; they are contributing to social norms about what constitutes a proper and respectable digital image.

The argument made by several industry representatives I spoke with—that the public intrinsically understands the importance of digital image management—is compelling. A 2010 Pew Survey found that 57 percent of American adult internet users use online search engines to find information about themselves.[58] The survey also found that younger adults were particularly likely to take steps to limit the availability of personal information by adjusting privacy settings on social network sites, deleting comments, or untagging themselves in pictures. To accept this argument, however, is to ignore the immense efforts on the part of those in the ORM industry to construct the risks posed by an unprotected online reputation, to educate the public about these risks, and to promote their tools as strategies for guarding against a negative digital image. Whether these efforts are supported through educational programs at universities, publishing editorials, doing interviews in response to incidents of online reputational damage, or simply "showing up" in advertisements when people are searching for ways to manage their online presence, this industry has aimed to shape the cultural understandings about the risks and value of visibility online.

Industry Ethics: Doing Business in the Gray Zone

Despite their shared orientation around the importance of protecting privacy and reputation online, combined with an overlapping set of strategies and tools for helping individuals to manage their online image, many in the field of online reputation management do not see themselves as part of a broader industry or community. In fact, when I asked respondents to talk about practices and ideologies shared across the industry, the conversation tended to move quickly to the features or services that set their companies and products apart. Just as they encourage individuals to think about what makes their own brand unique, representatives seemed eager to talk about the successes their companies had experienced in a field with few viable players.

During our interview, I asked Michael Fertik whether he saw Reputation.com as part of a broader industry. His response suggested ambivalence. "I don't know if there's much of a reputation community," he replied. "There are a series of companies in the reputation space that are small. Some of them are run by good people; some of them are run by very dastardly people." According to Reputation Hawk's Chris Martin, the absence of an industry community stems in part from the heavy competition and high turnover within the field. That doesn't mean, however, that firms are unaware of others in the reputation space. "Over the years," Martin reported, "there's kind of a group of us that have developed this small circle where we all trust each other and know we're good guys just trying to do a good job for clients."

Fertik and Martin's comments suggest that a possible impediment to the construction of a broader industry community may be a desire to avoid being lumped in with "bad" industry players. Consistent with other aspects of the digital world, the rules and norms governing the manipulation of the online environment to enhance one's image can be murky. The result is that some industry practices take place in what might be referred to as an ethical gray area with few agreed-on best practices to guide those in the field. During my conversations, I witnessed a deep awareness and engagement with the complex ethical questions facing the online reputation management industry. Some companies, for example, described thinking carefully about how they select their clients. Martin explained to me that Reputation Hawk's decision to stay small is a consequence of the company's desire to handpick the clients with whom it works. "We basically prescreen to kind of decide which campaigns we want to take on and which we don't," he said. "Occasionally we'll have someone request our services where the situation could be like they have some child abuse in the past and so we don't really want to take on that kind of campaign." Others in the industry make similar calculations. Reputation.com reportedly will not take on clients who wish to suppress violent crimes, but will work with individuals who have been falsely accused of crimes or those who have paid fines for white-collar misconduct.[59]

The approach of turning down clients whose digital imprint contains elements deemed to have crossed an ethical or legal line is not, however, an industry-wide practice. Just as online content platforms—such as Reddit and Twitter—prefer to position themselves as passive hosts rather than the referees of morality or decency,[60] some online reputation management firms prefer not to select clients based on what they observe to be an arbitrary set of ethical boundaries. Martin suggested that some companies will take on clients regardless of the nature of the content they are trying to suppress:

> You have a lot of companies in this industry who don't care. They'll take on anybody and their reasoning behind that, which you can understand, is basically someone did something ten years ago and now it's popping up in the top of their search results and they're like, "Hey, I've moved on and paid whatever price I paid for that mistake that I made and I don't want this just being at the top of Google every time someone searches for my name. So I want to promote the positive stuff that I'm doing now." And so that's what I would say is the big gray area in the industry. And it's different for different companies. I would say most of the companies out there don't pay too much attention to the actual, the case, you know, whatever the client doesn't want appearing at the top of the search results.

Martin's explanation of why a reputation management firm might be hesitate to turn down a client based on past actions resonates with an ideological perspective at the core of this industry: the internet's capacity to remember poses a problem for individuals who are looking to move on from their past. Stephen Hess told me that in meetings about Reputation.com's new products and services "the end of forgetting" is a frequent topic of discussion. He explained that "much of the work [Reputation.com] has done is targeted at the problem [of] the permanence of the internet."

Concerns about technologically facilitated memory structure an industry-wide belief that people should not necessarily be defined by the mistakes they've made in the past, particularly if they have atoned for their actions. A representative from one company stressed to me that there are no circumstances under which they would refuse to take on a client: "We believe everybody online has the right to control the way that they're perceived online. You know, of course, that means that we have to deal with some very difficult situations. But a helpful analogy might be a defense attorney who has to defend somebody who has committed a crime that they find objectionable, but they agree that they have the right to be represented, and we kind of feel the same way. We don't play judge and jury. We're here to provide a service." This comment, however, raises important questions about who has the right to determine which information is easily found and which is obscured. In the absence of effective legal mechanisms in the United States to erase outdated or false information from the web, this decision often falls to individual commercial firms, some of whom seem wary of taking on this responsibility.

The practice of cleansing the web to erase undesirable content is controversial. The public response to one large-scale online image management campaign reveals some of the tensions embedded in such practices. In April 2016, the *Sacramento Bee* reported that the University of California, Davis, had paid a public relations firm at least $175,000 to remove or bury online posts that referenced a 2011 incident in which a campus police officer had used pepper spray on a group of student protesters.[61] The online reputation management efforts were reportedly part of a broader university initiative to improve the institution's digital image and suppress content that was critical of the university's chancellor. While a university spokesperson described the campaign as part of efforts to ensure that the university and its chancellor were fairly portrayed online,[62] others argued that the efforts amounted to censorship.[63]

Responses to this incident reveal one of the ethical issues at the heart of online reputation management: who has the authority to decide what information is deserving of public attention? One firm contracted to design a search engine optimization strategy for UC Davis described its "primary goal" as to "achieve a reasonable balance of positive natural search results on common terms concerning UC Davis and Chancellor Katehi."[64] Conversely, a UC Davis student interviewed by *The Guardian* described the university's efforts as "trying to erase history" with the goal of "misleading people."[65] This line between information management and censorship is a thin one, and where it should be drawn is not always clear. For some, populating the internet with content that reflects positively on one's image is an essential part of contemporary self-presentation—no different from wearing professional clothing to the office.[66] Others, however, see the strategic use of promotional content to bury less favorable information as manipulative and dishonest.

Part of this concern about who has the authority to decide the information that is worthy of public attention is tied to the cost of reputation management services. Apart from the BrandYourself DIY platform, most online reputation management services are prohibitively expensive for individuals hoping to bury a news story or remove an image from the web.[67] The cost raises an important tension: what happens if everyone has an online reputation, but only some people can afford to protect or repair theirs? Viktor Mayer-Schönberger, as discussed in the previous chapter, has written that digital technologies make forgetting more expensive by driving down the cost of information storage and introducing tools for expedient access.[68] When it comes to digital content, it tends to be easier and less time-consuming to save artifacts, a task often carried out by default, than it is to selectively delete. The price of reputation management services introduces an additional monetary cost, thereby highlighting the disadvantages faced by those who cannot afford to effectively cleanse their digital image.

There is some consistency across the ORM industry regarding the difference between ethical and nonethical strategies for creating and optimizing content. As previously noted, many in the industry stress the creation of what they call "quality content" on behalf of clients. Not only will increasingly sophisticated search algorithms ignore repetitive content, but human audiences may also view material that appears to be scripted as inauthentic. Moreover, content that is interesting is more likely to generate page views, which, in turn, can bump it higher in the search results. The online reputation management industry, therefore, tends to define ethical content as being unique, well written, and consistent with the client's overarching narrative.

Those in the industry also differentiate between "black hat" and "white hat" methods of search engine optimization. White hat SEO strategies—such as the creation of engaging and high-quality content, strategic linking and web hosting patterns, and effective use of keywords—are considered to be legitimate methods of encouraging search engines to find and catalog content. Black hat techniques, on the other hand, refer to attempts to "trick" a search engine into indexing content. BrandYourself's Patrick Ambron describes commonly used black hat strategies including "keyword stuffing; cloaking, when the link in the search results is entirely different from the site you arrive at; and link buying, which is buying multiple links to drive traffic to your site."[69] The company representatives I spoke with tended to promote their use of white hat techniques as one strategy for signaling a commitment to ethical practices.[70]

Although they advertise the use of strategies that adhere to search engine rules, online reputation management companies have a complicated relationship with these digital publishers. Search engines act simultaneously as the primary platforms through which unwanted information is circulated and discovered, and as a key tool for suppressing that content. Regardless of whether they view Google and other search engines as allies, ORM companies recognize the socio-technical power of these platforms to shape how information is accessed. Accordingly, most companies attempt to work within, rather than against, the rules established by search platforms. This is partially due to ethical considerations, but is also a consequence of the practical problems with using black hat SEO practices. If content that uses manipulative strategies is discovered by a search engine it risks being "delisted" from the search index, possibly resulting in the resurfacing of content that had been previously suppressed.[71]

Some of those I spoke with expressed concern that the unethical behavior of some companies that claim to provide reputation management services has hurt the industry. Patrick Ambron described a lack of satisfaction with the approach offered by existing companies as the reason he decided to start BrandYourself. "To be frank," he told me, "I think the industry is very much broken. I don't think that the companies out there were catering to the right people or doing a very good job of what they claim they do." Like Fertik and Martin, Ambron lamented to me that companies who misrepresent themselves leave clients "with a bad taste in their mouths." To combat the skepticism the public may feel about the industry, Ambron said that his company focuses on demystifying the process. "Transparency is very important to us," he told me. "Even on the service side, it's always clear what we're doing, why it works, whether it will work or not." The company tries, he told me, not to create further confusion around an already complicated practice.

Efforts by companies in this field to position themselves as legitimate have been challenged by recent incidents in which agencies claiming to help victims of unwanted online content have exploited shame and embarrassment for commercial gain—incidents that have revealed a darker side of companies that make similar claims to online reputation management firms. Investigative news reports have revealed reciprocal relationships between content hosts and image management companies that both create and address issues of unwanted digital content. The cooperation between websites that display content and those that sell services to remove it ensures a continuing market for reputation management services. The proliferation of mug shot websites exemplifies this exploitative practice. Ambron drew my addition to these websites while describing the immense power search engines have to shape the online landscape. Such sites, which became highly visible in 2010, gather publicly available images from county sheriff's offices and courthouses and post them online. The professed purposes of the sites, as David Segal wrote in the New York Times, is to provide the public with easy and quick access to information about the problematic pasts of anyone, from a potential date to a youth softball coach.[72]

Mug shot websites, which once occupied prominent positions in some search results, present a problem for individuals looking to move on from interactions with law enforcement. The presence of these images at the top of an online search can feel particularly unfair for those who have had their criminal records corrected or amended, as well as for those never convicted of a crime. Legal systems built on principles of rehabilitation allow for the possibility that criminal records may be sealed or expunged after a period of service or as the result of treatment; however, the persistence and searchability of information online means, despite structural mechanisms in law that allow criminal records to effectively be "forgotten," related reports can live in search results even after the legal records have been deleted.[73]

The operators of mug shot websites position themselves as providing an important public service by giving people easy access to information about the criminal histories of those in their communities. The fact, however, that many of these sites offer services where people can pay a fee to have these images removed undermines these altruistic claims.[74] The partnership between host website and removal services is evident in reports that people who have paid to have mug shots removed often see the same images turn up on other websites accompanied by additional demands for removal fees. People's willingness to pay, often multiple times, to have mug shots taken down demonstrates the vulnerability of having these images define one's online existence.

The relationship between image removal services and platforms that host content has received attention from legislators who are concerned about the power these services exert over individuals who may be desperate to repair their online image. Lawmakers, however, are struggling to draft legislation that balances the public's right to know with individuals' desire to protect their reputations.[75] For now, the private sector has stepped in to provide a provisional solution. In 2013, Google announced that it had tweaked its algorithm to downgrade mug shot websites.[76] This change effectively erased these images from Google's search results. To disrupt the exploitative relationship between content hosting and removal services, some payment companies, including MasterCard, American Express, Discover, and PayPal, decided to terminate relationships with both the mug shot sites and the mug shot removal sites.[77] By refusing to accept payment for their services, these financial companies effectively cut off the leading source of funds. While these decisions by private companies help address the problem of predatory image management services in the short term, their actions also highlight the immense power commercial organizations exercise in determining the information that is visible online.

Revenge porn websites, which use a similar model to mug shot websites to exploit the vulnerability people feel when sensitive information is made public, offer another example of the complex political economy in which online reputation management services are embedded. Revenge porn websites are commercial repositories of sexual photos, shared without consent, usually posted by a former intimate partner.[78] These photos, originally intended for private viewing by a limited audience, are posted in tandem with identifying information such as names, social network account information, and offline addresses. Like mug shot websites, some revenge porn websites offer image removal for a fee. Others of these sites also post advertisements for online reputation management firms that promote information removal services.

Responses to nonconsensual image sharing reveal how the risks of unwanted or uninvited digital disclosures are not experienced equally across populations. The institutionalized shaming and efforts at humiliation and extortion facilitated through revenge porn sites disproportionally target women. The discourse around nonconsensual image sharing—as noted in the introduction's discussion of the "celebgate" scandal—can evoke the language of victim blaming, where those seen in the images are admonished for taking the pictures or failing to ensure their secure storage.[79] Writing about legal approaches to revenge porn, criminologist Michael Salter and legal scholar Thomas Crofts argue that a focus on individual responsibility and personalized responses ignores gender disparities in intimate relationships and reinforces cultural logics that blame women for gender-based violence.[80] Responses that cast blame on women when intimate sexual images are circulated without their consent rely on and reinforce persistent models of femininity rooted in values of modesty and chastity. This practice of attaching female decency to the ability of women to elude the efforts of those wishing to pry into their private affairs is, according to legal scholar Anita Allen, one of the persistent ways in which privacy is gendered.[81] These sites also support the strategies of humiliation that reside at the heart of the revenge porn industry. For a personal risk management approach to make sense, Salter and Crofts write, we must assume a contractual view of intimate relationships, one that not only fails to account for the realities of human behavior but "naturalizes male wrongdoing and gender power imbalances as the implicit backdrop to sexual negotiations that women must factor into their decision-making."[82]

As with mug shot websites, legislators have begun to turn their attention to addressing the exploitative nature of revenge porn sites.[83] As a
result, some of these sites have been shut down and some states have created laws to ban them altogether. In late 2017, the Ending Nonconsensual
Online User Graphic Harassment Act was introduced in the U.S. Senate
with bipartisan support. Moreover, social network sites have begun to introduce efforts to combat nonconsensual image sharing.[84] Some online
reputation management companies have issued statements specifically
condemning the practices of revenge porn sites and praising legislative
efforts to address this issue;[85] however, there is an undeniable tension in
an industry that is, by its nature, deeply embedded in a pervasive and
problematic culture of online shaming. Communication scholar Ganaele
Langlois and legal scholar Andrea Slane describe the online reputation
management industry as benefiting from an "affective economy of online
shame."[86] They point to the practice of targeting advertisements toward
individuals who are vulnerable—a more pernicious version of what Stephen Hess referred to as the targeting of acute pain points—as emblematic
of a capitalist system where human impulses are quantified, monetized,
and even exploited. The result, they argue, is that reputation management
services are invested in keeping online shaming flourishing to support
their business model.[87] Langlois and Slane write, "Overall, we see the
rise of an ecosystem of sorts: companies specializing in various forms of
shame feed reputation-management companies and vice versa."[88]

This is a problem for online reputation management firms who want
to distinguish themselves from those that prey on individuals in vulnerable situations. Speaking in general about "bad actors" in the online reputation management field, Michael Fertik described to me the
damage those types of sites can have for other ORM companies: "So,
there are actors on the reputation side who own websites where you are
slammed, and then try to sell you reputation services. That's very bad
and every so often . . . well, you get lumped in with them. So every so
often, someone will say, 'Oh, you are just like the rest.' It's taken us five or
six years since we started the company, most people now think of us as a
different thing, but you still have to always keep your nose super clean."
With all the ethical land mines, it is easy to imagine how transgressions
of self-imposed regulations may occur, particularly in the absence of
industry guidelines. About the practice of publishing negative content

that users can pay to have removed, Fertik noted, "At our scale, I'm sure were not perfect every day. But we don't do anything even close to like remotely one billion miles away from something like that. But that's bad, that's bad for 'this industry,' whatever you want to call it." While firms may avoid relationships with websites that exploit individuals through the publication of private or sensitive data, the ethical dilemmas here are difficult to escape. By providing a service that allows people to pay to have information buried or removed, these companies are part of a system that benefits from cultures of digital shaming.

Some industry players describe the need for self-regulation to help raise the profile of the entire online reputation management industry. Chris Martin, for example, suggested to me the introduction of standard practices, which "would help a lot because you have a lot of companies out there and some of the can be doing things that are, you know, not very ethical as far as how they are shaping search results in Google. So, yeah, I think if it were ever started it would be really important." Martin recalled efforts in 2009 by a few people to create the Online Reputation Management Association. When those people left the industry, Martin said, the initiative fell flat, leaving people to build their own networks. Others, like Patrick Ambron, view the lack of transparency in the field as an opportunity: "I do think there is not a strong industry ethic right now, which is why I think that is something we're trying to do just by doing things the right way."

Universal Threats, Limited Solutions

Borrowing from strategies refined in promotional fields, the online reputation management industry advocates for the application of commercial logics to individual self-presentation to assist clients in the creation of a digital image worthy of promotion. By incorporating tools associated with self-branding, the industry's method encourages people to think about themselves as a product with unique features and qualities that set them apart. Self-branding is commonly thought of as a set of practices crafted by microcelebrities—those who cultivate a public persona for online followers they view as fans, rather than friends[89]—that has trickled down to ordinary people. The evolution of the online reputation management industry offers a slightly different perspective: practices of self-branding by ordinary people have emerged as much out of a desire for self-protection as from aspirations of celebrity. The requirement of strategic visibility is cultivated both as a tactic for creating private spaces in an environment where it is easy to become overexposed, and as an approach to publicity that promises social and economic rewards based on the attention of others. This investment in visibility is an important component of an attention economy where self-production and display are fetishized and having an image for public consumption is an essential component of success.

The shift in thinking about digital reputations from protection to promotion underscores individual responsibilities for self-presentation and, accordingly, the social consequences for failures to safeguard one's personal image. Thinking about one's self-presentation as a strategic promotional project encourages practices of commodified self-reflexivity, where performances are rated and ranked according to the logics of a promotional culture that privileges values such as attention, popularity, and visibility, but penalizes those performances that are read as too visible, too self-promotional, or otherwise lacking taste. This framing of digital reputation operates simultaneously as a form of social and economic disciplining in which identities must be intentional and controlled in order to be profitable.[90] Although practices of digital identity construction are often presented as an empowering form of cultural production,[91] the project's deep commitments to promotional logics has the potential to limit discourses of the self and encourage the reproduction of familiar and socially accepted identities by favoring adherence to recognizable and uncontroversial narratives.[92]

Although industry discourse promotes identity management as essential, tools and services are not accessible by all those who may need or want them. Those with money, time, and facility with digital technologies are more likely to be able to take advantage of the tools to bury unwanted content and promote information that shows them in a positive light. Those with access to identities that conform to cultural norms regarding respectability—evaluations shaped by factors such as race, ethnicity, class, and gender—are invited to share more of themselves while others are encouraged to promote those parts of their identities that fit these cultural constructs and bury those that do not. Legal scholar Danielle Citron notes that criminal and tort law can address some of the damages of cyber abuse, including reputational harm, emotional distress, and privacy violations. She observes, however, the limits of these forms of redress, particularly in instances when attacks were perpetrated based on protected characteristics such as gender or race: "They fall short of a complete response because they fail to address the gender- and race-based nature of the damage."[93] The limits of the online reputation management approach are similar: they offer temporary solutions without comprehensive strategies to address the broader socio-technical structures that frame the problem.

Despite these limitations, the industry's discourse makes clear that the threats and possibilities of online reputation are universal. These assertions come in the form of warnings: "Thanks to rapid advances in digital technology," write Fertik and Thompson, "your reputation will become ubiquitous, permanent, and available worldwide—whether you like it or not."[94] But they also come in the form of empowering statements: "Thanks to the Internet," the authors continue, "*you* have the chance to take direct control of the way people see you."[95] Using a range of channels, from traditional news outlets to college programs, this industry has helped naturalize a set of expectations and responsibilities around online self-presentation. Discourse from the online reputation management industry dismisses strategies common among resisters that involve opting out of digital life and stresses the dangers of privacy strategies that rely on the absence of an online presence. Failure to fill one's digital space, the industry reasons, only invites others to occupy it on one's behalf.

By following a logic that demands visibility, this industry encourages strategies that entail capitulation to social and institutional monitoring. The next chapter examines a set of companies that responds to this requirement of visibility by providing tools that allow individuals to leverage the economic value that results from their digital presence. By resurrecting a version of the infomediary model introduced in chapter 3, these companies deliver tools that allow clients to collect and manage the sale of their personal data. This revised model, however, does not share with first-generation infomediaries an investment in opportunities for anonymity. Instead, it relies on an idea established and popularized by the online reputation management industry: that a visible online identity is an investment that, if carefully cultivated, can yield positive returns.

6

The Big Power of Small Data

A Revolution in Privacy

In May 2013, I attended the Internet Identity Workshop (IIW) at the Computer History Museum in Mountain View, California. This biannual conference brings together a range of people who share an interest in the way identity and identity architectures shape how users navigate and experience the web. During the three-day conference, two separate presentations referred to an imminent "revolution" in the personal data economy. Using similar historical metaphors, both presenters characterized the contemporary economic system as a form of "digital feudalism" in which individuals, acting as data serfs, toil in the service of powerful lords who profit from the information they collect.

The power of these lords notwithstanding, both presenters predicted a revolution that would overthrow "digital feudalism" in favor of a "digital enlightenment." Under this new economic order, the presenters anticipated, individuals would own their personal information. They would have cloud-based accounts—which would provide the foundation of a personal data ecosystem—from which they could facilitate the collection and storage of data on everything from finances and health to friendships and family.[1] Through the application of sophisticated analytic tools, individuals would be able to reveal and benefit from insights embedded in their data. Such a revolution in information access and ownership, the presenters argued, would fundamentally alter the relationship between data subjects and the institutional authorities that currently dominate the data economy.

These parallel presentations about an impending data revolution refer to a broader set of claims about the role of personal information in the contemporary global economy. Metaphors positioning personal data as a raw resource to be mined and refined are now commonplace as politicians and economists describe data as a new form of oil[2] or gold.[3] Positioned as a valuable economic resource, the data exhaust produced as a by-product of everyday interactions between people and their devices is treated as offering valuable insight in areas as diverse as health, education, finance, and urban planning. While companies make use of this information to analyze past behaviors, often in the hopes of predicting future preferences and practices, questions arise about the ethical implications of collecting and using personal information to shape everything from advertising to policing.[4]

There is an asymmetry inherent in metaphors that describe data as a raw resource that requires extraction and refining between those who *can know* and those *who are known*. When the IIW presenters distinguished between data lords and data serfs they did so to call attention to an imbalance between the near-ubiquitous availability of tools that produce personal data and the far more limited access to analytic technologies that aggregate, organize, and extract their meaning. As media scholar Mark Andrejevic points out, "The knowledge practices associated with big data represent a profoundly *un*democratic shift insofar as they are reliant upon access to huge and costly databases as well as to the processing power and technological know-how to make use of the data."[5] A data revolution, therefore, would require a redistribution of the tools that provide data with its economic value.

Several start-ups and established technology companies are taking aim at this asymmetry by building tools and technologies through which people can collect their own data and use analytic software and visualization tools to make sense of them. While some of these entrepreneurs are simply interested in providing individuals with data-driven insights into their own behaviors, others are motivated by a similar set of concerns to those that preoccupy academic critics and privacy advocates: opaque analytic tools are being used to identify individuals and applied in ways that shape their experiences and opportunities. By offering people the chance to engage in the capture and analysis of their personal data, these strategies aim to disrupt the hierarchical relationships between data subjects and the institutionalized agents that produce and use their information. Through these strategies, entrepreneurs allow individuals to feel empowered based on their access to personal data even as they engage with services that mandate personal information disclosure as a condition of access.

This premise of empowering individuals by giving them tools to access, store, and share their personal data revives an idea that was at the core of the infomediary model. Those who pioneered this approach at the end of the twentieth century observed that although personal information is valuable to third parties, individuals are well-positioned to collect and analyze this information in ways that generate unique insight and create new sources of value. Based on a similar set of ideologies, a collection of entrepreneurs have revived the infomediary model as inspiration for technical tools that would allow individuals to collect, manage, and leverage their digital data. Through these tools, these companies encourage individuals to quantify their behaviors, thereby converting visibility and participation into value.

This chapter considers the reemergence of the infomediary model as part of a personal data ecosystem—a network of tools that facilitates the collection, storage, and analysis of personal information—that embraces the power of "small data." While a growing number of "big data" initiatives promise to extract new forms of information and value hidden in massive troves of information,[6] advocates of "small data" programs offer strategies to undermine the hierarchies inherent in large-scale data projects that privilege those with access to immense data sets and powerful algorithms. Unlike the bird's eye view offered by big data projects, which tend to focus on trends and patterns, small data initiatives aim to offer personalized knowledge through tools deployed by individuals to help unearth the meaning in their personal information.

Those invested in the creation of a personal data ecosystem are aiming to build a new culture around personal information. By giving people the tools to engage with their data, they hope to build an economy where equal investments by consumers and companies will foster trust and facilitate a productive exchange of information. One of the central tasks is to build tools that will encourage individuals to take an interest in their data. Several small data start-ups are building personal data storage tools that allow users to fill their profiles with information from sources such as banks, personal tracking devices, and social media sites and apply visualization tools intended to reveal hidden meaning embedded in the data. Through the construction of these personal data platforms—alternatively referred to as data vaults, lockers, or stores—these companies encourage individuals to act as the central aggregators for their information, thereby facilitating the creation of a unique data set that is more comprehensive than anything commercial data brokers could build on their own.

The features each company provides through its personal data storage platform differ, but all the tools share the goal of educating people about the value offered by their information. In many ways, these virtual vaults closely parallel the tools provided by infomediaries at the end of the twentieth century. Moreover, the entrepreneurs behind the personal data ecosystem share with their predecessors a general perspective that endorses possibilities for individual empowerment through data control. There are, however, important differences between these two models. By juxtaposing the services offered by these two generations of companies, this chapter explores how a different political and social climate has altered frameworks for thinking about online privacy risks and solutions.

Reviving the Infomediary Model: Ownership, Knowledge, and Value

In 2011, Marc Guldimann founded Enliken, a personal data exchange platform designed to allow users to trade their personal data for compensation from interested companies. Guldimann's road to launching a personal data exchange platform parallels the paths taken by many of those who piloted infomediaries at the end of the twentieth century. As was the case for the entrepreneurs behind PrivaSeek and Privada, Guldimann's work in advertising had made him aware of the limits of industry-wide efforts to target consumers with messages tailored to their interests. While at Spongecell, an online display advertising company he co-founded, Guldimann observed efforts to target consumers with advertising content based on a combination of online context and past behavior. However, due to the "low quality" of the information Spongecell had purchased from data brokers, when we spoke in 2013 Guldimann described the company's efforts at addressable content as "an abject failure."

When he started Enliken, Guldimann was hoping to correct what he saw as behavioral advertising's central problem: unreliable consumer data. Based on his observation that "you get a lot further if you just involve the consumer," Guldimann established Enliken with the goal of introducing data collection strategies that combine transparency with usability. Rather than collecting information surreptitiously from unknowing consumers, Guldimann wanted to build a system that would yield better results by engaging individuals in the data collection process. By facilitating strategies for companies to go directly to the consumer and ask for their data, Guldimann hoped Enliken would promote what he saw as a more authentic conversation between consumers and companies, yielding higher-quality data that would benefit both parties.[7]

Throughout my interviews, I heard accounts from entrepreneurs concerned with the potential negative consequences facing an advertising industry that relied on the collection and use of personal information in the absence of consumer buy-in. Matt Hogan, for example, was motivated to start the personal data exchange platform Datacoup based on what he saw as persistent inequities and inefficiencies inherent in a digital economy where a range of players—including data brokers, ad agencies, and ad networks—have their hands in the pockets of consumers. "At the end of the day," Hogan told me during a 2013 conversation, "there's roughly $125 billion in revenues being generated annually on the backs of consumer data. The consumer gets largely nothing from all this content creation that we are doing every day, other than the targeted ads." Hogan—who, with Guldimann, ran a New York City–based meetup for those interested in the personal data economy—wanted to help individuals capture some of this value by providing them with the opportunity to "aggregate, visualize, and sell their own personal data."

Several of the entrepreneurs behind these start-ups join privacy advocates in pointing to the furtive collection of personal data as a breach of the presumption of privacy many people have when they go online. They also join the advocates in concerns about an economic system that relies on uncompensated consumer labor.[8] Most, however, do not challenge existing economic systems by calling for an end to data tracking or targeted advertising. Instead, they describe an economy where the needs of retailers, advertisers, and consumers are all met. Stemming from mutual respect and trust between retailers and consumers, they imagine an economic system where individuals can access and utilize the information that exists about them across public and private databases. While the focus of privacy advocates has largely considered options that would allow people to avoid pervasive surveillance regimes, the strategies offered by these companies aim to give individuals tools to collect and understand their own data—to engage in the system rather than be exploited by it.

These strategies involve the development of a personal data ecosystem in which individuals, armed with a personal data storage platform, become the central point of aggregation for information currently housed in silos spread across the digital landscape. These efforts to equip people with the tools to combine and analyze their information propose to give them an advantage over data brokers while also offering access to the insights allegedly hidden in a growing trove of personal data. By being able to tell a more holistic and accurate story about individuals through the aggregation of discrete data collected from a range of sources, those advocating for the construction of a personal data ecosystem pursue their goal of undermining the monopoly on knowledge held by those with the power to make sense of vast quantities of data: the data lords.

At the heart of the personal data ecosystem is an attempt to address concerns about an information economy that exploits data subjects while at the same time nurturing the optimism surrounding big data initiatives. To reconcile the tension existing between a culture that expects privacy and an economy that incentivizes disclosure and sharing, personal data brokers recruit individuals to act as the guardians of their information flows in the hopes that the resulting perception of autonomy and control will relieve anxieties about the potential for unwanted visibility. To do so, those behind the personal data ecosystem—like those behind anonymizers, infomediaries, and online reputation management companies—engage in a range of pedagogical activities to help individuals understand the latent value residing in their data trails through discourses of ownership, self-discovery, and rewards.

Seize the Data: Privacy through Ownership

In the 1997 book *Net Gain: Expanding Markets through Virtual Communities*, John Hagel III, one of the architects behind the infomediary model, suggested with co-author Arthur Armstrong that consumer concerns about privacy may limit the quantity and quality of information companies are able to collect. "The paradox," they wrote, "is that the better the technology becomes at capturing information, the more concern people will have about their privacy."[9] By offering the infomediary as a consumer-controlled repository of personal information, Hagel and Armstrong provided companies with a strategy for reducing individual anxieties while simultaneously allowing them to access more detailed information. They believed this strategy would only be successful, however, if individuals felt they owned and controlled their personal data. "The only way to resolve this paradox," they wrote "may be to acknowledge that users themselves are the rightful owners of their own usage and transaction information."[10]

By creating a set of ownership rights around personal data, they proposed that individuals would be encouraged to collect vast amounts of information about their own behaviors which they could then make available to third parties. Providing people with strategies to own their information, Hagel and Armstrong argued, would change the ways individuals engage with their data. "Privacy" they concluded, "disappears as an issue because information disclosure is at the discretion of the user."[11] Personal data brokers draw closely on the logic of information ownership and control outlined by Hagel and Armstrong more than two decades ago. Through personal data storage systems, they aim to empower individuals by giving them the tools to collect, analyze, and leverage the data that third-party companies have deemed valuable.

For the online data vault provider Personal,[12] the right of individuals to own their data has been a central component of the company's mission from the start. Founder Shane Green had been working at a global mobile device company when he founded Personal in 2009. An expert in location data and mapping software, Green decided he was not interested in the organization's goal of creating technologies that would monetize consumer data through increasingly pervasive forms of consumer tracking.[13] Green founded Personal based on an alternative model: a "private, personal network and data vault for individuals to manage and control access to their digital information."[14]

When I visited Personal's Washington, DC, offices in 2013, chief policy officer and general counsel Josh Galper told me that when the company began "there was no place you could aggregate your information from all the different places in your life and put it in that safe place where you could set permissions for sharing it, deciding how you want to use it, and get value from it." The company created its own data vault to fill this gap. Users, whom Personal prefers to call owners, could populate their data vault with information such as passwords, copies of their driver's license or birth certificate, and tax information. One of the services Personal provided was the ability to "pipe in" information from external sources by accessing an application program interface (API).[15] For example, a vault owner could access the API from their personal fitness tracker to fill their vault with information about their exercise habits. By allowing access to their bank's API, they could add information about spending habits. Galper described the platform as providing a way to help individuals ingest, organize, and reuse this information: "Whether it's use value, convenience, access, sharing it with someone else, using it to fill out forms, and even eventually monetizing your own data set so that you get the benefit."

Although Green talked publicly about the possibility of building a market where personal information could be bartered, shared, or exchanged with third-party services[16]—similar to the selling circle and personal datamart imagined by first-generation infomediaries iPrivacy and PrivaSeek—Galper told me helping people monetize content was part of the company's "roadmap," though it was not a service Personal was offering when we spoke. Nevertheless, the company has thought carefully about strategies to protect the claims of individuals to their data. This approach to ownership was operationalized in Personal's owner data agreement (ODA). This document was written to create legally enforceable protections for personal information and data—a key component of the company's mission to empower their clients. Galper described the ODA as a "very simple" but "unprecedented" legal agreement "because nobody has ever been asked to enter into a contract that empowers the user regarding their own data and that puts the person in charge." He explained the ODA as a reversal of the standard terms of service agreements that usually ask individuals to give up ownership of their information in exchange for access to a platform or service. Personal saw the ODA as a binding contract that all parties agreed to before information was exchanged. According to the document, if one party to the agreement was to misuse or lose that data, they would be in violation of the contract and could be held legally responsible.[17]

At the heart of this notion of data control is a belief, shared with those behind the early infomediaries, that individuals own their personal information. The twin issues of privacy and data ownership have become contentious in the digital moment in part because the terms governing information collection and use conflict with the relationship we instinctively feel with our personal information. In describing this connection, Galper told me, "You feel like you own it. It doesn't matter what the fine print says. There's this feeling that your digital identity is connected to you." This sense of ownership operates as the motivation behind Personal's ODA and is emphasized by the company's insistence that its clients be referred to as "owners" rather than "users."

Other members of the personal data community have developed their own strategies to help individuals assert ownership rights over their personal information. The Respect Network, a collective of companies that share the goal of building a user-centric internet through the creation and provision of a personal data ecosystem, has implemented a "promise" to protect the integrity of the information provided by all users in the network. Respect Network CEO Gary Rowe described the organization's goal to "re-establish trust between individuals and organizations through a platform that allows people to control their data and interaction."[18] As with companies like Personal, Enliken, and Datacoup, the Respect Network wants to leverage control over personal data, reputations, and social relationships to create value for users.[19]

Respect Network partners, a group that includes Personal, draw on a set of five principles that govern the collection and use of personal data in their ecosystem. Members of this coalition argue that these principles—promise, permission, protection, portability, and proof—improve on existing U.S. regulations (governed largely by the FTC's Fair Information Practice Principles) by doing more to engender trust between digital service providers and consumers. Promise, the first of the five principles, relates to what Drummond Reed, Respect Network founder, calls the "golden rule for data." This promise is a contractual obligation from each member of the network that states, "I agree to respect your right to control your identity and your data." Reed, who told me when we spoke in 2013 that he prefers the term "promise" over "contract," says this principle is at the heart of Respect Network's mission of facilitating trusting relationships online.

The Respect Network's promise gets at what may be the fundamental issue when it comes to digital privacy: respect. Although some people might want to opt out of third-party data collection and use altogether, those promoting the personal data ecosystem believe others are simply frustrated that their information is being collected and used in ways they have not explicitly consented to or do not understand. When privacy is assumed as a precondition for respect,[20] its violation can leave individuals feeling as though they are not valued. This lack of respect for individuals and their information may facilitate a hostile economic environment in which consumers feel they are being treated unfairly by data brokers and advertisers.

I introduced Reputation.com in previous chapters as a leading online reputation management company. Although it started with a mission of providing tools and strategies to help individuals repair and protect and eventually promote their digital image, more recently Reputation.com has turned its attention to the development of technologies to protect online privacy by facilitating control over data trails. Stephen Hess, a product manager at Reputation.com, explained to me the logic behind extending the company's reputation management services to include products that help people manage their personal data: "So we talk about privacy, which is about reputation. We talk about personal data. And at the end of the day, I think all of what those terms are getting at is that . . . you have a digital existence." At Reputation.com, Hess continued, "we seek to help you understand what your digital footprint is online, [to] control that information and what it presents." In fact, the strategies offered by the online reputation management companies and those behind the personal data ecosystem are not all that different: both are invested in helping clients understand and control their digital narratives, whether those stories are told through search results or data trails.

In the future, Hess explained, the company has plans to help its clients collect and leverage their digital information through the construction of a data vault. Like those data storage platforms introduced by other companies, the Reputation.com vault would allow clients to store information that could be shared selectively at the vault owner's request. Hess described the responsibility any third party with access to client data would have to abide by the terms of use set by the data owner when it negotiated the exchange of information through a vault. This arrangement, Hess argued, has the potential to empower the individuals to understand and manage the ways their data are being used. The strength of the data vault, Hess told me, is that it "is giving control over terms of use in a way that is first understandable to the consumer, but second is privacy-centered and consumer-centered."

In the era of big data, however, it is not always the initial or even secondary uses of personal data that concern people. Writing for the *New York Times Magazine*, Charles Duhigg described the efforts of retail giant Target to identify a particularly valuable consumer segment: pregnant women.[21] Analysts at Target looked for purchase patterns among customers who had enrolled in the company's baby-shower registry. By looking for similar patterns in the general population of consumers, Target began to assign shoppers a pregnancy score, indicating both how likely it was that each consumer was pregnant and their probable stage of pregnancy. This score informed company efforts to tailor advertisements and promotions to individuals in this consumer group. While people may be comfortable with a retailer collecting information about the brand of toilet paper they prefer in order to provide them with relevant coupons, they may object to that same retailer combining information about their toilet paper consumption habits with additional purchasing information to predict major life events such as pregnancy, retirement, marriage, or divorce.

When I visited the company's offices in 2013, Reputation.com was aiming to use its vault to prevent this kind of unwanted secondary and tertiary data use. Michael Fertik envisioned the construction of a platform that would include a sophisticated set of permissions to provide protections by limiting data use based on user-issued consent. These permissions would be paired with data and contractual information about when and how that information could be used. The goal of these permissions would be to provide the data owner with tools to control the flow of their information even as it is passes from one party to another. This idea of data permissions parallels efforts to promote privacy protection through data minimization. Introduced in chapters 2 and 3, data minimization works by limiting the information accessed during a transaction to that which is strictly relevant to that interaction. In the case of data permissions, the vault user would be able to determine the conditions under which the information they share could be used.

For example, a data vault owner may provide information about her age to a car insurance company. A contract would be attached to that piece of information that says her age can be used up to three times for actuarial purposes; however, that same contract would prevent the company from transferring the information to a third party or using the information a fourth time without seeking additional permissions. By attaching these consent protocols to the data to track and report use patterns, Fertik told me, misuse would be discoverable and the offending party could be held responsible and reprimanded for infractions. Reputation.com was also considering the potential for acting as a reputation broker—confirming with the auto insurance company whether the data vault owner met the conditions the insurance provider required without revealing any of the specific details.[22]

There are challenges, however, to frameworks that apply principles of ownership to personal data. For one thing, when a person choses to share information, their disclosures can contain details about other people who may not have consented to its release.[23] Consider the controversy surrounding the use of Facebook data by Cambridge Analytica, a political marketing firm most well-known for its work with Donald Trump's 2016 U.S. presidential campaign. The company claimed it could divide the electorate into psychographic segments—a strategy designed to identify and target individuals based on their personality traits. To build the data set necessary for this work, the company partnered with an academic from Cambridge University who paid hundreds of thousands of Facebook users to complete a personality test using an app called thisisyourdigitallife.[24] When Facebook users downloaded the app they were agreeing to its terms of service, which included having their information collected for the purposes of academic research. In violation of this agreement and Facebook's terms of service for third-party apps, Cambridge Analytica was provided the data for nonacademic use.

But this data set was not limited to information about the 270,000 individuals who had downloaded the app. The developer also gained access to data about the test takers' friends, a strategy that resulted in the creation of a database of over eighty million unique profiles.[25] At the time, this practice did not violate Facebook's rules for third-party apps, which were allowed to "scrape" data from the profiles of those who downloaded an app as well as from the profiles of their friends.[26] Given that most of the individuals represented in that database had not consented to have their information collected, the Cambridge Analytica incident points to the problem of thinking about privacy protections as a consequence of individuals making discrete decisions about how to share their own information. Legal scholar Lior Strahilevitz argues that collective privacy issues arise when "a single source of confidential information reveals something about multiple individuals, and these people disagree over whether the information should be disseminated."[27] In this instance, however, millions of people had no choice in deciding whether their profiles were accessed—for the purposes of an academic study or otherwise.

In her work on self-tracking, sociologist Deborah Lupton observes that contemporary practices tend to view data and the bodies to which they are connected as autonomous, self-knowing, and independently rational. These approaches tend not to recognize "the fact that the self is always inevitably sited within social, cultural, and political contexts; that people are always part of social groups and acculturated into specific cultural norms; and that their bodies are always experienced in relation to others' bodies."[28] With respect to information privacy, Lupton's observation raises concerns about frameworks that treat disclosure decisions as though consequences are localized and easily traced. danah boyd and Alice Marwick use the term "networked privacy" to describe the realities of a social world where information is routinely exposed through the connections people have with others.[29] The ability to access information about millions of Americans based only on their digital relations reveals the limitations of ownership models, which rely on individuals having full autonomy over their data.

Self-Discovery: Analysis, Visualization, and Personalized Knowledge

During one lunch at the IIW conference, I was sitting beside an app developer who was working on a program that would help users capitalize on their mobile location data. I told him about my research and asked if his current project had implications for consumer privacy. He chuckled and told me people aren't really interested in data privacy. They are interested, he said, in the insights data reveal about their everyday lives. By way of example, he offered the project he was working on that would allow people to map the location data from their mobile devices and visualize their movements over time. By sharing this information with those in their network, people would be able to see if their daily routines put them in proximity to any of their friends. I asked why anyone would want to know that. Because it's interesting, the developer responded. Maybe you always eat lunch on Wednesday two blocks away from a friend and you had no idea, he offered. Having that information might encourage you to meet up for lunch on Wednesdays. It was clear from our conversation, however, that even this potential social element was itself a secondary benefit of the platform.[30] The app, he believed, would be valuable because people are interested in what their information can reveal about their *own* activities and behaviors.

In *Net Gain*, Hagel and Armstrong briefly observed the potential for infomediaries to uncover patterns in clients' spending habits to help individuals make better financial decisions; however, for those currently building personal data storage technology, the ability to organize and analyze personal information is much more than a by-product of the service. Those in the personal information ecosystem see self-discovery as a crucial feature of data storage platforms. When first conceptualized, the infomediary model was based on the premise that marketers and advertisers recognized value in the data produced through various digital interactions. In the personal data ecosystem, vault developers stress that the users themselves are—or ought to be—interested in the knowledge generated through the capture and analysis of their personal data.

When Datacoup launched a test version of its platform, founder Matt Hogan was surprised by the extent of users' interest in the company's data visualization tools. Those who engaged with an early version of the product, Hogan told me, "wanted to see a kind of mirror image of themselves." Hogan wasn't sure what was behind this interest. "We don't know if this is for vanity purposes," he said. "We don't know if it's for self-tracking, self-measurement, self-improvement purposes . . . [but] this was something that overwhelmingly people wanted." Because of this feedback, the company made visualization tools, which let clients map and analyze their data, a core component of its service.

Those behind the personal data ecosystem are not the only ones trying to foster people's interest in the secrets hidden in their data trails. I will return for a moment to self-tracking as a useful lens through which to examine how the rhetoric of empowerment that often accompanies small data projects can be undone by the realities of conditions in which that tracking takes place. In 2009 Gary Wolf wrote in *Wired* magazine about a trend he had noticed taking root in his social network.[31] His friends, many of whom were deeply entrenched in geek and tech communities, were using digital tools to track various aspects of their lives by assigning numerical values to ordinary practices. By monitoring and quantifying their sleep, diet, and exercise habits, they were attempting to reveal previously untapped information about their daily lives. Of interest to Wolf, however, were the ways in which these practices were extending beyond the tech culture of Silicon Valley. Just as those in the cypherpunk community saw an interest in digital privacy expand as more and more people gained access to the internet, Wolf hypothesized that the shrinking size and increased sophistication of trackers was combining with the normalization of sharing encouraged by social media to expand the popularity of self-tracking beyond this niche community.[32]

To support the development of strategies and tools to help people make use of the growing streams of data they were producing, Wolf, with *Wired* editor Kevin Kelly, began a project called the Quantified Self.[33] Turning on its head the idea that self-knowledge was obtained through introspection and deep reflection, Quantified Selfers embrace the power of numbers—those that appear to be passively recorded and objectively reported—to reveal hidden information that could increase efficiency and be used in self-improvement projects. The movement's unofficial slogan—"Self-knowledge through numbers"—communicates this belief in the power of quantification to contribute to knowledge about individual and collective experience.[34] "Behind the allure of the quantified self," Wolf writes, "is a guess that many of our problems come from simply lacking the instruments to understand who we are."[35]

By applying digital tools to track our habits and behaviors, Wolf argues we can overcome the mental and physical limitations humans have when it comes to self-reflection.[36] By quantifying daily practices and applying analytic tools, both of which are presented as free from human bias, self-tracking tools promise answers to questions that users didn't even know they should be asking. These insights, Wolf says, can inform behavior, making the quantified selfer healthier, more productive, or thriftier. Self-tracking, then, is not done solely for the sake of knowledge; it's ultimate goal is self-actualization and improvement. The data vaults that are at the core of the personal data ecosystem are a source for this kind of personalized knowledge. The presentation of this information as objectively gathered and independently analyzed helps to construct the digital self as a project that can be understood, analyzed, and improved on.

The personal data ecosystem shares with the Quantified Self movement an interest in the use of numbers as a window through which to understand and analyze behavioral patterns. When I asked about his most memorable projects at Reputation.com, Stephen Hess described an application he built soon after arriving at the company. The tool analyzed users' Facebook profiles and reported the average number of people who "liked" their posts, status updates, and shares. It also provided some sentiment analysis so that the user could quickly understand the tone of the comments on their wall. For Hess, this application represented a small-scale version of Reputation.com's general mission. The company, Hess noted, wants to provide metrics on its clients' digital existence. "So you can imagine it as a heart rate monitor for your online life" he offered. "We collect information about what you are doing online," he continued, "and provide summaries of that information to help you better understand yourself and then hopefully make better decisions based on that data." Hess's tool combined opportunities for self-discovery and self-reflection with implicit messages about self-improvement—the same ideas behind the quantified self movement.

As is the case with the self-tracking technologies people use to evaluate their activity levels, sleep habits, or productivity, the tracking technologies offered by personal data services are sold using discourses of personal empowerment. Media scholar Gina Neff and anthropologist Dawn Nafus observe, however, that promises of empowerment often come up short. "The problem," they write in their book *Self-Tracking*, "is that many off-the-shelf tracking options, sold through appeals to 'empowerment,' do not actually help people figure out which questions they should be asking, much less how to ask the next question, test ideas, or make discoveries."[37] They generally do not encourage users to ask if the strategies for improvement built into these systems—take more steps, share more photos, gain more followers—are resonant with their own objectives. Appeals to empowerment through self-knowledge also tend to obscure the access enjoyed by others to these data and the conclusions they may draw as a result. Lupton makes a similar observation: the same tracking technologies that allow people to make claims about themselves are increasingly being used by others who draw their own assumptions about what the data reveal.[38] These conclusions may be invisible to the data subject and inconsistent with their self-image.

Empowerment through self-improvement is not, however, the only goal of the forms of data analytics provided through the personal data ecosystem's tools. By providing individuals with the instruments to capture and analyze their personal information, the personal data ecosystem hopes to educate users about the significance of this resource. Personal's Shane Green describes informing people about the value of their personal data and getting them interested in the stories it can tell as one of the most important and difficult tasks facing his company and other members of the personal data community.[39] By providing individuals with tools that reveal meaning embedded in their data trails, those building the personal data ecosystem hope people will begin to get a sense of the resource they are giving up when they provide this information to third parties for free. By raising awareness regarding the informational value of this content, those behind the personal data ecosystem aim to educate consumers about the practices of commodification and data transaction that support the digital economy. They are, in short, teaching individuals to view their personal information as an economic resource.

Reputation Rewards: Offers, Discounts, Cash, and Status

The hope driving those behind the personal data ecosystem—that giving people insight into the details hidden in their data trails will help start a conversation between consumers and marketers—revives an ambition of the first-generation infomediary projects. In *Net Gain* Hagel and Armstrong described how the infomediary would facilitate a shift in power from vendors to consumers and assist newly empowered users by allowing them to effectively manage and clearly communicate their interests to businesses. In addition to providing users with control to limit the access advertisers and retailers would have to their data, Hagel and Armstrong wrote that "the infomediary would help the member maximize the economic value of this information by auctioning the rights of controlled access to it, consistent with the privacy preferences of the member."[40] By giving individuals the opportunity to play a part in the commodification of their personal information, the personal data ecosystem maintains this goal of turning digital participation into economic reward.

Harnessing this value, however, requires that data are available for analysis. "Like money left under a mattress," the authors of a World Economic Forum (WEF) report titled *Unlocking the Value of Personal Data* write, "data is inert until it is used by someone for some purpose."[41] Some in the personal data community share with the WEF a concern about the dangers posed by the consequences of consumer efforts to opt out of data collection regimes. Datacoup's Marc Guldimann, for example, told me he worried that media reports about the use of digital data for practices ranging from advertising to national security have generated unnecessary public fear by conflating commercial data collection with government spying. Particularly in the aftermath of revelations by Edward Snowden in 2013, which exposed the extent of the U.S. government's domestic surveillance efforts, Guldimann contended these stories generate confusion that discourages people from sharing their personal information. This, he said, may threaten innovation in areas such as health and education, which rely on big data analytics.

Guldimann is not alone in his concern that mounting public fears about the misuse of personal information may result in unwillingness on the part of individuals to share their data. Liz Brandt is CEO of Ctrl-Shift, an organization based in the United Kingdom that brings together and advises people from a range of industries who share an interest in the personal information economy. When we spoke at Ctrl-Shift's London office in 2013, Brandt described an apprehension that people will respond to reports that corporations have misused data by refusing to share personal information. She warned about the disruptive potential of people "going dark." A widespread consumer decision to "turn off all their data sources and [not] let people have access to" their information, Brandt said, would "bring the economy to a halt."[42]

Part of the goal behind the personal data ecosystem is to create incentives that encourage people to participate in the data economy. Brandt described the "involvement, engagement, and education of the consumer" as "a massively important element of the future success of this market." One goal of some in the personal data community is to counterbalance fears about the misuse of information by irresponsible industry players by helping people to see the benefits of participating in the data economy. Alan Mitchell, Brandt's colleague at Ctrl-Shift, identifies the importance of building a culture around personal data. "The underlying goal," Mitchell says, "is to encourage economic growth by empowering individuals with their own data."[43] Providing people with the tools to engage with their personal information, he suggests, is fundamental to the broader industry objective. However, Mitchell notes, "customer demand for data will only really become manifest once there are services in place making using of it."[44]

Because they provide tools that allow individuals to collect, store, and share their own data, those in the personal data ecosystem frame their services as a necessary step in these efforts to democratize the benefits of the data economy. They emphasize people's ability to combine data from different platforms to create a singularly comprehensive and accurate profile—a data set that Personal's Shane Green refers to as "the golden copy." This profile is framed by the industry as an asset that gives people significant bargaining power with advertisers, whose efforts are hampered by partial and inaccurate data. Despite huge investments in data collection and analysis, digital advertising companies have not perfected the creation of personalized consumer profiles. For example, data brokers such as Acxiom, Experian, and BlueKai suffer from the problem of "dirty data"—the presence of errors, duplicate entries, and obsolete information in database records—as well as limits to the easy combination of information from independent data sets residing in different platforms across the web. By recruiting individuals to participate in the collection of their own information, the personal data ecosystem overcomes problems of messy and siloed data to create a level of specificity and, therefore, value that data brokers cannot achieve independently.

Through the Datacoup platform, Matt Hogan hopes to make more explicit to members the transaction that occurs when they take advantage of "free" content online. Hogan's description of a hypothetical conversation he has with prospective Datacoup clients reveals how the platform combines the language of insight and value to educate people about the promise of personal data: "Hey look. These behaviors that you're exhibiting, these patterns that you're creating in your life, these are the things that make you valuable. And these are the things that other people want to understand about you and that's why this should be leveraged; that's why you should take this asset and start to leverage it—because who you are is what makes you valuable, and this means the digital presentation of who you are is the way to do that in the most efficient form." In thinking about the possibilities of data visualization, Hogan told me he was inspired by Mint,[45] an app that accesses users' banking information to provide actionable information based on spending patterns. In 2013, Hogan was hoping to add a level of complexity to these types of services by integrating multiple streams of user data into the equation.

When I spoke with Hogan, Datacoup was in private beta mode—meaning it was accessible only to friends of the developers—while it ironed out the technology and worked with companies to determine how the data could be packaged and sold for maximum value to advertisers and revenue for the company and users. To create this advantage over traditional data brokers, Datacoup planned to encourage its users to combine information from financial institutions and social media platforms—a combination that would be difficult for data brokers to achieve on their own. Hogan describes the Datacoup approach as offering an "exchange platform" through which companies would be invited to indicate interest in a specific consumer profile. The example Hogan gave me was of a clothing company interested in advertising to women who fall into a defined age range and income class. The clothing company would buy access to a sample of one thousand women, ages twenty-five to thirty, with spending on their credit card above $3,000 per month. As the intermediary, Datacoup would use the data vault to identify people who fit this profile and distribute the clothing company's advertisement to those who matched the specifications. Datacoup would take a cut of the payment and the remainder would be distributed to individuals through their vaults.

For these efforts to be successful, the entrepreneurs supporting it believe they need to figure out how to facilitate discussions between consumers and vendors. Marc Guldimann's experience with Enliken demonstrates the difficulties of building an environment in which those conversations can occur. Between 2011 and 2014, Enliken revised its business model three times.[46] In its first iteration, Enliken enabled the sale of personal information in exchange for credits that clients could donate to a charity. Enliken users would download software that would track their online activity in a personal dashboard. They could indicate the information they were willing to make available to advertisers, with Enliken facilitating the exchange. Charities would receive 90 percent of the proceeds from the sale, and Enliken would pocket the rest.[47] After receiving seed funding, Enliken abandoned the charity-centered model in favor of a plan that allowed people to trade their data for content. This model, which Guldimann described as "kind of like a paywall," was eventually replaced by a third version that allowed users to trade their data for perks from participating vendors.

Reflecting on the company's multiple changes in direction, Guldimann said Enliken got ahead of itself when it decided to go out and simply ask people for their data. What they failed to understand, he told me, is that most companies were not interested in buying data directly from individuals: "In the end, the thing that we realized is that, as eager as people are to trade data for something of value, the businesses—as much as they want the data—weren't ready to have a conversation with people about data." More recently, Enliken has developed a tool Guldimann believes will help businesses begin that dialogue. When we spoke, the company was working on a software product that would allow consumers to see the information an online retailer has in their consumer profile. Guldimann referred to this approach as "transparency as a service," a phrase Enliken has used as its tagline. He suggested that as retailers become more responsible and transparent about the ways they are using personal information, they will be more willing to enter into direct negotiations with consumers for additional data. Creating transparency in the marketplace for data, Guldimann argued, will help facilitate a more honest and comfortable conversation between consumers and vendors. Similar to those behind the early infomediaries, this is a perspective that identifies consumer concern about data privacy as economic rather than social or political. By offering transparency in data use, these companies argue individuals will be less anxious that they are not being adequately compensated for its use.

The construction of transparency as a solution allows companies to flip the script on privacy; the position they present is not that companies should curtail the use of personal data, but rather that we need more transparency regarding the information companies know about us and how it is used. It is important to realize, however, that transparency does not always mean insight. This is particularly true in the era of what Frank Pasquale, an expert on the legal issues associated with digital technologies, calls "black box algorithms." In his book *The Black Box Society*, Pasquale reveals the work of complex analytic tools and big data to obscure the accuracy of conclusions.[48] One consequence, as legal scholar Paul Ohm writes, is that big data processes make it "difficult to know that we are in the presence of risky data, the kind of data that will likely lead to privacy harm."[49] As a result, merely gaining access to the information companies have about us does not by itself mitigate the potential for injury.

The personal data ecosystem promises agency and empowerment by allowing users to own, analyze, and leverage their data. These companies respond to prevalent public concerns about how personal data is created, accessed, and used by offering individuals a chance to be cut in on the profits generated through the collection and sale of their information. There are, however, barriers to the kinds of revenue sharing envisioned by this approach. The companies behind devices and platforms are much more likely to receive the benefits of data accrued through interactions with users. Whether this value comes from the actual sale of the data or from the perception of the company as data-rich, this value is rarely shared with the individuals who participate in its creation.[50] Moreover, the mechanisms that would govern the distribution of insight and revenue in the case of the personal data ecosystem have the potential to replicate existing inequities. Platforms like Datacoup and Enliken talk about compensating individuals for the data they share, thereby resolving the problem that advertisers have not generally demonstrated an interest in paying for information about a single person.[51] However, once that person's data is combined with those collected from hundreds of others, it is difficult to imagine that the individual would be appropriately compensated for the insights their own data reveal. The approach, moreover, is likely to compensate those identified by advertisers as valuable targets, thereby excluding those identified as less likely to be profitable.

A "New" Architecture for Privacy

The beliefs motivating the introduction of the infomediary model in the 1990s and more recent efforts to build a personal data ecosystem are remarkably similar. For an illustration of the parallels consider the following two statements, shared unprompted over the course of my research. The first is from Fred Davis, who founded Lumeria in the mid-1990s. The second is from Thomas Dignan of Reputation.com:

> So on MeBay you could be sharing your information and the more information you share the higher value offers you're going to get to do different things, like almost the reverse of the deals network, but it could be really customized deals and actually paying money for your attention. For example, we had a deal worked out with BMW. . . . It cost them $1,200 just to get somebody to walk through the door. . . . How about you offer somebody who's qualified to buy one of your cars $500 to walk through that door? They would be much more incentivized to come down. It's like, "Hey. Here's five hundred bucks if you come take a test drive on the new 328, because that's the one we think you can afford, or the 528 because that's the one we think you can afford based on your [FICO] score or whatever."

> For example, say we have a relationship with BMW, and BMW says, "Here are the criteria for people I want to market to." For example, they say, "We know that people who like red wine, or travel to Paris, or have bought BMWs in the past, or live in this zip code, are people we would like to market to." So what we would then do is, instead of saying, "Oh here is a list of people that enjoy red wine," instead of giving them the criteria, we give them a conduit to say, "Here's the pipe that you can pipe the marketing information that you want to send to people who have the criteria." And we never inform them of who that is, and then people can respond to them through the pipe, but [without] actually revealing any of their information.

Both the first-generation infomediaries and the personal data brokers respond to concerns about the inefficiencies created by a lack of trust in the online economy that results from companies that are not transparent about the ways they collect and use information about consumers. Both sets of companies also argue for the application of ownership rights to personal data and suggest that allowing individuals to control the flows of their information can address rising fears about the erosion of privacy online. They propose similar technical solutions—data vaults, private shipping, anonymous offers—to build a digital environment in which respecting individuals' rights to manage their personal information results in a more efficient marketplace.

The surface-level similarities between these methods, however, mask significant differences in approaches to privacy motivating the two models. While those behind the first-generation infomediaries were building integrated proxy servers and encryption technologies into their platforms to ensure opportunities for technical anonymity when their clients preferred it, services in the contemporary personal data community tend not to talk about privacy in terms of anonymity. Rather, they are inclined toward a definition of privacy operationalized through strategies of engaged visibility.[52] "A lot of people approach privacy with putting up walls and/or fences, and we don't believe that to be privacy," Matt Hogan told me. "Our definition of privacy is much more about control and channeling the resources that you have to the right paths." In the conversations that informed Datacoup's eventual approach, Hogan found that when people talk about privacy, they focus less on the visibility of their data and more on a feeling that they were being exploited. "The anger and indignation," he said, "is people saying, 'You know, I don't really care that my data is out there. I care that somebody else is profiting off of it, and that someone is not me.'"

In an interview with CNN, Marc Guldimann provided a similar definition of privacy as a strategy for managing the circulation of information rather than trying to limit its visibility. "I think there are a couple questions you have to ask," Guldimann told CNN's Jake Tapper:

> The first is what is privacy? A lot of people online today confuse anonymity with control. When people say privacy a lot of times they mean they want control over all of the information, which is being used to target them with ads. They want visibility and they want transparency. They don't mean that they want to be totally anonymous. In fact, when you

look at social media and you look at a lot of the mobile tools people are using they're broadcasting lots and lots of information about themselves. The only difference is they have total control over it.[53]

When Hogan, Guldimann, and other advocates of the personal data ecosystem talk about privacy, they describe a tension between concerns about the economic consequences of giving up access to a valuable resource and an acceptance that sharing digital information has not only become normalized but is expected and beneficial. The solutions companies like Enliken and Datacoup offer encourage people to take a more active role in the collection and analysis of their personal data to generate insights that can be used to engender self-knowledge or be leveraged for economic compensation. Although this approach does little to limit the creation and collection of personal information it allows individuals insight into how that information is being used. This line of thinking suggests that participation in one's own observation undermines the power of others to control the conditions of visibility and turns disclosure into an empowering act.[54]

An initiative by the activist and academic Steve Mann illustrates this perspective that the creation and exposure of information on an individual's own terms can be empowering. In 1994, Mann pioneered a series of projects that utilized wearable technologies and video streaming devices to publicize his everyday life. Mann argues that these examples of self-display, which he calls "lifecasting," enable a form of observation that upends traditional hierarchies of looking. Referred to as "sousveillance," or observation from below,[55] these practices of disclosure do not eliminate the top-down power of surveillance regimes. Mann argues, however, that distributed forms of observation can rebalance power in a mediated society.[56] Information captured by ordinary people, he reasons, can become part of the official record and supplement or challenge authoritative discourses.[57] According to this reasoning, turning oneself into a recording device makes it possible to undermine exploitative practices of observation. With new media technologies, "we become," Mann writes with Joseph Ferenbok, "sousveillance-enabled individuals able to contribute to a broader social responsibility of undersight."[58] By engaging the strategies of observation that serve to monitor and discipline, Mann argues it is possible to empower individuals through the subversion of dominant institutional power: empowerment through transparency and visibility rather than obscurity and anonymity.

Arguments that empowerment can be realized through a willingness to offer one's body and data up for display reflect what feminist scholar Rachel Hall has called "voluntary transparency."[59] The willing disclosure of the self, Hall writes, operates as a strategy for asserting innocence. Therefore, insofar as voluntary transparency operates to establish one's belonging, its benefits are disproportionately available to those who are understood to belong. As with the model of privacy through strategic transparency described in the previous chapter, this approach encouarges people to make themselves known to systems that reward the visiblilty of those deemed valuable. It therefore offers little recourse to those whose existence is unacknowledged or undervalued. Whereas the online reputation management industry acknowledges the consequences of being "invisible" within digital infrastructures, but not the systems of power that cultivate this discrepancy, the personal data ecosystem offers limited solutions for those who are systematically ignored by big and small data systems. This oversight is consistent with definitions of privacy that, as noted in the previous chapter, have more often been focused on problems of inclusion while overlooking contrasting concerns related to exclusion.[60]

When thinking about solutions to privacy concerns, it is essential to consider strategies that secure a balance between invisibility and obscurity. As noted in chapter 4, approaches that focus on inclusion risk ignoring the challenges facing those on the social margins who go unnoticed by contemporary surveillance systems. "Big data," writes Jonas Lerman, "poses risks also to those persons who are *not* swallowed up by it—whose information is not regularly harvested, farmed, or mined."[61] Lerman notes that when decisions about where to put a new bus route or open a new grocery store are informed by data from transit cards or credit card purchases, they overlook the needs of those who rely on cash—those who use less traceable currency not because they are intentionally opting out of surveillance infrastructures, but because they lack the economic capital to enter them. In crafting privacy protections that address the dangers of information already available to institutionalized surveillance systems, solutions can work to define privacy in ways that disregard the very real concerns of those who are less visible to these systems.[62] The focus in the personal data community on unwanted data collection makes sense when we consider that many of those who are part of the tech communities where these projects originate are more likely to experience the effects of big data inclusion. For those who carry smartphones, make purchases using debit or credit cards, or surf the web, privacy concerns are often framed as questions about how the data produced from those activities will be captured, stored, and used.

By providing individuals with tools to manage when and how their data are shared with digital vendors, the personal data ecosystem promotes what computer scientist Alex Pentland has called a "new deal on data."[63] Like the idea behind the revolution in data, this shift introduces ownership rights and profit sharing to democratize the value created when personal information is harvested, refined, and used. This deal does not, however, challenge the fundamental principles of an online commercial system in which personal data is the dominant mode of commerce—the entrance fee for digital life. The model of empowerment offered by the personal data ecosystem, which is framed in terms of freedom and control, assumes that those choices are in fact equally available and freely made. This provision of an impression of control communicates a perspective on privacy that avoids the ways digital infrastructures measure, evaluate, and segment populations they are designed to see, while ignoring those who find themselves on the margins of the surveillance environment.

What's more, by framing digital privacy as an economic issue—one that revolves around managing corporate access to personal data—the personal data ecosystem risks turning privacy from a civic concern to a consumer preference.[64] In so doing, it replicates the inequalities built into capitalist systems, where power is inextricably tied to consumer capital. The choice offered through the data vault is not *if* users want to engage in an economic system driven by personal information, but *how* they want to do so. The approach taken by the personal data ecosystem, like Mann's, does not directly confront practices of institutionalized surveillance. Instead, strategies that describe financial rewards in exchange for opting into surveillance systems risk diluting arguments about the political and social function of privacy in favor of those demanding fair compensation. Assuming that anxieties around surveillance are related to unfair compensation practices risks minimizing fears that privacy violations will result in physical dangers and social damages. Further, by assuming that information privacy concerns are based on fears that data use will fail to explicitly benefit the data subject, they may ignore the potential social and political harms generated by both data inclusion and exclusion.

Digital Enlightenment: Revolution or Evolution?

Much of the discussion I observed at the Internet Identity Workshop focused on the possibilities for the personal data ecosystem to revolutionize the relationship between individuals and their information. Workshop participants talked about using this transformation to effect a broader shift in the digital economy. Participants drew connections between themselves and members of the Homebrew Computer Club—a group of hobbyists and hackers that gathered in Silicon Valley in the 1970s and 1980s to work on projects, some of which form the basis of contemporary digital media.[65] Such allusions emphasize the community's commitment to working outside of powerful commercial and political systems to develop technologies that will disrupt the status quo. A blog entry by Personal CEO Shane Green reflects this outsider status: "I love big, disruptive ideas that can make the world a better place— and have spent much of my life building 'double bottom line' companies that can pursue such win-win outcomes. 'Democratizing data' through accessible tools and interfaces to help people create and manage complex data sets has been a focus of mine now for over a decade."[66] The language of disruption, empowerment, and even revolution, were common in discussions about the future of the personal data economy. For example, during our interview, Personal's Josh Galper made repeated reference to the company's commitment to "data liberation," and Personal joins other companies in positioning itself as part of a "consumer revolution."[67]

Meeco, a founding partner of the Respect Network, which describes itself as a data independence platform, employs similar revolutionary claims. Written by company co-founder and CEO Katryna Dow, the Meeco Manifesto begins, "Up until now the power to capture, analyse and profit from personal data has resided with business, government and social networks. What if you and I had the same power?"[68] Companies in the personal data community enjoy their status as interlopers working to change an unfair system. Datacoup motto's references this outsider status. The company slogan—"Reclaim your personal data"— celebrates the possibilities of an empowered consumer. The Datacoup tagline is seemingly a response to the reported motto for data brokerage firm BlueKai: "Carpe Datum" or "seize the data."[69] Hogan is quick to point out, however, that what could be understood as a purely altruistic mission to empower individuals is more of a "by-product" of the company's approach than a motivating ideology.

In speaking with other members of the personal data community, I found that what is sold as a revolution to upend the current economic order may turn out to be more of a slow evolution toward greater transparency and deeper efforts to engage consumers in the collection of personal information. Some IIW participants responded to presenters' use of the enlightenment metaphor by noting a lack of public fervor necessary to spark a true revolution. Based on her work with Ctrl-Shift, Liz Brandt shared with me her observation that consumers need to see a viable and convenient alternative to the existing arrangement before they attend to their personal information. "Some people kind of think there will be an uprising and people will claim back their data. I just don't see it," she told me. "I think it will be an iterative move to empower the consumer." This movement, Brandt noted, will take shape as individuals are confronted with instances where their information was misused and they are offered frictionless opportunities to harness and manage their information, which fit neatly into their routines.

While the proposed personal data ecosystem might educate people about the online economy, it seemingly does little to change that system. By drawing on the ideology behind the infomediary model described by John Hagel and his colleagues, the personal data ecosystem fits comfortably within the now-entrenched economic logics of the digital world. For example, describing his company's goals in a report, Shane Green notes that Personal is not meant to compete with social network sites and other platforms; rather, it is meant to complement them. "It will become easier and easier to decide whether social networks or private networks are appropriate to a given context. I don't think," Green continues, "it will be one or the other. . . . People will learn to effortlessly switch between them."[70] Extrapolated further, it is possible to view these efforts as shoring up the dominance of an approach that views personal data as a valuable currency within an increasingly powerful surveillance system. It is, therefore, important to consider the boundaries of this revolution. By encouraging individuals to take ownership over their personal data, companies urge them to invest in themselves—to embrace a more powerful role as the owner and operator of a holistic version of an identity derived through data. The revolution comes from a shift in control, but not from a radical restructuring of the systems in which value, importance, or status are defined.

Arguments that individuals can alleviate concerns about the misuse of their data by participating in its collection and use risks accepting a version of privacy experienced as an expense rather than a right. The commodification of privacy that results from expressions of consumer empowerment resting on economic benefits promotes rational decision making with the aim of maximizing personal profits. Critics have observed the creeping costs associated with online privacy protection.[71] Journalist Julia Angwin, for example, describes the fees she incurred while attempting to have personal information removed from various digital databases.[72] Similarly, digital industry critic Evgeny Morozov argues that privacy has ceased to be a freely accessible good and is instead a project that necessitates resources expenditure. "Those resources could be money, patience, attention—you might even hire a consultant to do all this for you—but the point is that privacy is becoming expensive," Morozov writes.[73] The costs associated with privacy, however, extend beyond the time and money required to create private spaces. The price of privacy includes the social and economic benefits individuals forego when they decide not to disclose personal information on a social network site or exchange their personal data for monetary incentives offered by online retailers. In the current digital environment, if personal data is the dominant currency, privacy can come at the cost of sociality and economic participation.

As the politics of visibility shift with the introduction of online architectures and economic models that habituate us to the inevitable realities of personal disclosure, there is some evidence that we are becoming accustomed to the idea that privacy is expensive. While describing Personal's move from a free product to a paid subscription model, Josh Galper told me the decision was made in part because consumers were skeptical about the company's business model. Without having to pay, Galper told me, consumers assumed the company was making money from their personal information. Personal concluded that consumers would rather pay for the product than be the product. The concern expressed about the integrity of a free service suggests both a growing understanding about the economics of many online platforms as well as a sense of resignation that there is no such thing as "free" content or services online.[74] Galper's anecdote suggests that consumers have internalized the well-worn saying "if you aren't paying for the content, you are the content."[75] In other words, we may be increasingly resigned to the idea that privacy comes with a cost.

Rather than focusing on ways to disrupt the capture of personal information online, companies behind the personal data ecosystem generally look for ways to tweak the existing arrangement to benefit individuals. Instead of emphasizing anonymity, the contemporary model focuses on the value of disclosure: how much is the data citizen willing to reveal and for what price? The personal data ecosystem operates within a digital culture that has evolved immensely over the past two decades. In this environment, choices to opt out seem to be rapidly disappearing. The remaining options reflect the extent to which individuals are willing to embrace practices of data sharing using tools that allow them to take advantage of their disclosures. While opportunities to build a "golden profile" are described as empowering, questions remain about whether the resulting sense that one is in control is in fact an illusion. Left largely unasked is the question of whether this new position as governor of one's data empire—without corresponding changes in practices that consider how data are valued and whose data are valued—is a benefit or a burden.

Conclusion

Optimism or Amnesia? Looking Forward, Looking Backward

During the 1970s energy crisis, the economist E. F. Schumacher published a collection of essays titled *Small Is Beautiful: Economics as If People Mattered*. In these essays, he challenged the conventional wisdom regarding the economics of environmentalism. In the opening pages Schumacher wrote, "The illusion of unlimited powers, nourished by astonishing scientific and technological achievements, has produced the concurrent illusion of having solved the problem of production."[1] Society's focus on the material gains facilitated by scientific advances, Schumacher continued, had fostered a collective ignorance about the deep environmental damage accompanying massive technological progress. Schumacher's *Small Is Beautiful* proposed the use of "small-scale technology" or "technology with a human face" to address the Western world's overinvestment in destructive technological systems.[2] Langdon Winner, a leading thinker on the political and social dynamics of technology, argues that *Small Is Beautiful* served as a guiding text for environmental activists, but resonated particularly with the scientists who made up the appropriate technology movement—a group that advocated for technological intervention to address such environmental problems as pollution, energy costs, and natural resource depletion.[3]

The efforts of the appropriate technologists, and the environmental movement more generally, provide an instructive framework through which to consider the efforts of the consumer privacy industry. Like the appropriate technologists, those behind many consumer-oriented privacy tools are responding to concerns that rapid technological innovation is pressing forward without adequate consideration of the broader social, economic, and political implications brought by these changes. Environmentalists and privacy advocates face the similar challenge of balancing complex interests and varying levels of acceptance within systems where individual decisions have networked consequences. Those in the consumer privacy industry share with the appropriate technologists an optimism that the implementation of people-centric technologies—an approach driven by the belief that development should meet users' needs rather than encouraging individuals to construct their preferences and desires around available technologies—will help address these complex issues. For the appropriate technologists, such efforts included the use of small-scale applications that, although labor intensive, were energy efficient.[4] For the consumer privacy industry, commitments to user-centric technologies are visible in solutions that minimize data sharing, shield identity markers, and emphasize individual choice and control.

During the research for this book, I encountered repeated allusions to the environment and the environmental movement in interviews, casual conversations, and media texts.[5] It is not, for example, uncommon for privacy advocates to draw from the challenges and lessons of the environmental movement as they make the case for vigilance around digital privacy. In a 2000 keynote address Austin Hill, then CEO of the anonymizer Zero-Knowledge Systems (ZKS), predicted privacy concerns would define the twenty-first century the way environmental issues and civil rights had defined the previous century.[6] Stephanie Perrin, ZKS's chief privacy officer, told me that she started using the term "Privacy Chernobyl" in the 1990s to signal the importance of securing information online. Perrin's term—a reference to the 1986 disaster at a Ukrainian power plant that raised questions about the safety of nuclear power and catalyzed thinking about the need for alternative sources of safe and sustainable energy—makes the argument that "a privacy meltdown" was necessary to force a public conversation about the issues raised by encroaching surveillance technologies. Although there have been several privacy incidents over the past two decades, including the disclosure by NSA contractor Edward Snowden regarding the U.S. government's surveillance activities and several massive database breaches, when we spoke in 2013 Perrin observed that none has been catastrophic enough to force organizations or governments to take decisive action to address digital privacy.

A clear articulation of the relationship between privacy and environmental issues comes from well-known cryptographer and cybersecurity expert Bruce Schneier. In contrast with popular claims that data is the raw resource that defines the digital era, Schneier describes data as a contaminant. "Data is the pollution of the information age," Schneier writes. "It's a byproduct of every computer-mediated interaction; all processes produce it. It stays around forever, unless it's disposed of. It can be recycled, but it has to be done carefully. And, like physical pollution during the early decades of the industrial age, most people completely ignore the problem."[7] Schneier predicts that, just as we now look back at the lack of attention paid to environmental pollution by titans of industry who were racing toward innovation, future generations will wonder about the decisions we made as we built the architecture and infrastructure that define the internet.

Throughout this book, I have pointed to metaphors and language as indicative of the strategies representatives from this industry employ to stress the importance and risks of privacy in the digital age. I have argued that these metaphors are important, not only for their discursive power, but also for what they reveal about the ideologies guiding industry efforts to help people manage their online images. Whether is it the use of terms such as "digital doppelgänger," "digital shadow," and "digital footprint" by the online reputation management industry to signal the dangers of an unattended online image, or the preference for the terms "owners" rather than "users" and "promises" instead of "contracts" by proponents of the personal data ecosystem, these linguistic decisions have symbolic power. The use of environmental metaphors is similarly instructive, in that it attempts to use a now-familiar framework to clarify the challenges of building privacy into digital systems and the need for public awareness and buy-in around these issues.

Privacy and environmental activism, however, share more than a rhetorical approach. The trend toward commodification, detailed throughout this book with respect to the privacy industry, closely parallels the trajectory of the environmental movement during the 1980s and 1990s. Beginning in the 1960s and 1970s, environmentalists—including the appropriate technologists—focused on the combined efforts of government and industry as a catalyst for changing the unsustainable environmental policies and practices wreaking havoc on the planet. In the 1980s, however, as neoliberal policies gained popularity, greater emphasis was placed on the role individuals could play in protecting the environment. This shift was consistent with a broader move toward a political agenda in Western countries—particularly the United States and United Kingdom—which promoted deregulation, privatization, and individual responsibility.[8] This included the development of environmentally friendly consumer products that would allow people to actualize their concerns about the environment through their purchase decisions. This approach, which environmental studies scholar Michael Maniates describes as the individualization of responsibility around environmentalism, located accountability for sustainable practices among individuals in their role as consumers.[9] It was a shift that also allowed environmental degradation to be framed not as the consequence of industrial systems, but as the outcome of poor consumer choices. It is a perspective which "asks that individuals imagine themselves as consumers first and citizens second."[10] This shift, Maniates notes, leaves "little room to ponder institutions, the nature and exercise of political power, or ways of collectively changing the distribution of power and influence in society."[11]

Powerful neoliberal ideologies helped promote a version of environmentalism in which technological advances and consumer education could effectively reconcile industry profit with conservation efforts. Consequently, the work of environmental advocates to bring about political change was interrupted by a version of conservationism situated squarely within the economic and political structures that were partially responsible for the havoc created by such unsustainable environmental practices as overproduction and conspicuous consumption. This experience of depoliticization in the environmental movement, achieved through the application of neoliberal practices including commodification and individualization, shares many similarities with evolving perspectives on privacy protection that have shaped, and been shaped by, the consumer privacy industry.

A discussion I had in 2013 with Kaliya Hamlin, executive director of the Personal Data Ecosystem Consortium (PDEC)—a group of organizations working collaboratively to build the infrastructure to support a personal data ecosystem—illustrated the blending of social and economic interests taking place in the fields of environmental and privacy activism. Hamlin, who prefers to be referred to by her handle "Identity Woman," described PDEC's commitment to socially responsible entrepreneurship. At one point in the conversation, she pointed to the Social Venture Network (SVN) and its founder, Josh Mailman, as one of PDEC's primary inspirations. The SVN was formed in 1987 with a vision of creating a "platform to connect, inspire, and support influential entrepreneurs who wanted to use business to create a values-driven and sustainable world."[12] Both SVN and PDEC aim to bring together entrepreneurs looking to address social issues through consumer-oriented solutions. Identity Woman pointed to Odwalla, a juice retailer committed to environmental sustainability, as an example of a company that has successfully merged an investment in civic engagement with its business interests. She told me she envisioned PDEC as building a similar network of entrepreneurs with a specific interest in values-based technology—people she described as committed to changing the world *through* technology, not *despite* it. The PDEC start-up members, Identity Woman told me, are those that "see the power of technology and they see the dark side, and they say, 'Look . . . we can just flip it and do good and do technology and have viable businesses.'"

One of the unifying goals shared by companies across the consumer privacy industry over the past two decades has been to disrupt powerful systems that define reputation and identity on behalf of individuals. This vision is resisted by digital media companies that are hesitant to modify their services to provide individuals with more control over the collection, use, and presentation of their personal information. Search engines, built on the notion of organic and unbiased results, have framed efforts to remove or obscure content as a form of censorship and an assault on free speech.[13] Industries that rely on personal information and behavioral data to fund their services are wary of efforts that would make it more difficult to leverage the latent value of raw data, and some in the advertising industry go so far as to refer to the use of ad-blocking software as a form of theft.[14] Governments have challenged the use of strong encryption, citing national security concerns. The consumer privacy industry has pushed back against these challenges in their efforts to find strategies that would provide people with the authority and autonomy to manage their digital profiles. Through efforts to educate people about the value of their personal information and image coupled with the provision of tools to help manage them, these companies have turned to strategies of user control and personal choice. Through their services, individuals are invited to make seemingly autonomous decisions about the collection, use, and display of their personal information. While doing so, they are tasked with striking a delicate balance between the risks of exposure and the rewards of disclosure.

Fears about the erosion of privacy tend to occur when people feel unable to manage access to their information, to themselves, and to the spaces they occupy. As philosopher of technology Helen Nissenbaum writes, "Intuitions behind both the constraint and control conceptions [of privacy] are sound; namely that control over information about oneself is an important dimension of privacy, but so is the degree of access that others have to this information, irrespective of who is in control."[15] The consumer privacy industry's focus on creating technologies that implore individuals to take control over personal information resonate with the perspective that a sense of autonomy (or lack thereof) is essential for understanding the lived experience of privacy and surveillance. Where these approaches fall short, however, is when the promotion of individual empowerment works to obscure the larger social and economic structures that undermine efforts to make these strategies widely accessible or effective.

What limits strategies for privacy protection that rely on individuals to exercise control is that so many of the breaches that concern us— secondary uses of data; nonconsensual information sharing; the loss of context as content is replicated, shared, and reproduced—reside outside the purview of personal autonomy. While understanding privacy as a condition that results from personal choices fits nicely with strategies and tools that rely on an active and informed user, definitions that rely on discourses of control also influence how we understand accountability. By selling tools that *empower* individuals by providing them with access to their digital data, this industry runs the risk of discounting the persistence of information asymmetries. By accepting arguments that we have a responsibility to *control* our identities—whether by producing and promoting an authentic image or by managing our personal data—we risk overlooking the ways cultural expectations and technological features mediate how narratives are displayed, encountered, and read.

The services offered by the consumer privacy industry provide practical strategies to combat the unwanted circulation of information; however, any approach that treats privacy violations as a personal rather than social issue risks isolating individual concerns from this broader set of issues. By embracing a model consumer–citizen who makes informed choices about the costs and benefits of disclosure, this approach has helped normalize privacy as an individual responsibility with discrete and personalized consequences—an outlook that makes the Privacy Chernobyl described by Stephanie Perrin far less likely. When privacy violations are treated as the result of risk calculations evaluated at the individual level, and the consequences of unwanted disclosure are viewed as harming individuals rather than society, the sense of widespread destruction Perrin's phrase was meant to evoke is improbable. Not only can this lead to us to assign blame to individuals for poor choices or failures to erect proper protection, but it may also obscure systemic social issues that inform how we access and experience privacy.

As we rely on for-profit companies to solve the problems of privacy in the digital environment, we reframe the debate around issues of consumer rights. The engagement of commercial systems as the primary avenue through which we safeguard privacy risks restricting protections to those who have long enjoyed more opportunities for privacy. This focus narrows discussions of privacy to questions of personal data, individual reputation, and the fair exchange of information, a move that may negate important conversations about ways in which strong privacy protections benefit communities. Not only, as Priscilla Regan writes, does robust privacy support democratic processes and institutions, but individuals are unlikely to benefit from privacy protections that are not widely shared.[16] Approaches that frame privacy as a commodity minimize the need for collective, citizen-based action to defend it. Through a celebration of free market structures and technological tools to overcome existing challenges, these companies have positioned the ownership of the self—one's image, reputation, and data—as a strategy for mitigating economic and social risk. These companies do important work to draw attention to the mechanisms of the digital world that shape visible and invisible profiles and to offer immediate solutions to address *individual* privacy violations online; however, without additional intervention from regulators, we are looking to these companies to solve a *societal* problem.

Over the past two decades, companies in the consumer privacy industry have responded to and shaped what we mean when we assert rights to privacy in the digital world. It has moved from an environment that dismissed the need for a unified or consistent identity, to one that emphasizes opportunities for managed disclosure and strategic self-presentation to capitalize on visibility. One result of this reorientation has been to help blur the conceptual boundaries between identity exploration and reputation management by recasting spaces that might be used for identity experimentation or self-discovery for the construction and evaluation of permanent digital personae. In the face of limited strategies for truly opting out of information disclosure, the online privacy industry has offered an alternative: own the data and control the narrative. By helping individuals to construct the defining version of their identity—whether that is a near-complete collection of their data trails or the most visible content in a search result—the consumer privacy industry offers tactics focused on managed visibility and strategic transparency. These approaches aim to balance a need for privacy with socioeconomic incentives that favor visibility. By acknowledging the current realities of the online economy, this approach offers opportunities for individuals to benefit from participation in a market for information that would otherwise be exploiting their data with little personal return, taking an "if you can't beat them, join them" approach to the surveillance economy.

The efforts of the consumer privacy industry tend to privilege the efficacy of market mechanisms over government intervention. I have noted concern across digital media industries that regulation will stifle innovation and impose unnecessary restrictions on the technology industry. The consumer privacy industry presents solutions described as commensurate with opportunities for both economic growth and individual protection. This version of techno-solutionism that inscribes superior problem-solving abilities to the work of algorithms, code, and strong network structures[17] helps absolve governments of a responsibility to implement unpopular regulations. By choosing to work alongside the prevailing contract at the heart of the digital economy—one that provides content and services in exchange for personal information—companies in the consumer privacy industry offer a solution that readjusts rather than reforms the existing commercial order. Framing this shift in terms of a restructuring of economic power from the company to the consumer—a data revolution—enables an approach that employs radical rhetoric without the need for commensurate political, economic, or social change.

Preparing for a Revolution: Confidence in the Consumer Privacy Industry

In 2000, Austin Hill described the difficulty of creating a sense of urgency about personal privacy through allusions to the struggles of the environmental movement. "Ask people 'Are you concerned about the environment?' and they'll say 'Yes,'" Hill observed. But, he continued, ask them, "'Are you willing to give up your gas-guzzling SUV for an electric car?' 'No.'"[18] When we spoke in 2013, Stephanie Perrin drew a similar parallel between privacy and environmentalism, but offered a more optimistic vision of the movement's future. "Back in the seventies, we didn't think we'd ever get to the point where people would be willing to wash out our food cans and recycle them," Perrin observed. "Now . . . people sort all their garbage, they have their plastic all washed and stacked over here and the cat food tins over there. That took thirty years, but it finally happened. I think that's the kind of change we're looking at." Privacy protections, in other words, must become routine and accessible if they are to become effective. But for that to happen, the barriers must be reduced and the stakes made clear. For the past two decades, this has been part of the mission of the consumer privacy industry.

While privacy has proven easy to commodify, it has been harder to sell. A persistent question across this industry has been whether individuals are willing to pay to protect their privacy. Given the challenges faced by commercial privacy-enhancing technologies at the turn of the twenty-first century, it is reasonable to question the optimism among those behind the current generation of privacy products. Why do companies in this industry's second generation believe they can succeed where their predecessors failed? Does this optimism reflect an institutional amnesia regarding the fate of previous businesses, or has something really changed? Personal's Josh Galper described what he sees as an inevitable shift in the online economic landscape. "I think privacy is an area that's been ripe for disruption for a long time," he told me. "Since the internet became commercially viable in the nineties, we've seen various attempts by companies to disrupt it in favor of the individual with varying degrees of success." Galper recalled a series of efforts at digital privacy intervention by for-profit companies. "When Shane [Green] and the founders came up with this idea, it was not new," he observed. "It had been around for ten or so years, as detailed in [the books] *Net Worth* and *Net Gain*; however, the model just hadn't worked until then. We're now in a much different time for technology and privacy where it's possible for it to work." Galper's references to works by Hagel, Rayport, and Armstrong that introduced the infomediary model were unique among those I spoke with, but he was not alone in his assertion that the public was more concerned about privacy today and, therefore, more receptive to strategies and tools to defend it than they had been in the two previous decades.

A common refrain among many of those I spoke with was that the earlier companies—the infomediaries and anonymizers—were ahead of their time. But what has changed in less than twenty-five years to make those in the industry believe they are no longer ahead of the curve? A number of industry representatives pointed to the technological limitations of 1990s digital infrastructure as a central reason for the failure of early consumer privacy tools. The proliferation and sophistication of digital and mobile devices since the turn of the twenty-first century has fueled industry optimism about a growing interest in privacy protection. Ctrl-Shift's Liz Brandt described the rise of smartphones and associated application platforms as a trigger that has increased the amount of data collected, the potential for those data to generate value, and correspondingly the desire to protect those data. Contemporary companies in the privacy industry argue that digital and mobile technology was neither pervasive enough nor sufficiently powerful the late 1990s to provide a useful service to consumers. As digital technologies have become more integrated into our lives, however, the value of a service that protects against privacy invasions and helps collect and organize the vast quantity of data exhaust we generate may become more widely appreciated. Thomas Dignan of Reptuation.com described to me "a convergence of ubiquity of the internet, that didn't exist ten years ago," with "the ability to store data." This has, according to Dignan, facilitated a moment where consumer privacy protection is both feasible from a technological perspective and worthwhile from a consumer perspective.

In addition to new technical capabilities, those in the privacy industry observe a social concern about digital privacy driven by a growing awareness regarding the collection and analysis of personal information by companies and governments. Michael Fertik, CEO of Reputation. com, described a "low-level anxiety" about privacy and reputation that exists today that he argued did not exist two decades ago. Similarly, others in the industry pointed to extensive coverage of high-profile privacy events to justify claims about rising public awareness. During interviews, I heard about the public fallout from Facebook's frequent revisions to its privacy policies, Edward Snowden's disclosures, and other privacy events to explain arguments that public concern about consumer and government surveillance is at an all-time high. The year 2013 was "historic . . . for privacy," observed Josh Galper. "From Snowden to the massive data breaches of the last year to all the attention that the media and political leaders have focused on the issue, what we've been witnessing is remarkable and a real sea change." Those I spoke with agreed that there is currently greater public understanding regarding the ways in which personal data drives the online economy and an increasing sense of injustice as individuals recognize the value their information is generating for others. Matt Hogan pointed to the success of companies such as Google and Facebook, both of which profit from the collection and use of personal data, as responsible for driving "a lot more awareness of what's going on with personal data and the value of personal data."

There was also a sense among my respondents that the political environment would be supportive of industry efforts to enhance personal privacy online. Citing mounting pressure on governments in North America and Europe to protect online privacy, they lamented past regulatory efforts that failed to provide people with adequate notice or offer suitable mechanisms for consent. Liz Brandt described a "transparency agenda" being driven through in Western societies and pointed to the Open Government Initiative in the United States and the Midata program in the United Kingdom as two examples of public programs that are encouraging citizens to manage and capitalize on their personal information. Similarly, Josh Galper praised the Obama Administration's Open Government Initiative as one indication of a new political and regulatory climate around personal data that mirrors the empowerment discourse characteristic of the consumer privacy industry. "When you look at how today's laws and regulations about personal data are written," Galper observed, "they operate with the presumption that organizations, like companies and government, are the data collectors and controllers. Individuals are merely passive in their data relationships with entities, simply vessels from whom data is collected." This view of privacy, Galper noted, is beginning to change: "Our view is that this is an antiquated approach and that individuals should be at the center of their own data flows and in control of it. This view is starting to take hold in the public and private sectors in a variety of different policy efforts and business offerings."

Based on these trends—the technological landscape that facilitates the creation of vast quantities of data, a consumer class that is increasingly aware and concerned about how these data are being used, and a legislative environment poised to implement user-friendly privacy regulations—there is a sense across the industry that businesses are becoming more open to adapting their practices to allow for increased user control over personal information. Companies engaged in these practices, members of the consumer privacy industry argue, may soon be subject to a consumer revolt or legislation to restrict the collection or use of personal information online. During our conversation, Identity Woman recalled a conference on user-centric platforms in 2010 that included participants from large data brokerage firms. She remembered asking them why they had attended an event about user-centric tools and privacy. Many of the representatives from various data brokerage firms, Identity Woman told me, gave the same response: "We see the writing on the wall and if we don't change our practices, we are going to get regulated out of existence within seven years."

Those in the consumer privacy industry present their services as meeting consumers' needs at the same time as they offer opportunities for the types of disclosure necessary for social and economic engagement. Matt Hogan's assertion, discussed in chapter 6, that the value of information increases when individuals are given a seat at the bargaining table, was echoed in various ways throughout my interviews. Josh Galper told me that companies are beginning to accept the argument that they can benefit when they cede power to the individual. "The key," he said, "is to put the customer in charge by empowering them with their own information and, through that, foster even closer engagement with the individual." Across the industry, people talk about how the trust generated through the respectful treatment of consumer information can lead to a more efficient marketplace in which individuals offer marketers and retailers more comprehensive information about their personal preferences and behaviors. The industry presents this as a win-win for businesses and consumers, and Liz Brandt says some companies are starting to come around to this idea. She recalled for me a point in the recent past where it was common to hear marketers, advertisers, and business people say, "Over my dead body is anybody going to get more control over my data and over this relationship. It's my data and it's our relationship with our customers and they don't have anything to do with it." That perspective, Brandt observed, "is definitely shifting, and more and more organizations are willing to consider sharing more and more information, and starting to see the benefits of efficiencies and an upside on revenues." There is a sense that businesses are beginning to recognize the benefit of building relationships with consumers around data to capitalize on the trust that comes from the respectful and transparent treatment of personal information.

The Profitability of Studying Industry Failure

The fact that the consumer privacy industry comprises private companies makes it difficult to gauge its economic viability. Some of the companies within the privacy industry are backed by venture capitalists, meaning they are funded in exchange for private equity. The result is an economic landscape of which it is difficult to get a clear picture, even for industry analysts. Another challenge is the industry's volatility. In the time since I conducted my interviews, some of the companies have changed direction. For example, Personal rebranded as TeamData as part of its efforts to shift its focus away from personal data management to networked data and information sharing.[19] The company later joined with personal data platform Digi.me to provide strategies for individuals to securely store, share, and visualize their personal information.[20] In 2015, Reputation.com's founder and longtime CEO Michael Fertik stepped away from that position, although he remained on the company's board in the executive chairman position.[21] For those interested in the sociopolitical dimensions of privacy, however, the importance of this industry is not tied exclusively to its economic successes. The first chapters of this book are in fact focused primarily on companies that were commercially unsuccessful. But this failure to make a long-term economic impact does not signal irrelevancy. Together, the companies in the consumer privacy industry have had a significant cultural influence: through the circulation of discourses that frame the risks and rewards of online visibility, they have helped shape how we think about privacy online. Their efforts have influenced public discourse about such seemingly commonsense ideas as authenticity, identity, reputation, and anonymity. Through their pedagogical efforts, which include relationships with regulators and journalists, as well as colleges and universities, these companies have promoted a framework for defining the benefits and dangers of visibility in the digital age in ways that have influenced our understandings about digital self-presentation.

If attention to past economic, social, or political efforts can reveal important details about the circumstances that led to failures, the experience of environmentalism in the late twentieth century may prove instructive for those interested in building privacy into technological systems. Consider, once again, Winner's reflection on the appropriate technology movement.[22] These scientists recognized the need for research to be conducted outside existing knowledge structures to effectively address environmental concerns. Ultimately, however, the appropriate technology movement faced resistance from predictable sources—those with significant investment in the maintenance of the status quo—and failed to achieve its utopian vision. In his reflection on the now apparent naïveté of the appropriate technologists, Winner notes a flaw in the movement's revolutionary visions. "Most of those active in the field were willing to proceed as if history and existing institutional technical realities simply did not matter," he writes. "That proved to be a serious shortcoming. It meant that many of their projects were irrelevant to the technical practices they hoped to challenge."[23] Attempts by the appropriate technologists to spur a revolution did not consider how the social, political, and economic histories of the industries they were trying to change would shape the types of interventions that were possible. By failing to incorporate these considerations into their own efforts, Winner suggests, the appropriate technologies were unable to predict how contemporary sociopolitical agendas might influence and ultimately hinder their success.

An appreciation of the successes and failures of previous intervention efforts is, therefore, essential to understanding the important and ongoing shifts within the consumer privacy industry. Considering privacy-enhancing technologies within their historical context helps correct a tendency to overemphasize the uniqueness of the political, cultural, and economic characteristics of the present moment. The challenges faced by companies in the 1990s have not disappeared in the intervening years. Moreover, claims from contemporary companies about a climate that has the technological resources coupled with the political and public appetite to change how we address digital privacy echo the claims made at the end of the twentieth century. Examining the industrial failures of the 1990s, therefore, may highlight the likely challenges confronting contemporary industry players. There is, however, another benefit of examining the two generations of consumer privacy services side by side. Looking at the similarities and differences in industry ideology and discourse helps clarify how sociocultural approaches to privacy have evolved.

When comparing the first and second generations of the consumer privacy industry similarities are revealed, but so, too, are important differences. For some involved in the industry in the late 1990s, privacy was an ideological project. Although the nature of this project was articulated differently depending on the motivations of those behind each company, there was an investment in privacy—achieved through anonymity or pseudonymity—as a fundamental part of digital life. In the 1990s, the industry was advocating for the development of web platforms that did not rely on the provision of personally identifiable information. It pushed for a right to privacy enabled by opportunities for anonymity that were accessible beyond communities of hackers and coders. To support the construction of this anonymous digital environment, the consumer privacy industry sought strategies of authentication that did not require the use of stable identity markers. For many at these companies, privacy was a holistic project—one that extended beyond the commercial realm to create protections for a wide variety of interactions.

Those in the second generation of the consumer privacy industry reside in a different socio-technical environment from their predecessors and, as a result, have different notions about how to define and protect privacy online. Given the ubiquity of practices of online self-presentation and digital sharing, those without an online presence are often viewed in the contemporary moment as suspect or at the very least odd. The consequence is an industry that largely asks individuals to invest in safe strategies of disclosure rather than seek opportunities to remain outside systems of surveillance. As the value of online engagement has increased and corresponding opportunities to opt out of the digital environment have declined, the consumer privacy industry has looked for ways to help users optimize their efforts at managed self-presentation. As a result, privacy in the current context is defined not only as the ability to control the circulation of personal data, but also to capitalize on this information in a world where all networked activities are imagined as contributing to an ever-expanding digital résumé.

A defensive posture that seeks to manage personal narratives and obscure information is an understandable reaction to the realities of the current digital ecosystem—an environment in which powerful companies work to create economic and cultural incentives for visibility, effectively narrowing opportunities for anonymity. This interpretation of privacy as controlled disclosure creates chances to hide elements of a digital image so long as there is a public persona that is recognizable, findable, and unassuming. Versions of privacy that embrace the construction and display of a unified, authentic, and socially palatable self may fall short of securing the infrastructures necessary for intimate social engagement and identity experimentation. This framework for understanding privacy, one that encourages approaches to identity as a strategic project, does not encourage risks in self-presentation nor does it provide much space for mistakes. Instead, this perspective reinforces a picture of identity that is valuable insofar as it is consistent and unchallenging.

Responses to the contemporary surveillance environment do little to address the inequalities fostered and exacerbated by capitalist systems and their embedded assumptions for consumer culture. The right to privacy has historically been more accessible to those wealthy enough to build walls that shield them from public view and for those whose identities—deemed "normal" or "acceptable"—allow them to escape public observation and scrutiny. And while mass surveillance efforts watch and analyze the behaviors of entire populations, not everyone experiences those observations or their consequences in the same way.[24] The application of a price tag to these services does not introduce costs for privacy—those have long been established—but it does make the economics of privacy more explicit. Whether people are paying for services that help them create and promote their preferred personal narrative or investing in tools that make them invisible to advertisers, these solutions do little to change the social and economic structures that allocate access to private spaces.

Redefining Privacy Online

The vision guiding the privacy industry in the twentieth century was the creation of a digital world where anonymity and pseudonymity operated as the default. Companies in this first generation were working to build an online world where engagement in the data economy was a matter of personal choice. Rather than assuming people were willing to give up access to their digital information, these companies advocated for data collection practices that presumed people wanted to opt out unless they made the decision to share their information. In the current environment, companies in the privacy industry no longer present opting out as a wise option or even a possibility. Companies like Anonymizer, Zero-Knowledge Systems, and iPrivacy sought to broaden options for strong privacy protection to accommodate a diversifying population of internet users. While plenty of services do exist to support anonymous engagement with the digital world, the idea that the broader public is interested in complete anonymity has been largely dismissed, replaced by a sense that a willingness to participate in economic transactions that exchange information for services is essentially a precondition for digital engagement. The result is that options for individuals—and for companies in the consumer privacy industry—have contracted. Contemporary privacy services are forced to confront an environment in which anonymity is assumed to be an unattractive option for most people. These companies are involved in renegotiating the definition of privacy to fit this new reality.

Lance Cottrell, founder of one of the first commercial anonymization companies, has observed the challenge of creating privacy tools for a digital culture that places a high value on transparency and openness. "I think it's getting even more complicated and I'm spending a lot of time thinking about what the next generation of privacy tools should look like," Cottrell told me. "When you talk to real users, they say 'I want to protect my privacy on the Internet,' and simultaneously they'll say, 'I want to use social media and be on Facebook and share things with my friends.' And so I think that fundamentally we need to rethink what we even mean when we say 'internet privacy' and what kind of tools may be available." Cottrell's insight points to a tension reflected in different ways throughout this book: how to reconcile methods of interaction that seem to conflict with an enduring social need for moments of invisibility and spaces of anonymity. This tension is manifest in the confusion of parents and educators when they find young people—who appear to share every aspect of their lives on social networking sites—are indignant about adults infringing on their privacy by monitoring their online activity. This tension is also reflected in the persistent interpretation of personal disclosure as the implicit surrender of privacy. It is embedded in Cottrell's rhetorical question, "You know, if you are using Facebook, what exactly are you still hiding?" This perceived inconsistency is at the heart of contemporary digital culture.

Over the past two decades, consumer privacy companies have sought to gain headway in a competitive digital environment. In the process of trying to become financially successful, the companies in this industry have had an important cultural impact. The industry's role in supporting the renegotiation of fundamental sociological terms over the course of just over two decades highlights the cultural complexity of these issues. Debates over the meaning of privacy are, however, far from settled. The industrial forces I've outlined in this book have offered a framework for privacy focused on individual efforts to control information that is publicly available. Recent trends, however, suggest another shift in how popular digital and mobile platforms are approaching privacy.

In 2014, legal scholar Tim Wu reflected on the resurgent popularity of online anonymity and ephemeral content.[25] The swell in mobile apps that allow users to engage friends or strangers in anonymous communication or to exchange content that would disappear after being received, Wu argued, stems from the fact that "you can share as much as you like, but nothing sticks to the 'real' you."[26] In 2013, Snapchat, an app that allows users to send content that disappears from recipients' phones within seconds, was the sixth most popular smartphone app in the iOS App Store with more downloads than Twitter, Instagram, and Facebook.[27] Although the app does not *prevent* the unwanted circulation of photos—recipients can take screenshots before the images disappear from their phones—by adding friction between receiving and storing a photo Snapchat aims to encourage spontaneous sharing that is not hindered by fears that content will *automatically* become part of a persistent digital record.

Another recent trend is the popularity of apps, which encourage users to post content anonymously or under a pseudonym. Examples of networks that have allowed people to anonymously interact within and outside existing social networks include Whisper, Secret, and Yik Yak. On Whisper, users post anonymous messages, which appear over arbitrary backgrounds and are visible to other app users. Yik Yak, which also allowed users to post anonymous messages, was location-based, meaning messages could be seen and interacted with only by those nearby. Secret, which required access to an address book, allowed users to see anonymous comments posted by those in their existing social networks. Wu suggested the popularity of these apps was driven by a generation of young people in need of a break from the calculated self-performance required on social platforms. "If Facebook is like a never-ending high school reunion, and Twitter serves up water-cooler chatter," Wu wrote, "the anonymous spaces promise some mixture of drunken party talk, group therapy and the confession booth, absent the hangovers, scheduled meetings and Hail Marys."[28]

Even Mark Zuckerberg, Facebook's founder who in 2010 declared that "having two identities for yourself is an example of a lack of integrity,"[29] has revisited his position on anonymity. Ten years after Facebook was founded, the company, which has played an important role in shaping dominant norms that favor a single, authentic, online identity, began rethinking some aspects of its platform. After Snapchat reportedly turned down a $3 billion acquisition offer, Facebook began working on new applications, some of which were rumored to allow users to log in and communicate privately.[30] Zuckerberg acknowledged the "pressure" and "burden" of continuously operating under a "real identity," adding that society is "at the point where we don't need to keep on only doing real identity things."[31]

Technologies that introduce ephemerality or anonymity into digital content are not new. During the late 1990s and early 2000s, Hushmail, ZipLip, Anonymizer, and Zero-Knowledge Systems offered anonymous messaging, and companies like Disappearing and TigerText experimented with vanishing content. More recently, apps such as Wickr and Signal have been introduced to provide encrypted messaging options. The protections offered by these tools differ, however, in important ways from the information privacy provided in the popular social apps described by Wu. While companies such as Anonymizer and ZeroKnowledge Systems used sophisticated encryption and message routing to create anonymous spaces where individuals were undiscoverable—often even by the companies themselves—apps like Yik Yak and Whisper facilitate anonymity only among users: what might be called social anonymity. While users may be unknown to other individuals using the service, those behind the apps are able to see detailed information about the device used to access the platform.

Observers, concerned about claims to anonymity and ephemerality, have raised questions about the privacy of content shared through these apps. Photos sent through Snapchat, for example, may be saved on company servers,[32] a practice that has allowed the platform to comply with warrants requiring that pictures be handed over.[33] Reports have also revealed that Whisper tracks user behaviors and has considered implementing targeted advertising.[34] Anonymous messaging apps—which Wu correctly predicted would be short lived—are at least as interesting for what they suggest about the evolution of digital culture as for the technological innovations they offer. As technical objects these popular apps are imperfect guarantors of anonymity. Through their use of digital address books and storage practices, they offer a far less comprehensive version of anonymity than services designed to ensure information is undiscoverable. As cultural objects, however, they provide a way for individuals to signal a desire for content to be treated as private or at least temporary. Moreover, an interest in social anonymity reveals desire for interactions that do not become part of a permanent online biography or inform a reputation score.

The popularity of these apps signals an interest in pumping the brakes on a culture that has been careening toward transparency and the inescapable responsibility of identity management. These tools are celebrated for offering authenticity, but not a version of authenticity based on the continual disclosure of information or the creation of content that is recognizable to search engine algorithms. Rather, in the context of these services, authenticity is based on the forms of disclosure and self-presentation supported by anonymous spaces. Consider the following statement from Whisper's blog regarding its "mission to make the world a more authentic, compassionate, understanding and connected place":

> We launched Whisper in the Spring of 2012 out of a deep belief that the way people share and interact with each other is changing. We felt that the next iteration of the social web would not solely be focused around reputation management. And while we knew what we created would always be a unique place to express yourself authentically, Whisper quickly exploded to become much more than that. It is now a fast-growing, constantly evolving community of millions of people bound by sharing stories, expressing unvarnished moments, revealing honest emotions and connecting with the world around them.[35]

These platforms signal an interest in online engagement that does not depend on practices of strategic transparency. Instead, they offered individuals a chance to escape from the obligations of an internet environment in which any comment or action may be connected to a permanent reputation.

In 2004, media scholar Gina Neff and sociologist David Stark described internet design as being in a constant state of flux they called "permanently beta." "Permanently beta," they wrote, "is a fluid organizational form resulting from the process of negotiation among users, employees, and organizations over the design of goods and services."[36] Although Neff and Stark's definition refers to the organizational processes that result from continuous technological change, it is perhaps useful to think about privacy and the industries that have emerged around this concept as similarly in constant beta: not a finished product, but rather the result of continual, unsettled, and ongoing negotiations that take place among various stakeholders in the face of a continually evolving technological, social, and political contexts. I began this book by stating this is not a story about the end of privacy. Rather, it is concerned with the role of an industry in shaping and responding to the ongoing conversations around this term. It is interested in how those engaged with this industry think about the problem of privacy online and the solutions it offered and continues to offer to address those issues. It examines the ways that new technologies introduce threats to those who previously felt comfortable in their ability to control the elements of their lives that were made public. At the same time, it considers how the introduction of commercial solutions that shape who is empowered to assert control may operate to reproduce existing inequalities in who gets to decide where the boundaries between public and private spaces are drawn and additionally who benefits from those divisions.

Technological Solutions in Context

Just as the consumer privacy industry should not be viewed outside the social and political worlds that shaped it, the tools and services offered by the companies introduced throughout this book should not be viewed as singular technical solutions. Instead, they should be treated as part of a shared set of social, legal, and technical structures that help to make the norms and consequences of digital disclosures clear and predictable. These tools offer technological approaches that, if carefully combined with thoughtful regulation to ensure equal access to protections, can serve as a necessary stimulus to engage in discussions around personal and collective privacy rights designed to facilitate shared understandings and expectations about the context and nature of respectful information practices. This approach to privacy borrows from Helen Nissenbaum's construction of contextual integrity in which she defines privacy as "a right to appropriate flow of personal information."[37] In this framework, technical tools become one leg of a three-legged stool[38] in which regulation, cultural norms, and technology facilitate and support shared expectations about information privacy. In this model, regulation such as the Right to Be Forgotten—the European Union's digital privacy effort which, among other things, gives individuals the right to request that erroneous or irrelevant content be delisted from search sites[39]—operates alongside applications that introduce ephemerality to digital content and offer strategies to remove or bury unwanted content. This toolbox approach to privacy protection does not remove agency from the individual, nor does it create a paternalistic system in which opportunities for sharing are removed. What it does is create opportunities to insert friction into a digital environment that has been designed to collect and remember. It also provides opportunities to deal with the forms of cultural bias that technological systems have proven ill equipped to eradicate.

To the extent that they offer individuals tools to assist in the management of personal information—including collection, analysis, and use—the companies in the consumer privacy industry have provided practical strategies for individual intervention into a deepening conflict over privacy that tends to be defined in terms of ownership and control; however, much as the appropriate technologists face challenges due to institutional and cultural investments in the status quo, these commercial providers are restricted by the socioeconomic realities of the cultures in which they reside. Few people seem to be looking to be completely and continuously anonymous or to opt out of digital systems all together. Rather, they are looking for strategies that are consistent with the concerns they have about unwanted visibility. They are seeking tools that help mitigate the unintended negative consequences that accompany the collection and use of personal information. In other words, they are looking to translate feelings of anonymity and obscurity experienced offline into their online lives. And, for those who lack the luxury of being anonymous in public spaces, they are searching for ways to improve on a physical world that focuses surveillance efforts on some bodies but not others.

One of the narratives throughout this book has been a consistent focus on empowerment through control. Given that companies—from anonymizers to infomediaries to online reputation management firms to the companies that make up the personal data ecosystem—have addressed privacy concerns through tools and services designed to enable individuals to exercise control over their personal information, it is essential to consider what the empowerment promised by these services looks like in the absence of control. Each of these chapters has pointed to instances in which efforts to control the circulation of information are challenged by the economic and political structures that demand visibility, the social networks that encourage disclosure, and the technical tools that generate and collect data. How then do we conceive of autonomy—over one's reputation, image, and data—when control is an untenable proposition?

The notion of relational autonomy is instructive here. We have seen, throughout this consumer privacy industry, a definition of *personal* responsibility related to *individual* choices. Relational autonomy, which has its roots in feminist theory, focuses on collective responses as a strategy for addressing social problems.[40] Unlike constructions of autonomy that are deeply tied to individualistic notions of rights and responsibilities, relational autonomy considers how embedded networks operate to shape and confine the range of available options. In their edited collection on the topic, philosophers Catriona Mackenzie and Natalie Stoljar write that relational autonomy is "premised on a shared conviction, the conviction that persons are socially embedded and that agents' identities are formed within the context of social relationships and shaped by a complex of intersecting social determinants, such as race, class, gender, and ethnicity."[41] Applied to issues of privacy, relational autonomy asks us to consider how political and economic structures, social networks, and technical artifacts support and constrain efforts to manage the circulation and visibility of our information. As a theoretical perspective, it considers the possibility of empowerment through shared obligations. Approaches that decentralize responsibility, treating privacy as a shared obligation, have the potential to reduce the stigma that follows some types of privacy breaches. It encourages us, based on the recognition that autonomy cannot be achieved through independent action alone, to be generous in our evaluations of others. Consequently, it offers something that the tools and services in this industry rarely do: it offers a framework for taking privacy out of the realm of individual choice and reimagining it as a set of mutual obligations.

As I have argued throughout this book, the tools and services offered by companies across the consumer privacy industry have implications beyond privacy. As they encourage us to create a single account in which all our data and personal information is stored—for both ease of protection and effective self-promotion—they implicate ways that we think about notions of authenticity, identity, and self-presentation. As they encourage us to track and submit data from online interactions, they support the growth of a reputation society in which our value is based on the rankings and ratings assigned to us by others—a system that currently enjoys little of the regulatory guidance of existing reputation systems, such as those that supervise financial institutions and credit reporting agencies. As they encourage self-tracking, data visualization, and content sharing, they promote linear narratives of identity formation that privilege consistency over experimentation.

These services provide clients with tools to manage and make sense of their digital data. Through these tools, and by offering individuals the chance to sell their personal information, these companies draw attention to the underlying economic forces that drive the online economy. They also offer practical solutions to those suffering from the consequences of a negative digital image and have the time, finances, and technical skills to capitalize on their services. These commercial solutions alone cannot, however, address the problems of pervasive digital surveillance or the complex range of privacy violations that people face in their daily lives. Approaches that assign an economic value to privacy also allow existing industry practices to be insulated from debates about the social and communal importance of privacy. In so far as this commodification serves to shift privacy from a right to an expense, it neutralizes the need for collective political action by focusing on the responsibility individuals have to ensure that their own privacy is protected and their identity is effectively managed. These limitations should cause us to hesitate before turning to industrial approaches as an *exclusive* means of solving the problems digital privacy. They should instead inspire a rethinking of the value of privacy—particularly as it relates to collective rights—and encourage conversations about solutions that combine the strengths of technological, regulatory, and cultural approaches.

ACKNOWLEDGMENTS

My first published book was featured in a corner of Mrs. Arnott's elementary school classroom under the sign "Books by Local Authors." Between that publication and this one have been myriad acts of generosity—singular and sustained—for which I am deeply indebted and eternally grateful.

My elementary and high schools offered teachers who were passionate about the value of reading and the importance of writing, none more so than Baruch Zohar. At Carleton University, my professors—particularly Eileen Saunders, Susan Whitney, and Josh Greenberg—saw me as an academic long before the thought occurred to me. That the research for this book received generous support from the Social Sciences and Humanities Research Council of Canada is a result of their guidance and encouragement.

At the University of Pennsylvania, the faculty, administration, and students in the Annenberg School for Communication provided the scholarly communities and emotional networks that made writing more collaborative and less isolated than is its tendency. I am exceedingly grateful that many of my classmates are now better described as colleagues, collaborators, mentors, and friends.

The efforts of my graduate supervisors and mentors to challenge my thinking and improve my scholarship balanced shrewd critique with assurances that I was up to the challenge. The sharp insights and thoughtful questions offered by Barbie Zelizer and Sharrona Pearl enhanced my work, while their professional and personal integrity have provided models to which I continue to aspire. My choice of graduate programs was driven by a desire to work with Joe Turow, whose dedication, attentiveness, and encouragement has been instrumental in building my research agenda and career. My research was further nuanced and refined through discussions with Katherine Sender, Keith Hampton, Peter Decherney, and Helen Nissenbaum.

At the University of New Hampshire I joined a group of colleagues deeply committed to the public mission of teaching and scholarship. I am grateful to my supportive and inspiring colleagues, particularly those in the Department of Communication. I feel uniquely privileged to be part of this community.

I am thankful to the team at NYU Press—Eric Zinner, Lisha Nadkarni, Dolma Ombadykow, Aswin Punathambekar, Nina Huntemann, Adrienne Shaw, and especially Jonathan Gray—for their early enthusiasm and sustained commitment to this project. Thanks as well to the anonymous reviewers for generously sharing their time and expertise to provide detailed comments and encouragement. While errors in this work are entirely my own, I am indebted to the work of Cathy Hannabach and her team at Ideas on Fire for their efforts to minimize their occurrence. My work has benefited immensely from the intellectual efforts of each of these individuals and their teams.

I am also indebted to the generosity of my interviewees—those who took time from their schedules and invited me into their offices and community spaces. Their thoughtful reflections on failure, success, and the importance of privacy in the digital world made this work possible.

I have had the good fortune throughout my life of being surrounded by wonderful friends. Sharing my academic careers with Chris Ali and Katherine Wong created much-needed feelings of comfort, belonging, and perspective in a world where those things can be rare. Despite their persistent efforts to repatriate me to Toronto, Ilvana Montgomery and Wei-Ting Harrison's willingness to spend their vacations in whichever city I'm currently calling home has been one of the greatest pleasures of my life. More recently, Mike McWhirk has shared with me the day-to-day frustrations and excitements that come with writing and publishing a book. I am as grateful for our mutual passion for privacy and security as I am for his insistence that we occasionally discuss something else.

Though we are geographically distant, my family are my most dependable and valuable confidantes, and their support and insight are present in all that I do. I am indebted to my mom, Susan; my dad, David; and my sister, Audrey, for their guidance, their enthusiasm for my work, and for always taking my calls. It is impossible to express how much their support means—I can only hope that they know.

I often hear it said that as academics, the most valuable things we possess are our ideas. In researching and writing this book, I've come to consider time an equally precious resource. For all those who have generously shared their time with me—and for all those who share their time with others—thank you.

Portions of earlier versions of this work have appeared in the journal *Media Industries* in the article "Fail Fast: The Value of Studying Unsuccessful Technology Companies" and in the journal *Policy & Internet* in the article "From Privacy Pragmatist to Privacy Resigned: Challenging Narratives of Rational Choice in Digital Privacy Debates," © 2016 Policy Studies Organization.

NOTES

INTRODUCTION

1 "Why Privacy Is Our 2013 Word of the Year," *Dictionary.Com Blog* (blog), December 17, 2013, http://blog.dictionary.com.

2 "Oxford Dictionaries Word of the Year: 2013," *OxfordWords Blog* (blog), November 19, 2013, http://blog.oxforddictionaries.com.

3 Teresa M. Senft and Nancy K. Baym, "What Does the Selfie Say? Investigating a Global Phenomenon," *International Journal of Communication* 9 (2015): 1588–1606.

4 Adrienne Massanari, "#Gamergate and The Fappening: How Reddit's Algorithm, Governance, and Culture Support Toxic Technocultures," *New Media & Society* 19, no. 3 (2017): 329–46, http://doi.org/10.1177/1461444815608807.

5 Alice E. Marwick "Scandal or Sex Crime? Gendered Privacy and the Celebrity Nude Photo Leaks," *Ethics and Information Technology* 19, no. 3 (2017): 177–91, http://doi.org/10.1007/s10676-017-9431-7.

6 Michael Warner, *Publics and Counterpublics* (New York: Zone Books, 2002), 28.

7 Zizi Papacharissi, "Privacy as a Luxury Commodity," *First Monday* 15, no. 8 (August 2, 2010), http://dx.doi.org/10.5210/fm.v15i8.3075.

8 Nick Bergus, "How I Became Amazon's Pitchman for a 55-Gallon Drum of Personal Lubricant on Facebook," *Nick Bergus: Thoughts on Things* (blog), February 23, 2012, http://nbergus.com.

9 Somini Sengupta, "So Much for Sharing His 'Like,'" *New York Times*, May 31, 2012.

10 I use the term "commercial web" to refer to the post-browser internet, which is characterized in part by the presence of companies online and the growth of e-commerce.

11 This industrial grouping does not include a set of companies engaged in the adjacent field of information security—those, for example, that sell identity and credit monitoring tools. This grouping also leaves out free and open source software—such as Tor—that provides opportunities to surf the web anonymously.

12 I use the term "proto-industry" when referring to the collection of companies invested in providing commercial solutions to concerns regarding personal privacy. This term is intended to signal the emergent nature of this community, the members of which are often aware of one another but tend not to view themselves as part of a cohesive industry that is bound by shared ethics or best practices.

13 For a more detailed argument about the study of failed technology companies and industries, see Nora Draper, "Fail Fast: The Value of Studying Unsuccessful Technology Companies," *Media Industries* 4, no. 1 (2017), http://doi.org/10.3998/mij.15031809.0004.101.

14 Kenneth Lipartito, "Picturephone and the Information Age: The Social Meaning of Failure," *Technology and Culture* 44, no. 1 (2003): 50–81, http://doi.org/10.1353/tech.2003.0033.

15 See, e.g., Mark Andrejevic, "The Work That Affective Economics Does," *Cultural Studies* 25, nos. 4–5 (2011): 604–20, http://doi.org/10.1080/09502386.2011.600551; Daniel J. Solove, *The Digital Person: Technology and Privacy in the Information Age* (New York: NYU Press, 2004); Joseph Turow, *The Daily You: How the New Advertising Industry Is Defining Your Identity and Your Worth* (New Haven, CT: Yale University Press, 2011); José van Dijck, *The Culture of Connectivity: A Critical History of Social Media* (Oxford, UK: Oxford University Press, 2013).

16 Colin J. Bennett and Charles D. Raab, *The Governance of Privacy: Policy Instruments in Global Perspective* (Cambridge, MA: MIT Press, 2006).

17 Colin J. Bennett, *The Privacy Advocates: Resisting the Spread of Surveillance* (Cambridge, MA: MIT Press, 2008).

18 But see Philip E. Agre and Marc Rotenberg, eds., *Technology and Privacy: The New Landscape* (Cambridge, MA: MIT Press, 1997); John Edward Campbell and Matt Carlson, "Panopticon.Com: Online Surveillance and the Commodification of Privacy," *Journal of Broadcasting & Electronic Media* 46, no. 4 (2002): 586–606; Arvind Narayanan, Solon Barocas, Vincent Toubiana, Helen Nissenbaum, and Dan Boneh, "A Critical Look at Decentralized Personal Data Architectures," February 21, 2012, http://arxiv.org; David J. Phillips, "Privacy Policy and PETs: The Influence of Policy Regimes on the Development and Social Implications of Privacy Enhancing Technologies," *New Media & Society* 6, no. 6 (2004): 691–706; Ira R. Rubinstein, "Regulating Privacy by Design," *Berkeley Technology Law Journal* 26, no. 3 (2011): 1409–56.

19 I draw here from Torin Monahan's notion of "built pedagogy" as "the lessons taught by technological systems and spaces." See Monahan, *Globalization, Technological Change, and Public Education* (New York: Routledge, 2005), 9.

20 Helen Nissenbaum, *Privacy in Context: Technology, Policy, and the Integrity of Social Life* (Stanford, CA: Stanford Law Books, 2010), 2.

21 Timothy Havens, Amanda D. Lotz, and Serra Tinic, "Critical Media Industry Studies: A Research Approach," *Communication, Culture and Critique* 2, no. 2 (2009): 235, http://doi.org/10.1111/j.1753-9137.2009.01037.x.

22 Havens, Lotz, and Tinic, 234.

23 Hugh Gusterson, "Studying Up Revisited," *Political and Legal Anthropology Review* 20, no. 1 (1997): 114–19; see also Joseph Turow, *Media Systems in Society: Understanding Industries, Strategies, and Power*, 2nd ed. (New York: Longman, 1997) for a discussion of "power roles."

24 Marie Hicks, *Programmed Inequality: How Britain Discarded Women Technologists and Lost Its Edge in Computing* (Cambridge, MA: MIT Press, 2017); Nathan Ensmenger, *The Computer Boys Take Over: Computers, Programmers, and the Politics of Technical Expertise* (Cambridge, MA: MIT Press, 2010).

25 This is not to suggest women are not engaged in this space. The organization Women in Security and Privacy was founded in 2014 to provide support and mentorship for women working in these fields.

CHAPTER 1. THE CONSUMER PRIVACY SPACE

1 Joshua Quittner, "Invasion of Privacy," *Time*, August 25, 1997.

2 Quittner, 30.

3 Quittner, 32–33.

4 Quittner, 28.

5 danah boyd, *It's Complicated: The Social Lives of Networked Teens* (New Haven, CT: Yale University Press, 2014).

6 Daniel J. Solove, "Introduction: Privacy Self-Management and the Consent Dilemma," *Harvard Law Review* 126, no. 7 (2013): 1880–1903.

7 Nick Bergus, "How I Became Amazon's Pitchman for a 55-Gallon Drum of Personal Lubricant on Facebook," *Nick Bergus: Thoughts on Things* (blog), February 23, 2012, http://nbergus.com.

8 Samuel D. Warren and Louis D. Brandeis, "The Right to Privacy," *Harvard Law Review* 4, no. 5 (1890): 193–220.

9 Warren and Brandeis.

10 Nicholas A. John and Benjamin Peters, "Why Privacy Keeps Dying: The Trouble with Talk about the End of Privacy," *Information, Communication & Society* 20, no. 2 (2017): 284–98, http://doi.org/10.1080/1369118X.2016.1167229.

11 Carolyn Marvin, *When Old Technologies Were New: Thinking about Electric Communication in the Late Nineteenth Century* (New York: Oxford University Press, 1990), 67–68.

12 David M. Henkin, *The Postal Age: The Emergence of Modern Communications in Nineteenth-Century America* (Chicago: University of Chicago Press, 2006).

13 For details of the case, see Christie Blatchford, "Tender Youth, Terrible Crime, Compelling Case," *The Globe and Mail*, November 19, 2004.

14 Joseph Breen, "Johnathan Mistrial: Judge Says Post Story Casts Doubt on Witness," *National Post*, February 16, 2005.

15 Christie Blatchford, "Johnathan Trial Aborted," *The Globe and Mail*, February 16, 2005.

16 Quoted in Breen, "Johnathan Mistrial."

17 Sherry Turkle, *Life on Screen: Identity in the Age of the Internet* (New York: Simon & Schuster, 1995), 12.

18 boyd, *It's Complicated*.

19 Anthony Giddens, *Modernity and Self-Identity: Self and Society in the Late Modern Age* (Stanford, CA: Stanford University Press, 1991), 5.

20 Giddens, 81.

21 Giddens, 28–29.

22 Ulrich Beck and Elizabeth Beck-Gernsheim, *Individualization: Institutional Individualism and Its Social and Political Consequences* (London: SAGE Publications, 2002).

23 Beck and Beck-Gernsheim, 3.

24 Beck and Beck-Gernsheim.

25 Matthew Adams, "The Reflexive Self and Culture: A Critique," *British Journal of Sociology* 54, no. 2 (June 2003): 221–38, http://doi.org/10.1080/0007131032000080212.

26 Erving Goffman, *Presentation of Self in Everyday Life* (New York: Anchor Books, 1959).

27 Goffman, 48.

28 danah boyd's various discussions of context collapse explain how digital technologies complicate audience segmentation strategies. See boyd, *It's Complicated*; and boyd, "Why Youth (Heart) Social Network Sites: The Role of Networked Publics in Teenage Social Life," in *Youth, Identity, and Digital Media Volume*, ed. David Buckingham, MacArthur Foundation Series on Digital Media and Learning (Cambridge, MA: MIT Press, 2007), 119–42.

29 boyd, *It's Complicated*, 31.

30 José van Dijck, *The Culture of Connectivity: A Critical History of Social Media* (Oxford, UK: Oxford University Press, 2013).

31 See Robert Hackett, "What to Know about the Ashley Madison Hack," *Fortune*, August 26, 2015, www.fortune.com.

32 James Hamblin, "My Outrage Is Better Than Your Outrage," *The Atlantic*, July 31, 2015, www.theatlantic.com.

33 Irwin Altman, "Privacy: A Conceptual Analysis," *Environment and Behavior* 8, no. 1 (1976): 7–29.

34 Altman, 12.

35 Anita L. Allen and Erin Mack, "How Privacy Got Its Gender," *Northern Illinois University Law Review* 10 (1991): 441.

36 Allen and Mack; see also Anita L. Allen, *Uneasy Access: Privacy for Women in a Free Society* (Totowa, NJ: Rowman & Littlefield, 1988).

37 Judith Wagner DeCew, "The Feminist Critique of Privacy: Past Arguments and New Social Understandings," in *Social Dimensions of Privacy: Interdisciplinary Perspectives*, ed. Beate Roessler and Dorota Mokrosinska (New York: Cambridge University Press, 2015), 85–103.

38 Larry Gross, "Privacy and Spectacle: The Reversible Panopticon and Media-Saturated Society" in *Image Ethics in the Digital Age*, ed. Larry P. Gross, John Stuart Katz, and Jay Ruby (Minneapolis: University of Minnesota Press, 2003), 95–113.

39 Anita L. Allen, "Gender and Privacy in Cyberspace," *Stanford Law Review* 52 (2000): 1175–1200.

40 Allen, 1177.

41 Youth Criminal Justice Act, S.C. 2002, c. 1, http://laws-lois.justice.gc.ca.

42 Christie Blatchford, "A Boy, One Last Lovely Time," *The Globe and Mail*, December 6, 2003.

43 Quoted in Armina Ligaya, "Johnathan's Mother Struggles to Forgive," *The Globe and Mail*, September 22, 2006.

44 Michele Gilman and Rebecca Green, "The Surveillance Gap: The Harms of Extreme Privacy and Data Marginalization," *NYU Review of Law and Social Change* 42 (forthcoming).

45 Rosemarie Garland-Thomson, "The Politics of Staring: Visual Rhetorics of Disability in Popular Photography," in *Disability Studies: Enabling the Humanities*, ed. Sharon L. Snyder, Brenda Jo Brueggemann, and Rosemarie Garland-Thomson (New York: Modern Language Association of America, 2002), 56.

46 Tarleton Gillespie, "The Relevance of Algorithms," in *Media Technologies: Essays on Communication, Materiality, and Society*, ed. Tarleton Gillespie, Pablo J. Boczkowski, and Kirsten A. Foot (Cambridge, MA: MIT Press, 2014), 167–93.

47 Lisa Nakamura, *Cybertypes: Race, Ethnicity, and Identity on the Internet* (New York: Routledge, 2002), 120.

48 Rena Bivens, "The Gender Binary Will Not Be Deprogrammed: Ten Years of Coding Gender on Facebook," *New Media & Society* 19, no. 6 (June 2017): 880–98, http://doi.org/10.1177/1461444815621527.

49 Larry Gross, "The Contested Closet: The Ethics and Politics of Outing," *Critical Studies in Mass Communication* 8, no. 3 (1991): 357.

50 Gross.

51 See Jonathan Cohn, "My TiVo Thinks I'm Gay: Algorithmic Culture and Its Discontents," *Television & New Media* 17, no. 8 (December 2016): 675–90, http://doi.org/10.1177/1527476416644978.

52 José van Dijck, "'You Have One Identity': Performing the Self on Facebook and LinkedIn," *Media, Culture & Society* 35, no. 2 (2013): 199–215.

53 Valeriya Safronova, "Facebook Confronts Gender Identity Issue," *New York Times*, September 24, 2014.

54 Lil Miss Hot Mess, "Let Me Be Lil Miss Hot Mess: Facebook Took Away My Stage Name," *Salon*, September 24, 2014, www.salon.com.

55 Vauhini Vara, "Who's Real Enough for Facebook?" *New Yorker*, October 2, 2014, www.newyorker.com.

56 Paul M. Schwartz and Daniel J. Solove, "The PII Problem: Privacy and a New Concept of Personally Identifiable Information," *New York University Law Review* 86, no. 6 (2011): 1814–95.

57 Vincent Mosco, *The Political Economy of Communication*, 2nd ed. (Los Angeles: SAGE Publications, 2009), 128.

58 Mosco, 127.

59 See, for example, Mark Andrejevic, *Infoglut: How Too Much Information Is Changing the Way We Think and Know* (New York: Routledge, 2013); Christian Fuchs, "Labor in Informational Capitalism and on the Internet," *Information Society* 26,

no. 3 (2010): 179–96; Oscar Gandy Jr., *The Panoptic Sort: A Political Economy of Personal Information* (Boulder, CO: Westview, 1993).

60 Alan F. Westin, *Privacy and Freedom* (New York: Atheneum, 1967).

61 For a thorough history of the Privacy Act of 1974, see Priscilla Regan, *Legislating Privacy: Technology, Social Values, and Public Policy* (Chapel Hill: University of North Carolina Press, 1995).

62 Dallas Smythe, "Communications: Blindspot of Western Marxism," *Canadian Journal of Political and Social Theory* 1, no. 3 (1977): 1–27.

63 Joseph Turow, *Niche Envy: Marketing Discrimination in the Digital Age* (Cambridge, MA: MIT Press, 2006).

64 Lizabeth Cohen, *A Consumers' Republic: The Politics of Mass Consumption in Postwar America* (New York: Vintage Books, 2004), chap. 7.

65 Mark Andrejevic, "The Work of Being Watched: Interactive Media and the Exploitation of Self-Disclosure," *Critical Studies in Media Communication* 19, no. 2 (2002): 230–48.

66 Joseph Turow, *The Daily You: How the New Advertising Industry Is Defining Your Identity and Your Worth* (New Haven, CT: Yale University Press, 2011).

67 Oscar Gandy Jr., "Coming to Terms with the Panoptic Sort," in *Computers, Surveillance, and Privacy*, ed. David Lyon and Elia Zureik (Minneapolis: University of Minnesota Press, 1996), 132–55. See also, David Lyon, *Surveillance as Social Sorting: Privacy, Risk, and Digital Discrimination* (New York: Routledge, 2003).

68 John Cheney-Lippold, "A New Algorithmic Identity: Soft Biopolitics and the Modulation of Control," *Theory, Culture & Society* 28, no. 6 (2011): 164–81, http://doi.org/10.1177/0263276411424420.

69 Michel Foucault, *Discipline and Punish: The Birth of the Prison*, 2nd ed. trans. Alan Sheridan (New York: Vintage Books, 1995).

70 Shoshana Zuboff, "Big Other: Surveillance Capitalism and the Prospects of an Information Civilization," *Journal of Information Technology* 30, no. 1 (2015): 75, http://doi.org/10.1057/jit.2015.5.

71 Bergus, "How I Became Amazon's Pitchman."

72 Daniel J. Solove, "Speech, Privacy, and Reputation on the Internet," in *The Offensive Internet: Speech, Privacy, and Reputation*, ed. Saul Levmore and Martha Craven Nussbaum (Cambridge, MA: Harvard University Press, 2010), 22.

73 Andrejevic, "Work of Being Watched," 245.

74 Daniel J. Solove, *The Digital Person: Technology and Privacy in the Information Age* (New York: NYU Press, 2004).

75 Westin, *Privacy and Freedom*, 7.

76 Westin also argued that privacy allows for emotional release, self-evaluation, and protected communication.

77 Cheney-Lippold, "New Algorithmic Identity."

78 Cheney-Lippold, 177.

79 Gillespie, "Relevance of Algorithms."

80 Torin Monahan, "Editorial: Surveillance and Inequality," *Surveillance & Society* 5, no. 3 (2008): 217.

81 Gillespie, "Relevance of Algorithms," 167.

82 Gillespie, 172.

83 Monahan, "Editorial," 217.

84 A. Michael Froomkin, "The Death of Privacy?" *Stanford Law Review* 52 (2000): 1461–43; see Lori B. Andrews, *I Know Who You Are and I Saw What You Did: Social Networks and the Death of Privacy* (New York: Free Press, 2012); Simon Garfinkel, *Database Nation: The Death of Privacy in the 21st Century* (Sebastopol, CA: O'Reilly, 2000).

85 Josh Lauer, "Surveillance History and the History of New Media: An Evidential Paradigm," *New Media & Society* 14, no. 4 (2011): 567, http://doi.org/10.1177/1461444811420986.

86 Jerry M. Rosenberg, *The Death of Privacy* (New York: Random House, 1969), 4–5.

87 Rosenberg, 5.

88 John and Peters, "Why Privacy Keeps Dying."

89 John and Peters, 2.

90 John and Peters, 13.

91 Katherine Sender describes a similar position taken by those behind the construction of the gay market. See Sender, *Business, Not Politics: The Making of the Gay Market* (New York: Columbia University Press, 2004).

92 Gina Neff, "The Changing Place of Cultural Production: The Location of Social Networks in a Digital Media Industry," *ANNALS of the American Academy of Political and Social Science* 597, no. 1 (2005): 134–52; Hortense Powdermaker, *Hollywood: The Dream Factory: An Anthropologist Looks at the Movie-Makers* (Boston: Little, Brown, 1950).

93 Jennifer Holt and Alisa Perren, eds., *Media Industries: History, Theory, and Method* (Oxford, UK: Blackwell Press, 2009).

94 Gaye Tuchman, *Making News: A Study in the Construction of Reality* (New York: Free Press, 1978); Barbie Zelizer, "Journalists as Interpretive Communities," *Critical Studies in Mass Communication* 10, no. 3 (1993): 219–37.

95 Thomas Donaldson and Thomas W. Dunfee, *Ties That Bind: A Social Contracts Approach to Business Ethics* (Cambridge, MA: Harvard Business Review Press, 1999), 3.

CHAPTER 2. DIGITAL PRIVACY GOES MAINSTREAM

1 Peter H. Lewis, "Of Privacy and Security: The Clipper Chip Debate," *New York Times*, April 24, 1994, www.nytimes.com.

2 A. Michael Froomkin, "The Metaphor Is the Key: Cryptography, the Clipper Chip, and the Constitution," *University of Pennsylvania Law Review* 143, no. 3 (1995): 709–897.

3 Colin J. Bennett, *The Privacy Advocates: Resisting the Spread of Surveillance* (Cambridge, MA: MIT Press, 2008), 149.

4   Bennett, 147; for a full description of the concerns regarding the Clipper Chip program, see Froomkin, "Metaphor Is the Key."

5   Froomkin; the Clipper Chip initiative, which was introduced under president George H. W. Bush and continued under president Bill Clinton, was fully abandoned by 1996. See Bennett.

6   Toby Lester, "The Reinvention of Privacy," *The Atlantic*, March 1, 2001, www.theatlantic.com. Lester's piece provided a comprehensive description of the privacy space as it existed in 2001. I revisited several of the key players he introduced and am indebted to his framing of the field.

7   For a typology of PETs, see David J. Phillips, "Privacy Policy and PETs: The Influence of Policy Regimes on the Development and Social Implications of Privacy Enhancing Technologies," *New Media & Society* 6, no. 6 (2004): 691–706; "Privacy Enhancing Technologies: A Review of Tools and Techniques," Office of the Privacy Commissioner of Canada, November 2017, www.priv.gc.ca.

8   Sociologist Manuel Castells describes the introduction of the web browser as "the main event that led to the constitution of the internet in its current form." See Castells, *The Internet Galaxy: Reflections on the Internet, Business, and Society* (New York: Oxford University Press, 2001), 10.

9   Fred Turner, *From Counterculture to Cyberculture: Stuart Brand, the Whole Earth Network, and the Rise of Digital Utopianism* (Chicago: University of Chicago Press, 2006).

10 "Internet Adoption, 1995–2013," Pew Internet & American Life Project, 2013, www.pewinternet.org.

11 "Usage over Time: Trend Data (Adults)," Pew Internet & American Life Project, 2013, www.pewinternet.org.

12 Susannah Fox, "Trust and Privacy Online," Pew Internet & American Life Project, August 20, 2000, www.pewinternet.org.

13 Saul Levmore, "The Internet's Anonymity Problem," in *The Offensive Internet: Speech, Privacy, and Reputation*, ed. Saul Levmore and Martha Craven Nussbaum (Cambridge, MA: Harvard University Press, 2010), 50–51.

14 John W. Kingdon, *Agendas, Alternatives, and Public Policies*, 2nd ed. (Boston: Longman, 2011), 165.

15 Kingdon, 168.

16 Kingdon, 166.

17 Richard Shelby, "Congress: Freedom from Behavioral Profiling Act of 2000," Pub. L. No. S. 536 (2001), www.govtrack.us.

18 Raymond Green, "Consumer Online Privacy and Disclosure Act.," Pub. L. No. H.R. 5430 (2000), www.govtrack.us.

19 Christine Varney, "Testimony of Christine Varney, Partner Hogan & Harston," Senate Commerce, Science, and Transportation Committee Hearing on Internet Privacy (2000), www.gpo.gov.

20 Robert G. Torricelli, "Internet Privacy," Senate Commerce, Science, and Transportation Committee Hearing on Internet Privacy (2000), www.gpo.gov.

21 Torricelli.

22 Bill S. 2063 was referred to the Senate Committee on the Judiciary but advanced no further. Jeffrey Rosen argues it was "vigorously and successfully resisted by the e-commerce lobby." Jeffrey Rosen, "The Eroded Self," *New York Times Magazine*, April 30, 2000, www.nytimes.com.

23 Lester, "Reinvention of Privacy"; Andrea Petersen, "E-Commerce (A Special Report): Industry by Industry—Privacy—Private Matters: It Seems That Trust Equals Revenue, Even Online," *Wall Street Journal*, February 12, 2001.

24 Tyler Hamilton, "Privacy Mishaps Can Sink Firms: Report on Privacy," *Toronto Star*, January 8, 2001.

25 Jan Fernback and Zizi Papacharissi, "Online Privacy as Legal Safeguard: The Relationship among Consumer, Online Portal, and Privacy Policies," *New Media & Society* 9, no. 5 (2007): 715–34.

26 Mary J. Culnan and George R. Milne, "The Culnan–Milne Survey of Consumers and Online Privacy Notices," Isenberg School of Management, University of Massachusetts Amherst, 2001, http://intra.som.umass.edu.

27 Joseph Turow, *Americans and Online Privacy: The System Is Broken* (Philadelphia: Annenberg School for Communication, University of Pennsylvania, 2003), http://repository.upenn.edu; Joseph Turow, Lauren Feldman, and Kimberly Meltzer, *Open to Exploitation: American Shoppers Online and Offline* (Philadelphia: Annenberg School for Communication, University of Pennsylvania, 2003), http://repository.upenn.edu; Joseph Turow, Jennifer King, Chris Jay Hoofnagle, Amy Bleakley, and Michael Hennessy, "Americans Reject Tailored Advertising and Three Activities That Enable It," September 29, 2009, available at SSRN, http://dx.doi.org/10.2139/ssrn.1478214; Joseph Turow and Nora Draper, "Advertising's New Surveillance Ecosystem," in *Routledge Handbook of Surveillance Studies*, ed. David Lyon, Kevin D. Haggerty, and Kirstie Ball (New York: Routledge, 2012), 133–40; Joseph Turow, Michael Hennessy, and Nora Draper, *The Tradeoff Fallacy: How Marketers Are Misrepresenting American Consumers and Opening Them Up to Exploitation* (Philadelphia: Annenberg School for Communication, University of Pennsylvania, 2015), www.asc.upenn.edu.

28 A 2012 Carnegie Mellon study determined that if internet users read every privacy policy they encountered online, they would spend twenty-five days a year engaged in this activity. Aleecia M. McDonald and Lorrie F. Cranor, "The Cost of Reading Privacy Policies," *I/S: A Journal of Law and Policy for the Information Society* 4, no. 3 (2008), http://lorrie.cranor.org.

29 Lance Cottrell, quoted in Reid Kanaley, "Privacy Policies on Web Sites Are Only for the Gullible," *Philadelphia Inquirer*, November 19, 2000.

30 Jonathan A. Obar and Anne Oeldorf-Hirsch, "The Biggest Lie on the Internet: Ignoring the Privacy Policies and Terms of Service Policies of Social Networking Services," Information, Communication & Society (2018), doi.org/10.1080/13 69118X.2018.1486870.

31 George R. Milne and Mary J. Culnan, "Using the Content of Online Privacy Notices to Inform Public Policy: A Longitudinal Analysis of the 1998–2001 U.S.

Web Surveys," *Information Society* 18, no. 5 (October 2002): 345–59, http://doi. org/10.1080/01972240290108168.

32 Curtis Frye, *Privacy-Enhanced Business: Adapting to the Online Environment* (Westport, CT: Quorum Books, 2001), 156.

33 An article in the *Journal of the Academy of Marketing* argued, "To the extent that consumers look for the seal of approvals from these authenticators and choose to do business with only reputed organizations that respect their privacy, their privacy is protected." Roland T. Rust, P. K. Kannan, and Na Peng, "The Customer Economics of Internet Privacy," *Journal of the Academy of Marketing* 30, no. 4 (2002): 462.

34 Joel R. Reidenberg, "E-Commerce and Trans-Atlantic Privacy," *Houston Law Review* 38, no. 3 (2001): 717–49.

35 Reidenberg, 727–28.

36 Sean Doherty, "Keeping Data Private," *Network Computing*, June 25, 2001.

37 Frye, *Privacy-Enhanced Business*, 177.

38 Tyler Hamilton, "Web Founder Pushes Privacy Technology," *Toronto Star*, June 20, 2002.

39 Jaclyn Easton, *Going Wireless: Transforming Your Business with Mobile Technology* (New York: Harper Business, 2002).

40 Rick Whiting, "Companies Get Public with Privacy: As Executives Hammer Out Privacy Policies, Vendors Vie for Attention with Tools and Services," *Information-Week*, January 7, 2002.

41 Reuters, "IBM, AT&T Release Free Privacy Tools," April 4, 2002.

42 Leslie Walker, "Cloaking Devices Designed for Wary Web Shoppers," *Contra Costa Times*, November 5, 2000.

43 Federal Trade Commission, *Self-Regulation and Privacy Online* (Washington, DC: Subcommittee on Communication of the Committee on Commerce, Science, and Transportation, July 27, 1999), 4, www.ftc.gov.

44 Eric Hughes, "A Cypherpunk's Manifesto," March 9, 1993, www.activism.net.

45 Steve Kenny and John Borking, "The Value of Privacy Engineering," *Journal of Information, Law & Technology* 1 (2002), http://www2.warwick.ac.uk.

46 Frye, *Privacy-Enhanced Business*.

47 Ann Cavoukian and Tyler Hamilton, "Whither Privacy, Post-9/11?" *Toronto Star*, September 9, 2002.

48 Julio Ojeda-Zapata, "Privacy Concerns Feeding Growth of Protective Technology, Laws," *St. Paul Pioneer Press*, April 12, 1999, www.highbeam.com.

49 Jeri Clausing, "Want More Online Privacy? Join the Crowd," *New York Times*, August 22, 1998, www.nytimes.com.

50 Steven Bonisteel, "Zero-Knowledge Offers Web Surf-Cloaking Software," *Newsbytes*, December 13, 1999.

51 Quoted in Clausing, "Want More Online Privacy?"

52 Andy Riga, "Prophets Zero in on Profits: Zero-Knowledge Revises Approach to Sales in Bid to Cash In on Privacy Market It Helped Create," *Montreal Gazette*, March 28, 2001.

53 Anick Jesdanun, "Privacy Program Back, Less Anonymous," Associated Press, March 12, 2002.

54 John Schwartz, "As Debate on Privacy Heats Up, Sales Don't," *New York Times*, November 5, 2001.

55 Anita L. Allen, *Uneasy Access: Privacy for Women in a Free Society* (Totowa, NJ: Rowman & Littlefield, 1988), 18.

56 This example is drawn from Andrew Clement, Brenda McPhail, Karen Louise Smith, and Joseph Ferenbok, "Probing, Mocking, and Prototyping: Participatory Approaches to Identity Infrastructuring," in *Proceedings of the 12th Participatory Design Conference: Research Papers, Volume 1* (New York: ACM Press, 2012), 27, http://doi.org/10.1145/2347635.2347639.

57 Clement et al.

58 ID Lab, "What Does Your ID Reveal about You?" Prop ID: Toward a Citizen-Centric ID System, n.d., http://propid.ischool.utoronto.ca.

59 Clement et al., "Probing, Mocking, and Prototyping."

60 Hughes, "Cypherpunk's Manifesto."

61 Kanaley, "Privacy Policies on Web Sites."

62 Federal Trade Commission, "FTC Announces Settlement with Bankrupt Website, Toysmart.Com, regarding Alleged Privacy Policy Violation," July 21, 2000, www.ftc.gov. Should a suitable buyer be found, they would be bound by the terms of the Toysmart privacy statement and would have to seek user consent to use information in ways not already outlined in the policy. News coverage noted that this case had been particularly embarrassing for the Walt Disney Company, which owned 60 percent of Toysmart and had been aggressively lobbying the FTC against broader privacy laws covering websites' use of consumer information. See "FTC Approves Toysmart Plan to Sell Its Customer List, with Conditions," *Wall Street Journal*, July 21, 2000, www.wsj.com. Several state attorneys generals objected to this decision and, in August 2000, a Massachusetts bankruptcy court denied Toysmart's motion to approve the FTC. See Gary Anthes, "Toysmart, FTC Overruled on Sale of Customer Data," *Computerworld*, August 17, 2000, www.computerworld.com. In January 2001, the FTC reported that Toysmart would be paid $50,000 to destroy their data and the money would be used to pay its creditors. Associated Press, "Toysmart to Destroy Data, Be Paid," *Los Angeles Times*, January 10, 2001, http://articles.latimes.com.

63 Jason Catlett, "Profiling: Comments to the Dept. of Commerce and Federal Trade Commission," Feedback to Federal Trade Commission, October 18, 1999, www.ftc.gov.

64 Frye, *Privacy-Enhanced Business.*

65 Rosen. "The Eroded Self," *New York Times Magazine*, April 30, 2000, www.nytimes.com.

66 When it was launched in the 1990s, online retailer Amazon allowed those shopping on its website to indicate their preference that data collected by the site be kept confidential. In a 2000 revision to its privacy policy, however, Amazon

described consumer data as an asset that may be sold or transferred to other companies. The Digital Convergence Corporation launched a creative campaign to capitalize on consumer data in which it gave away more than one million barcode scanners called CueCats. When users plugged these devices into their internet-enabled computers, they could open an advertiser's webpage simply by scanning barcodes that appeared in magazines and newspapers. Unbeknownst to many users, the CueCat scanner was equipped with a unique identification chip that would track and store users' shopping habits and generate a database of consumer data the Digital Convergence Corporation could sell to interested third parties. These increasingly common practices revealed a business model widely used by online retailers: the creation of profiles that combined personal information and online activities to track, analyze, and eventually predict consumer preferences and behaviors.

67 Privacy advocate and legal expert Joel Reidenberg pointed to a Forrester Research study which concluded that inadequate privacy protections had led American consumers to spend $12 billion less online than they might otherwise have in 2000. Reidenberg, "E-Commerce and Trans-Atlantic Privacy," 725.

68 Marcia Stepanek, quoted in Perri Peltz, Bruce Francis, and Fionnuala Sweeney, "Protecting Your Privacy Online," *CNN Insight*, April 3, 2000.

69 D. Crowe, "Advertisers Tackle Online Privacy," *Australian Financial Review*, May 15, 2000.

70 Ann Cavoukian and Tyler Hamilton, *The Privacy Payoff: How Successful Businesses Build Customer Trust* (Toronto: McGraw-Hill Ryerson, 2002).

71 Cavoukian and Hamilton, "Whither Privacy, Post-9/11?"

72 EarthLink, "EarthLink Debuts New Privacy-Focused Ad Campaign," February 26, 2001, www.earthlink.net.

73 Les Seagraves, "Need for Internet Privacy Legislation," Pub. L. No. 107-1151, Committee on Commerce, Science, and Transportation (2001), 64, www.gpo.gov.

74 Seagraves.

75 Michel Gondry, "Privacy," TBWA\Chiat\Day, 2001, www.youtube.com/watch?v=f7T9B7Y4ET0.

76 Stephanie Olsen, "EarthLink Promises 'Anonymous' Web Surfing," *CNET*, March 8, 2001, www.news.cnet.com.

77 EarthLink, "EarthLink Debuts New Privacy-Focused Ad Campaign."

78 EarthLink.

79 Rich Siegel and John Shirley, "Harris," TBWA\Chiat\Day, 2002, www.tvspots.tv.

80 Michael McCarthy, "Critics Target 'Omnipresent' Ads: Advertising Spreads into Non-traditional Venues, Sites," *USA Today*, March 16, 2001.

81 McCarthy.

82 John Schwartz, "As Big PC Brother Watches, Users Encounter Frustration," *New York Times*, September 5, 2001.

83 Quoted in Olsen, "EarthLink Promises 'Anonymous' Web Surfing."

84 Schwartz, "As Big PC Brother Watches, Users Encounter Frustration."

85 Olsen, "EarthLink Promises 'Anonymous' Web Surfing."

86 Mary Koelbel Engle, "Re: EarthLink, Inc., Matter No. 002 3258," May 31, 2002, www.ftc.gov.

87 Engle.

88 Frye, *Privacy-Enhanced Business*.

89 Polly Sprenger, "Sun on Privacy: 'Get Over It,'" *Wired*, January 26, 1999, www.wired.com.

90 Scott McNealy, "The Case against Absolute Privacy," *Washington Post*, May 29, 2001.

91 McNealy.

92 Lawrence Lessig, *Code: And Other Laws of Cyberspace, Version 2.0*, 2nd ed. (New York: Basic Books, 2006), 2.

93 Lessig, 3.

94 Lessig, chap. 1.

95 Turner, *From Counterculture to Cyberculture*, chap. 1.

96 John Perry Barlow, "A Declaration of the Independence of Cyberspace," EFF Projects, February 8, 1996, http://projects.eff.org.

97 Jeffrey H. Reiman, "Driving to the Panopticon: A Philosophical Exploration of the Risks to Privacy Posed by the Highway Technology of the Future," *Santa Clara Computer and High Technology Law Journal* 11, no. 1 (1995): 27–44.

98 Michel Foucault, *Discipline and Punish: The Birth of the Prison*, 2nd ed. trans. Alan Sheridan (New York: Vintage Books, 1995).

99 Reiman, "Driving to the Panopticon."

100 Jeroen van den Hoven, "Privacy and the Varieties of Informational Wrongdoing," in *Readings in CyberEthics*, ed. Richard. A. Spinello and Herman. T. Tavani (Sudbury, MA: Jones and Bartlett, 2001), 488–500.

101 Clausing, "Want More Online Privacy?"

102 Turner, *From Counterculture to Cyberculture*, 16.

103 Bradley Johnson, "Software Developer Zeroes In on Privacy," *Advertising Age*, April 24, 2000, www.adage.com.

104 Michael Bazeley, "Internet Users Who Want to Reclaim Some of Their Privacy," *San Jose Mercury News*, May 1, 2003.

CHAPTER 3. OPT OUT FOR PRIVACY, OPT IN FOR VALUE

1 John Hagel III and Jeffrey. F. Rayport, "The Coming Battle for Customer Information," *Harvard Business Review* 75, no. 1 (1997): 5–11. See also, James Glave, "The Dawn of the Infomediary," *Wired*, February 24, 1999.

2 Hagel and Rayport, 6.

3 Quoted in Reid Kanaley, "Privacy Policies on Web Sites Are Only for the Gullible," *Philadelphia Inquirer*, November 19, 2000.

4 "Lumeria Ad Network Demos at Red Herring's Venture 2000 Conference," *PR Newswire*, May 22, 2000.

5 Equifax–Harris, *Equifax–Harris Mid-Decade Consumer Privacy Survey* (New York: Louis Harris and Associates, 1995).

6 Ponnurangam Kumaraguru and Lorrie Faith Cranor, *Privacy Indexes: A Survey of Westin's Studies* (Pittsburgh: Institute for Software Research, 2005), http://repository.cmu.edu.

7 Chris J. Hoofnagle and Jennifer M. Urban, "Alan Westin's Privacy Homo Economicus." *Wake Forest Law Review*, 49 (2014): 261–317.

8 Equifax–Harris, *Equifax–Harris Mid-Decade Consumer Privacy Survey*, 13.

9 Quoted in L. Miller and E. Weise, "Keeping 'Pry' out of the Privacy Debate," *USA Today*, March 31, 1999.

10 See Priscilla Regan, "Privacy and the Common Good: Revisited," in *Social Dimensions of Privacy: Interdisciplinary Perspectives*, ed. Beate Roessler and Dorota Mokrosinska (New York: Cambridge University Press, 2015), 50–70. See also, Julie E. Cohen, "Turning Privacy Inside Out." *Theoretical Inquiries in Law* 20, no. 1 (forthcoming); Valarie Steeves, "Reclaiming the Social Value of Privacy," in: *Privacy, Identity and Anonymity in a Network World: Lessons from the Identity Trail*, ed. Ian Kerr, Valarie Steeves, and Carole Lucock. (Oxford: Oxford University Press, 2009), 191–208.

11 Although PrivaSeek was renamed Persona in June 2000, it will be referred to as PrivaSeek throughout this book.

12 Hagel and Rayport, "Coming Battle for Customer Information," 6.

13 Jennifer Lach, "The New Gatekeepers," *American Demographics*, June 1999.

14 Catherine Greenman, "Efforts to Keep the Web from Getting Too Personal," *New York Times*, April 27, 2000.

15 Lach, "New Gatekeepers."

16 "Privada(TM) Delivers Personal Privacy with New Anonymous Email Service; Privada's Messaging Incognito(TM) for Consumers Provides Industry's Most Effective POP3 Anonymous Email Solution," *PR Newswire*, November 2, 1999.

17 Helen Nissenbaum, *Privacy in Context: Technology, Policy, and the Integrity of Social Life* (Stanford, CA: Stanford Law Books, 2010), 117–18.

18 Charles Duhigg, "What Does Your Credit-Card Company Know about You?" *New York Times Magazine*, May 12, 2009, www.nytimes.com.

19 Ann Cavoukian, *Privacy by Design . . . Take the Challenge* (Toronto: Office of the Privacy Commissioner of Ontario, 2009), 73.

20 Doc Searls, *The Intention Economy: When Customers Take Charge* (Boston: Harvard Business Review Press, 2012).

21 Erving Goffman, *The Presentation of Self in Everyday Life* (New York: Anchor Books, 1959).

22 danah boyd, "Why Youth (Heart) Social Network Sites: The Role of Networked Publics in Teenage Social Life," in *Youth, Identity, and Digital Media Volume*, ed. David Buckingham, MacArthur Foundation Series on Digital Media and Learning (Cambridge, MA: MIT Press, 2007), 119–42.

23 Dallas Smythe, "Communications: Blindspot of Western Marxism," *Canadian Journal of Political and Social Theory* 1, no. 3 (1977): 1–27.

24 Sut Jhally and Bill Livant, "Watching as Working: The Valorization of Audience Consciousness," *Journal of Communication* 36, no. 3 (1986): 124–43.

25 Jennifer Jones, "Cashing In on Privacy," *Network World*, September 18, 2000, www.networkworld.com, emphasis added.

26 Nate Zelnick, "Is It Privacy That Users Want, or Does Everyone Have a Price?" *Internet World*, March 15, 1999.

27 Quoted in Zelnick.

28 Simon G. Davies, "Re-Engineering the Right to Privacy: How Privacy Has Been Transformed from a Right to a Commodity," in *Technology and Privacy: The New Landscape*, ed. Philip E. Agre and Marc Rotenberg (Cambridge, MA: MIT Press, 1997), 143.

29 John Edward Campbell and Matt Carlson, "Panopticon.Com: Online Surveillance and the Commodification of Privacy," *Journal of Broadcasting & Electronic Media* 46, no. 4 (2002): 586–606.

30 Oscar Gandy Jr., "Coming to Terms with the Panoptic Sort," in *Computers, Surveillance, and Privacy*, ed. David Lyon and Elia Zureik (Minneapolis: University of Minnesota Press, 1996), 148.

31 Joseph Turow, *The Daily You: How the New Advertising Industry Is Defining Your Identity and Your Worth* (New Haven, CT: Yale University Press, 2011).

32 See, for example, Richard A. Posner, "The Right of Privacy," *University of Georgia Law* 12, no. 3 (Spring 1978): 393–422.

33 Ann Cavoukian and Don Tapscott, *Who Knows: Safeguarding Your Privacy in a Networked World* (New York: McGraw-Hill, 1997), 99.

34 Beate Roessler, "Should Personal Data Be a Tradable Good?: On the Moral Limits of Markets in Privacy" in *Social Dimensions of Privacy: Interdisciplinary Perspectives*, ed. Beate Roessler and Dorota Mokrosinska (New York: Cambridge University Press, 2015), 141–61.

35 Andrew Clement, Brenda McPhail, Karen Louise Smith, and Joseph Ferenbok, "Probing, Mocking, and Prototyping: Participatory Approaches to Identity Infrastructuring," in *Proceedings of the 12th Participatory Design Conference: Research Papers, Volume 1* (New York: ACM Press, 2012), 21, http://doi.org/10.1145/2347635.2347639.

36 Daniel J. Solove, "Introduction: Privacy Self-Management and the Consent Dilemma," *Harvard Law Review* 126, no. 7 (2013): 1880.

37 Jeffrey H. Reiman, "Driving to the Panopticon: A Philosophical Exploration of the Risks to Privacy Posed by the Highway Technology of the Future," *Santa Clara Computer and High Technology Law Journal* 11, no. 1 (1995): 29.

38 Reiman, 29.

39 Mark Andrejevic, "The Work of Being Watched: Interactive Media and the Exploitation of Self-Disclosure," *Critical Studies in Media Communication* 19, no. 2 (2002): 230–48.

40 Jennifer R. Whitson and Kevin D. Haggerty, "Identity Theft and the Care of the Virtual Self," *Economy and Society*, 37, no. 4 (2008): 572–94, https://doi.org/10.1080/03085140802357950.

41 Davies, "Re-engineering the Right to Privacy," 143.

42 Ellen Riordan, "Commodified Agents and Empowered Girls: Consuming and Producing Feminism," *Journal of Communication Inquiry* 25, no. 3 (2001): 282.

43 David Harvey, *A Brief History of Neoliberalism* (Oxford, UK: Oxford University Press, 2005), 2.

44 Andrejevic, "Work of Being Watched," 245.

45 Orrin G. Hatch, *Know the Rules, Use the Tools: Privacy in the Digital Age* (Washington, DC: U.S. Senate Judiciary Committee, 2000), 9.

46 Susan Barnes, "A Privacy Paradox: Social Networking in the United States," *First Monday* 11, no. 9 (September 2006), http://dx.doi.org/10.5210/fm.v11i9.1394.

47 Toby Lester, "The Reinvention of Privacy," *The Atlantic*, March 1, 2001, www.theatlantic.com.

48 Lester.

49 Orrin G. Hatch and Herbert Kohl, both in "Privacy in the Digital Age: Discussion of Issues Surrounding the Internet," Pub. L. No. J-106-19, § Committee on the Judiciary (1999), www.gpo.gov.

50 Siva Vaidhyanathan, *The Googlization of Everything (and Why We Should Worry)* (Berkeley: University of California Press, 2011), 75. This same principle is referred to by Evgeny Morozov as "technological solutionism." See Morozov, "Why We Are Allowed to Hate Silicon Valley," *Frankfurter Allgemeine Zeitung*, November 11, 2013, www.faz.net. Tarleton Gillespie uses the term "technological fixes." See Gillespie, *Wired Shut: Copyright and the Shape of Digital Culture* (Cambridge, MA: MIT Press, 2007).

51 Gillespie, 2.

52 Harvey, *Brief History of Neoliberalism*, 165.

53 Cavoukian, *Privacy by Design*, 24.

54 Quoted in Anne Colden, "Privacy Comes into Full View," *Denver Post*, July 30, 2000.

55 Steve Lucas, "Prepared Testimony of Statement of Mr. Steve Lucas, Chief Information Officer and Senior Vice President, Industry Government Affairs before the House Commerce Committee Telecommunications, Trade, and Consumer Protection Subcommittee," *Federal News Service*, July 13, 1999, www.gpo.gov.

56 Hatch, *Know the Rules, Use the Tools*.

57 Harvey, *Brief History of Neoliberalism*, 165.

58 Davies, "Re-engineering the Right to Privacy."

59 Lisa Guernsey, "Secrecy for All, as Encryption Goes to Market," *New York Times*, May 18, 2000.

60 Anonymizer continues to offer privacy-enhancing tools to a consumer market, but the company has adjusted its strategy to meet the realities of the contemporary environment. At this time, the bulk of the company's revenues have shifted away from user-implemented tools to government departments and companies willing to invest in strong privacy technology on behalf of the end user.

61 Andy Riga, "Prophets Zero in on Profits: Zero-Knowledge Revises Approach to Sales in Bid to Cash in on Privacy Market It Helped Create," *Montreal Gazette*, March 28, 2001 sec. Technology.

62 Susan Smith, "Hamnett Hill, 36," *The Globe and Mail*, May 5, 2008, www.theglobeandmail.com.

63 David Atkin, "Zero-Knowledge Learns Its Lesson," *The Globe and Mail*, May 13, 2002, www.theglobeandmail.com.

64 Smith, "Hamnett Hill."

65 There was some media speculation that Zero-Knowledge Systems faced pressure from U.S. authorities to abandon any products that assisted individuals in hiding their identity and communications online. The company, however, insisted their decision was motivated purely by economic concerns. See Anick Jesdanun, "Privacy Program Back, Less Anonymous," Associated Press, March 12, 2002; John Schwartz, "As Debate on Privacy Heats Up, Sales Don't," *New York Times*, November 5, 2001.

66 In 2005, ZKS rebranded as Radial Point. It its new incarnation, the company worked primarily with internet service providers (ISP) to provide security features to consumers including virus protection, firewalls, and parental controls.

67 Daniel J. Solove, *Nothing to Hide: The False Tradeoff between Privacy and Security* (New Haven, CT: Yale University Press, 2011), 14.

68 "Montreal Firm Closes Anonymity Service," Reuters, November 5, 2001.

CHAPTER 4. REPUTATION DEFENDERS

1 Tarleton Gillespie, "Algorithmically Recognizable: Santorum's Google Problem, and Google's Santorum Problem," *Information, Communication & Society* 20, no. 1 (2017): 63–80, http://doi.org/10.1080/1369118X.2016.1199721; Siva Vaidhyanathan, *The Googlization of Everything (and Why We Should Worry)* (Berkeley: University of California Press, 2011).

2 However, on important debates regarding the term "algorithm," see Nick Seaver, "Algorithms as Culture: Some Tactics for the Ethnography of Algorithmic Systems," *Big Data & Society* 4, no. 2 (December 2017): 1–12, http://doi.org/10.1177/2053951717738104.

3 Tom McNichol, "Fixing the Reputations of Reputation Managers," *Bloomberg Businessweek*, February 2, 2012, www.businessweek.com. Nora A. Draper, "The New Reputation Custodians: Examining the Industrialization of Visibility in the Reputation Society," in *Challenging Communication Research*, ed. Leah A. Lievrouw (New York: Peter Lang), 157-71.

4 Helen Kennedy, "Beyond Anonymity, or Future Directions for Internet Identity Research," *New Media & Society* 8, no. 6 (December 1, 2006): 859–76, http://doi.org/10.1177/1461444806069641.

5 Jon Ronson, *So You've Been Publicly Shamed* (New York: Riverhead Books, 2015).

6 Steve Inskeep, "'Publicly Shamed:' Who Needs the Pillory When We've Got Twitter?" *Morning Edition*, March 31, 2015, www.npr.org.

7 Nancy K. Baym, "The Emergence of On-Line Community," in *CyberSociety 2.0: Revisiting Computer-Mediated Communication and Community*, ed. Steven Jones (Thousand Oaks, CA: SAGE Publications, 1998), 35–68; Lori Kendall, *Hanging Out in the Virtual Pub: Masculinities and Relationships Online* (Berkeley: University of California Press, 2002).

8 Kennedy, "Beyond Anonymity."

9 José van Dijck, "'You Have One Identity': Performing the Self on Facebook and LinkedIn," *Media, Culture & Society* 35, no. 2 (2013): 199–215; Alice Marwick and danah boyd, "I Tweet Honestly, I Tweet Passionately: Twitter Users, Context Collapse, and the Imagined Audience," *New Media & Society* 13, no. 1 (2010): 114–33.

10 van Dijck.

11 Mark Zuckerberg is quoted as saying that "people have really gotten comfortable not only sharing more information and different kinds, but more openly and with more people. That social norm is just something that has evolved over time." Ann Cavoukian, "Privacy Is Still a Social Norm," *The Globe and Mail*, March 12, 2010, www.theglobeandmail.com. Cavoukian notes, however, that his staff said his words were taken out of context.

12 Jeffrey H. Reiman, "Privacy, Intimacy, and Personhood," *Philosophy & Public Affairs* 6, no. 1 (1976): 26–44.

13 danah boyd and Nicole B. Ellison, "Social Network Sites: Definition, History, and Scholarship," *Journal of Computer-Mediated Communication* 13, no. 1 (October 2007): 211, http://doi.org/10.1111/j.1083-6101.2007.00393.x.

14 boyd and Ellison.

15 See, for example, Amanda Holpuch, "Victory for Drag Queens as Facebook Apologises for 'Real-Name' Policy," *The Guardian*, October 1, 2014, www.theguardian.com.

16 Robert Bodle, "The Ethics of Online Anonymity or Zuckerberg vs. 'MOOT,'" *Computers and Society* 43, no. 1 (2013): 22–30.

17 van Dijck, "You Have One Identity"; Alice Marwick, "Selling Your Self: Online Identity in the Age of a Commodified Internet," University of Washington, 2005.

18 Joseph Turow, *The Daily You: How the New Advertising Industry Is Defining Your Identity and Your Worth* (New Haven, CT: Yale University Press, 2011).

19 danah boyd, *It's Complicated: The Social Lives of Networked Teens* (New Haven, CT: Yale University Press, 2014).

20 Quoted in Jeffrey Rosen, "The Web Means the End of Forgetting," *New York Times*, July 21, 2010, www.nytimes.com.

21 This story is related by Daniel Solove in *The Future of Reputation: Gossip, Rumor, and Privacy on the Internet* (New Haven, CT: Yale University Press, 2007), 144.

22 Bruce Bimber, Andrew J. Flanagin, and Cynthia Stohl, "Reconceptualizing Collective Action in the Contemporary Media Environment," *Communication Theory* 15, no. 4 (2005): 365–88.

23 Jo Napolitano, "Hold It Right There, and Drop That Camera," *New York Times*, December 11, 2003.

24 Erving Goffman, *Behavior in Public Places: Notes on the Social Organization of Gatherings* (New York: Free Press, 1966).

25 Helen Nissenbaum, *Privacy in Context: Technology, Policy, and the Integrity of Social Life* (Stanford, CA: Stanford Law Books, 2010), 117–18.

26 Viktor Mayer-Schönberger, *Delete: The Virtue of Forgetting in the Digital Age* (Princeton, NJ: Princeton University Press, 2009).

27 Mayer-Schönberger.

28 Vaidhyanathan, *Googlization of Everything (and Why We Should Worry)*, 7.

29 Lucas D. Introna and Helen Nissenbaum, "Shaping the Web: Why the Politics of Search Engines Matters," *Information Society* 16 no. 3 (2000): 169–85.

30 Woodrow Hartzog and Evan Selinger, "Obscurity: A Better Way to Think about Your Data Than 'Privacy,'" *The Atlantic*, January 17, 2013, www.theatlantic.com; Michael Zimmer, "The Externalities of Search 2.0: The Emerging Privacy Threats When the Drive for the Perfect Search Engine Meets Web 2.0," *First Monday* 13, no. 3 (2008), http:// http://doi.org/10.5210/fm.v13i3.2136.

31 Communications Decency Act, 47 U.S.C. § 230 (1996).

32 Cass R. Sunstein, *On Rumors: How Falsehoods Spread, Why We Believe Them, and What Can Be Done* (Princeton, NJ: Princeton University Press, 2014), 82–85.

33 This Streisand effect is referenced in Michael Fertik and David Thompson, *Wild West 2.0: How to Protect and Restore Your Online Reputation on the Untamed Social Frontier* (New York: American Management Association, 2010), 229–30.

34 Andy Greenberg, "The Streisand Effect," *Forbes*, May 11, 2007, www.forbes.com.

35 For a detailed discussion of the role of online reputation management firms as an extralegal channel, see Ben Medeiros. "The Reputation-Management Industry and the Prospects for a 'Right to Be Forgotten' in the US," *First Amendment Studies* 51, no. 1 (2017), http://doi.org/10.1080/21689725.2017.1308262.

36 This is also referred to as a "name collision." See Fertik and Thompson, *Wild West 2.0*, 214–15.

37 Sally Wyatt, "Danger! Metaphors at Work in Economics, Geophysiology, and the Internet," *Science, Technology, & Human Values* 29, no. 2 (April 2004): 242–61, http://doi.org/10.1177/0162243903261947.

38 Steven L. Nock, *The Costs of Privacy: Surveillance and Reputation in America* (New York: Aldine de Gruyter, 1993).

39 Quoted in Andrea Gordon, "Want a Job? Scholarship? Watch What You Post," *Toronto Star*, August 30, 2008.

40 Judith Ireland, "Net Narcissism: The Essay," *Sydney Morning Herald*, February 5, 2011.

41 Anthony Giddens, *Modernity and Self-Identity: Self and Society in the Late Modern Age* (Stanford, CA: Stanford University Press, 1991), 5.

42 Giddens, 81.

43 Giddens, 58.

44 Tarleton Gillespie, "The Relevance of Algorithms," in *Media Technologies: Essays on Communication, Materiality, and Society*, ed. Tarleton Gillespie, Pablo J. Boczkowski, and Kirsten A. Foot (Cambridge, MA: MIT Press, 2014), 184.

45 A 2005 study from the Pew Research Center reported that 41 percent of Americans who use the internet—about fifty-nine million people—were using search engines daily. See Lee Rainie, *Big Jump in Search Engine Use* (Washington: Pew

Research Center, 2005), www.pewinternet.org. This put search ahead of email as the country's most prevalent daily internet activity, revealing the power of search engines to control access to digital content. For a discussion of the importance of algorithms in shaping the social world, see also Gillespie, "Algorithmically Recognizable."

46 However, some companies do work with "people finder" websites to have personal information removed.

47 Bernardo A. Huberman, Peter L. T. Pirolli, James E. Pitkow, and Rajan M. Lukose, "Strong Regularities in World Wide Web Surfing," *Science* 280, no. 5360 (April 1998): 95.

48 Fertik and Thompson, *Wild West 2.0*, 27, 88–89.

49 Ivy L. Lee, *Publicity: Some of the Things It Is and Is Not* (New York: Industries Publishing Company, 1925), 19.

50 Lee, 21.

51 Gillespie, "Relevance of Algorithms."

52 Adam Dachis, "LinkedIn, WordPress, Vimeo, and Other Sites You Should Join for a Better Online Reputation," *Lifehacker* (blog), August 2, 2012, www.lifehacker.com.

53 Ben Woods, "How to Stop Bad Press from Ruining Your Online Reputation," *TheNextWeb* (blog), June 21, 2013, www.thenextweb.com.

54 Reputation Changer, "Reputation Crisis: iPhone 4S Puts Businesses on High Alert Online," *GlobeNewswire*, January 5, 2012, www.globenewswire.com, emphasis added.

55 Sally Adee, "Keeping Up E-ppearances," *New Scientist*, February 19, 2011.

56 Nathan Olivarez-Giles, "How Google Penalized RapGenius," *Digits* (blog), December 27, 2013, http://get.digits.com.

57 Steve Henn, "Fixing Your Online Reputation: There's an Industry for That," *All Things Considered* (May 29, 2013), www.npr.org.

58 Henn.

59 Solove, *Future of Reputation*, 192. He refers specifically to Reputation.com, which at the time of his writing was called ReputationDefender.

60 Finn Brunton and Helen Fay Nissenbaum, *Obfuscation: A User's Guide for Privacy and Protest* (Cambridge, MA: MIT Press, 2015), 1.

61 Quoted in Eric Pfanner, "In a Wikileaks Era, Balancing Public and Private," *New York Times*, January 25, 2011.

62 Laura Portwood-Stacer, "Media Refusal and Conspicuous Non-Consumption: The Performative and Political Dimensions of Facebook Abstention," *New Media & Society* 15, no. 7 (2013): 1042, http://doi.org/10.1177/1461444812465139.

63 Quoted in Mary Callahan, "Experts: Your Online Trail Could Put Reputation at Risk," *Press Democrat*, June 16, 2013, www.pressdemocrat.com.

64 Michael H. Goldhaber, "The Attention Economy and the Net," *First Monday* 2, no. 4 (1997), http://doi.org/10.5210/fm.v2i4.519.

65 John Whitfield, *People Will Talk: The Surprising Science of Reputation* (Hoboken, NJ: John Wiley & Sons, 2012), 193.

66 Irwin Altman, "Privacy: A Conceptual Analysis," *Environment and Behavior* 8, no. 1 (1976): 7–29.

67 Michael Warner, *Publics and Counterpublics* (New York: Zone Books, 2002), 31.

68 Alice Marwick, *Status Update: Celebrity, Publicity, and Branding in the Social Media Age* (New Haven, CT: Yale University Press, 2013), 229.

69 boyd, *It's Complicated*, 60.

70 danah boyd and Alice Marwick, "Social Steganography: Privacy in Networked Publics" (paper presented at the International Communication Association Conference, Boston, 2011), www.danah.org.

71 Valeriya Safronova, "The Finstagram Rebellion," *New York Times*, November 19, 2015.

72 See also Brooke Erin Duffy and Ngai Keung Chan, "You never really know who's looking: Imagined surveillance across social media platforms," *New Media & Society* (2018), doi.org/10.1177/1461444818791318.

73 Rhodri Marsden, "How the Net Can Be a Permanent Reminder of Past Indiscretions," *Independent*, November 30, 2010, www.independent.co.uk.

74 Juliana Reyes, "Brand.Com Has Filed for Bankruptcy," *Technical.ly Philly*, May 4, 2015, www.technical.ly/philly.

75 Deirdre Davis, "The Harm That Has No Name: Street Harassment, Embodiment, and African American Women," *UCLA Women's Law Journal* 4, no. 2 (Spring 1994): 133–78; Cynthia Grant Bowman, "Street Harassment and the Informal Ghettoization of Women," *Harvard Law Review* 106, no. 3 (January 1993): 517–80.

76 Davis, "Harm That Has No Name," 136.

77 Andre Cavalcante, *Struggling for Ordinary: Media and Transgender Belonging in Everyday Life* (New York: NYU Press, 2018).

78 Alice Marwick and Ross Miller, *Online Harassment, Defamation, and Hateful Speech: A Primer of the Legal Landscape* (New York: Fordham University Center on Law and Information Policy, 2014), http://ir.lawnet.fordham.edu.

79 Marsden, "How the Net Can Be a Permanent Reminder."

80 Katharine O. Seelye and Liz Robbins, "Duke Winces as a Private Joke Slips Out of Control," *New York Times*, October 8, 2010.

81 Kashmir Hill, "The Privacy Landmine That Is Duke Graduate Karen Owen's 'Senior Thesis,'" *Forbes*, September 30, 2010.

82 Danielle Keats Citron, "Civil Rights in Our Information Age," in *The Offensive Internet: Speech, Privacy, and Reputation*, ed. Saul Levmore and Martha Craven Nussbaum (Cambridge, MA: Harvard University Press, 2010), 33–34.

83 For details on the threats associated with being invisible online, see Taina Bucher, "Want to Be on the Top? Algorithmic Power and the Threat of Invisibility on Facebook," *New Media and Society* 14, no. 7 (2012): 1164-80, http://doi.org/10.1177/1461444812440159.

84 Warner, *Publics and Counterpublics*, 26.

85 Jonas Lerman, "Big Data and Its Exclusions," *Stanford Law Review* 66 (2013): 56.

86 Lerman, 59.

87 For a discussion of the #IfTheyGunnedMeDown hashtag, see Roni Jackson, "If They Gunned Me Down and Criming while White: An Examination of Twitter Campaigns through the Lens of Citizens Media," *Cultural Studies ↔ Critical Methodologies*, March 3, 2016, http://doi.org/10.1177/1532708616634836.

88 Anna Everett, *Digital Diaspora: A Race for Cyberspace* (Albany: State University of New York Press, 2009).

89 Catherine Knight Steele, "Badges of Oppression, Positions of Strength: Digital Black Feminist Discourse and the Legacy of Black Women's Technology Use" (paper presented at the Berkman Klein Luncheon Series, Berkman Klein Center for Internet and Society at Harvard University, November 21, 2017), http://cyber.harvard.edu.

90 Safiya Umoja Noble, *Algorithms of Oppression: How Search Engines Reinforce Racism* (New York: NYU Press, 2018).

91 Taina Bucher, "The Algorithmic Imaginary: Exploring the Ordinary Affects of Facebook Algorithms," *Information, Communication & Society* 20, no. 1 (January 2017): 30–44, http://doi.org/10.1080/1369118X.2016.1154086.

92 Latanya Sweeney, "Discrimination in Online Ad Delivery," *ACM Queue* 11, no. 3 (March 2013): 1–19.

93 Sweeney, 9.

94 Citron, "Civil Rights in Our Information Age," 31–32. She observes that, in the case of cyber harassment, over 50 percent of incidents involve male attackers and female targets: "Cyber mobs often target lesbian and/or nonwhite women with particular virulence. They also focus on men of color, religious minorities, and gay men."

95 Consider, for example, Adrienne Massanari's observations about the reproduction of discriminatory or "toxic" cultures in digital spaces. See Massanari, "#Gamergate and The Fappening: How Reddit's Algorithm, Governance, and Culture Support Toxic Technocultures," *New Media & Society* 19, no. 3 (2017): 329–46, http://doi.org/10.1177/1461444815608807.

96 Ryan Erskine, "How to Protect Your Online Reputation in 2017," *Entrepreneur*, January 23, 2017, www.entrepreneur.com.

97 This point is well-developed by Matthew Adams in "The Reflexive Self and Culture: A Critique," *British Journal of Sociology* 54, no. 2 (June 2003): 222–23, http://doi.org/10.1080/0007131032000080212.

98 Anthony Giddens, "Living in a Post-Traditional Society," in *Reflexive Modernization: Politics, Tradition, and Aesthetics in the Modern Social Order*, ed. Ulrich Beck, Anthony Giddens, and Scott Lash (Stanford, CA: Stanford University Press, 1994), 75.

99 Sarah Banet-Weiser, *AuthenticTM: The Politics of Ambivalence in a Brand Culture* (New York: NYU Press, 2012).

100 Adams, "Reflexive Self and Culture," 234.

101 Martha Craven Nussbaum, *Hiding from Humanity: Disgust, Shame, and the Law* (Princeton, NJ: Princeton University Press, 2004).

102 Martha Craven Nussbaum, "Objectification and Internet Misogyny," in *The Offensive Internet: Speech, Privacy, and Reputation*, ed. Saul Levmore and Martha Craven Nussbaum (Cambridge, MA: Harvard University Press, 2010), 82.

103 Nussbaum, *Hiding from Humanity*, 298.

104 Nussbaum, "Objectification and Internet Misogyny," 81–83.

105 Alec Baldwin, "Alec Baldwin: Good-Bye, Public Life," *New York*, February 24, 2014, www.nymag.com.

106 Baldwin.

107 Baldwin.

CHAPTER 5. REPUTATION PROMOTERS

1 Michael Fertik and David Thompson, *Wild West 2.0: How to Protect and Restore Your Online Reputation on the Untamed Social Frontier* (New York: American Management Association, 2010), 2.

2 Fertik and Thompson, 2.

3 Michael Fertik and David Thompson, *The Reputation Economy: How to Optimize Your Digital Footprint in a World Where Your Reputation Is Your Most Valuable Asset* (New York: Crown Business, 2015), 2.

4 Fertik and Thompson, 16.

5 Steven L. Nock, *The Costs of Privacy: Surveillance and Reputation in America* (New York: Aldine de Gruyter, 1993).

6 Daniel J. Solove, *The Future of Reputation: Gossip, Rumor, and Privacy on the Internet* (New Haven, CT: Yale University Press, 2007).

7 E. L. Godkin, "The Rights of the Citizen to His Own Reputation," *Scribner's Magazine* 8, no. 1 (1890): 58–67.

8 Godkin, 66.

9 Nock, *Costs of Privacy*.

10 Nock, 7.

11 Nock, chap. 3. See also, David Lyon, *Identifying Citizens: ID Cards as Surveillance* (Cambridge: Policy Press, 2009).

12 Howard Rheingold, *Smart Mobs: The Next Social Revolution* (Cambridge, MA: Perseus Publishing, 2003), xix.

13 See Sherry Turkle, *Life on the Screen: Identity in the Age of the Internet* (New York: Simon & Schuster, 1995).

14 "You Own Your Own Words," The WELL, n.d., www.well.com.

15 Gary Alan Fine describes how the good and bad reputations of famous historical figures reveal complex cultural assumptions and shared social values. See Fine, *Difficult Reputations: Collective Memories of the Evil, Inept, and Controversial* (Chicago: University of Chicago Press, 2001).

16 "You Own Your Own Words."

17 Consider, however, Danielle Citron's argument that the YOYOW philosophy is also a libertarian strategy to absolve web hosts from responsibility for comments made by those posting on their site. See Citron, "Civil Rights in Our Information Age,"

in *The Offensive Internet: Speech, Privacy, and Reputation*, ed. Saul Levmore and Martha Craven Nussbaum (Cambridge, MA: Harvard University Press, 2010), 37.

18 Chrysanthos Dellarocas, "Designing Reputation Systems for the Social Web," in *The Reputation Society: How Online Options Are Reshaping the Offline World*, ed. Hassan Masum and Mark Tovey (Cambridge, MA: MIT Press, 2011), 3–11.

19 Alessandro Gandini, *The Reputation Economy* (London: Palgrave Macmillan UK, 2016), 28, http://doi.org/10.1057/978-1-137-56107-7_3.

20 Paul Resnick, "Beyond Bowling Together: SocioTechnical Capital," in *Human-Computer Interaction in the New Millennium*, ed. John M. Carroll (Boston: Addison-Wesley, 2001), 647–72.

21 Cliff Lampe, "The Role of Reputation Systems in Managing Online Communities," in *The Reputation Society: How Online Options Are Reshaping the Offline World*, ed. Hassan Masum and Mark Tovey (Cambridge, MA: MIT Press, 2011), 77–87.

22 Alessandro Gandini, "Digital Work: Self-Branding and Social Capital in the Freelance Knowledge Economy," *Marketing Theory* 16, no. 1 (2016): 123–41, http://doi.org/10.1177/1470593115607942.

23 Fertik and Thompson, *Wild West 2.0*, 189; Patrick Ambron, "Why You Can't Just Ignore Personal Branding—Even If You Really Want To," *LinkedIn* (blog), April 6, 2017, www.linkedin.com.

24 Randy Farmer has written that online reputations, which tend to be based on numerical scores and small snippets of text, lack the nuance of "real world" reputations. See Farmer, "Web Reputation Systems and the Real World," in *The Reputation Society: How Online Options Are Reshaping the Offline World*, ed. Hassan Masum and Mark Tovey (Cambridge, MA: MIT Press, 2011), 13–24.

25 Alice Marwick, *Status Update: Celebrity, Publicity, and Branding in the Social Media Age* (New Haven, CT: Yale University Press, 2013).

26 Alison Hearn, "Structuring Feeling: Web 2.0, Online Ranking and Rating, and the Digital 'Reputation' Economy," *Ephemera* 10, nos. 3–4 (2010): 422.

27 Brooke Duffy and Jefferson Pooley examine the application of promotional logics to academia through their examination of Academia.edu. See Duffy and Pooley, "'Facebook for Academics': The Convergence of Self-Branding and Social Media Logic on Academia.edu," *Social Media + Society* 3, no. 1 (January 2017): 1–11, http://doi.org/10.1177/2056305117696523.

28 Hearn, "Structuring Feeling."

29 Marwick, *Status Update*.

30 Hearn, "Structuring Feeling."

31 Tom Peters, "The Brand Called You," *Fast Company*, September 1997, www.fastcompany.com.

32 Peters.

33 Although see Alison Hearn, "'Sentimental "Greenbacks" of Civilization': Cartes de Visite and the Pre-History of Self-Branding," in *The Routledge Companion to Advertising and Promotional Culture*, ed. Matthew P. McAllister and Emily West

(New York: Routledge, 2013), 24–38, for a discussion of cartes de visite and the history of promotional self-presentation.

34 Lionel Wee and Ann Brooks, "Personal Branding and the Commodification of Reflexivity," *Cultural Sociology* 4, no. 1 (2010): 45–62, http://doi.org/10.1177/1749975509356754.

35 Paul du Gay, *Consumption and Identity at Work* (London: SAGE Publications, 1996), 56.

36 Wee and Brooks, "Personal Branding and the Commodification of Reflexivity."

37 Du Gay, *Consumption and Identity at Work*; Peter Miller and Nikolas Rose, "Governing Economic Life," *Economy and Society* 19, no. 1 (February 1990): 1–31, http://doi.org/10.1080/03085149000000001; Alison Hearn, "'Meat, Mask, Burden': Probing the Contours of the Branded 'Self,'" *Journal of Consumer Culture* 8, no. 2 (2008): 197–217.

38 Wee and Brooks, "Personal Branding and the Commodification of Reflexivity," 46.

39 Susan Chritton, *Personal Branding for Dummies* (Hoboken, NJ: Wiley & Sons, 2012).

40 Anthony Giddens, *Modernity and Self-Identity: Self and Society in the Late Modern Age* (Stanford, CA: Stanford University Press, 1991); Anthony Giddens, "Living in a Post-Traditional Society," in *Reflexive Modernization: Politics, Tradition, and Aesthetics in the Modern Social Order*, ed. Ulrich Beck, Anthony Giddens, and Scott Lash (Stanford, CA: Stanford University Press, 1994), 56–109; Ulrich Beck and Elisabeth Beck-Gernsheim, *Individualization: Institutional Individualism and Its Social and Political Consequences* (London: SAGE Publications, 2002); Ulrich Beck, Anthony Giddens, and Scott Lash, *Reflexive Modernization: Politics, Tradition, and Aesthetics in the Modern Social Order* (Cambridge, MA: Polity Press, 1994); Zygmunt Bauman, *Liquid Modernity* (Malden, MA: Polity Press, 2000).

41 Bauman, *Liquid Modernity*.

42 Chritton, *Personal Branding for Dummies*, 8.

43 Quoted in Judith Ireland, "Net Narcissism: The Essay," *Sydney Morning Herald*, February 5, 2011.

44 Jeremy l'Anson, "Career Coach: Job Hunters Are Being Tracked Online," *Telegraph*, March 7, 2013, www.telegraph.co.uk.

45 Michael H. Goldhaber, "The Attention Economy and the Net," *First Monday* 2, no. 4 (1997), http://doi.org/10.5210/fm.v2i4.519.

46 Hearn, "Structuring Feeling," 426.

47 Wee and Brooks, "Personal Branding and the Commodification of Reflexivity."

48 See Michael Zimmer and Anthony Hoffman, "Privacy, Context, and Oversharing: Reputational Challenges in a Web 2.0 World," in *The Reputation Society: How Online Options Are Reshaping the Offline World*, ed. H. Masum and M. Tovey (Cambridge, MA: MIT Press, 2011), 175–84.

49 Charles Lindholm, "Authenticity," in *The Wiley Blackwell Encyclopedia of Race, Ethnicity, and Nationalism*, ed. Anthony D. Smith, Rutledge M. Dennis, John

Stone, Xiaoshuo Hou, and Polly Rizova (Oxford, UK: John Wiley & Sons, 2015), 1–3.

50 Sarah Banet-Weiser, *AuthenticTM: The Politics of Ambivalence in a Brand Culture* (New York: NYU Press, 2012), chap. 2.

51 Banet-Weiser, 85.

52 Mark Andrejevic, *Infoglut: How Too Much Information Is Changing the Way We Think and Know* (New York: Routledge, 2013), 30.

53 Natasha Singer, "Toning Down the Tweets Just in Case Colleges Pry," *New York Times*, November 20, 2014.

54 Mary Beth Marklein, "Job Hunters: Polish That Online Image," *USA Today*, December 20, 2012.

55 Megan O'Neal, "Confronting the Myth of the 'Digital Native,'" *Chronicle of Higher Education*, April 21, 2014, www.chronicle.com.

56 "Promotions," BrandYourself, 2017, http://promotions.brandyourself.com.

57 "Promotions."

58 Mary Madden and Aaron Smith, "Reputation Management and Social Media," Pew Internet & American Life Project, May 26, 2010, www.pewinternet.org.

59 Susan Kinzie and Ellen Nakashima, "Calling In Pros to Refine Your Google Image," *Washington Post*, July 2, 2007.

60 Saul Levmore, "The Internet's Anonymity Problem," in *The Offensive Internet: Speech, Privacy, and Reputation*, ed. Saul Levmore and Martha Craven Nussbaum (Cambridge, MA: Harvard University Press, 2010), 50–67.

61 Sam Stanton and Diana Lambert, "UC Davis Spent Thousands to Scrub Pepper-Spray References from Internet," *Sacramento Bee*, April 13, 2016, www.sacbee.com.

62 UC Davis spokeswoman Dana Topusis, quoted in Stanton and Lambert.

63 Anita Chabria, "Pepper-Sprayed Students Outranged as UC Davis Tried to Scrub Incident from the Web," *The Guardian*, April 14, 2016, www.theguardian.com.

64 Quoted in Stanton and Lambert, "UC Davis Spent Thousands."

65 Quoted in Chabria, "Pepper-Sprayed Students Outranged."

66 BrandYourself's Patrick Ambron, for example, writes, "Choosing not to brand yourself is like letting someone else pick out your outfit—and we all know about the importance of first impressions." See Ambron, "Why You Can't Just Ignore Personal Branding."

67 Jon Ronson writes that, for a particularly challenging case, an online reputation management company such as Reputation.com might charge hundreds of thousands of dollars. See Ronson, *So You've Been Publicly Shamed* (New York: Riverhead Books, 2015), 225.

68 Viktor Mayer-Schönberger, *Delete: The Virtue of Forgetting in the Digital Age* (Princeton, NJ: Princeton University Press, 2009).

69 Louis Bedigian, "Is Your Google Reputation Ruined?" *Benzinga* (blog), March 14, 2012, www.benzinga.com.

70 Tarleton Gillespie has written critically about the distinction between coordinated efforts to game search algorithms and the publication of genuine content. He argues most efforts fall somewhere in the middle. See Gillespie, "Algorithmically

Recognizable: Santorum's Google Problem, and Google's Santorum Problem," *Information, Communication & Society* 20, no. 1 (2017): 63–80, http://doi.org/10.10 80/1369118X.2016.1199721.

71 "Consumer Alert: ReputationChanger.com Warns Consumers of Reputation Management Companies Who Engage in Black Hat SEO," *PR Newswire*, January 30, 2012, www.prnewswire.com.

72 David Segal, "Mugged by a Mug Shot Online," *New York Times*, October 6, 2013.

73 Bill Keller writes about the implications for journalists and news organizations when the legal record is changed such that it no longer reflects the historical record. When legal facts no longer align with the historical facts recorded in digitized news sources, the responsibility of news organizations remains unclear. Bill Keller, "Erasing History," *New York Times*, April 28, 2013, www.nytimes.com.

74 Segal does note that some sites report having a "courtesy removal service" that allows people who can proved they were exonerated, not charged, or have since turned their life around to have images removed free of charge. See Segal, "Mugged by a Mug Shot Online."

75 Segal.

76 Steven Musil, "Google Works to Demote Mug Shot Sites in Search Results," *CNET*, October 6, 2013, www.news.cnet.com.

77 Segal, "Mugged by a Mug Shot Online."

78 For more information on the business model and legal responses, see Michael Salter and Thomas Crofts, "Responding to Revenge Porn: Challenges to Online Legal Impunity," in *New Views on Pornography: Sexuality, Politics, and the Law*, ed. Lynn Comella and Shira Tarrant (Santa Barbara, CA: Praeger, 2015), 233–53.

79 Although see Caitlin Lawson for a discussion of the media's treatment of the female celebrities as victims. See Lawson, "Innocent Victims, Creepy Boys: Discursive Framings of Sexuality in Online News Coverage of the Celebrity Nude Photo Hack," *Feminist Media Studies*, July 19, 2017, 1–17, http://doi.org/10.1080/146 80777.2017.1350197.

80 Salter and Crofts, "Responding to Revenge Porn."

81 Anita L. Allen, *Uneasy Access: Privacy for Women in a Free Society* (Totowa, NJ: Rowman & Littlefield, 1988).

82 Salter and Crofts, "Responding to Revenge Porn," 236. See also, Adele Hasinoff, *Sexting Panic: Rethinking Privacy, Criminalization, and Consent* (Urbana, IL: University of Illinois Press, 2015).

83 Jacob Kastrenakes, "California Becomes First State to Convict Someone for Operating a Revenge Porn Website," *The Verge*, February 3, 2015, www.theverge.com.

84 Niraj Chokshi, "Facebook Unveils Tools to Root Out Revenge Porn," *New York Times*, April 6, 2017.

85 See, for example, "The End of Revenge Porn?" *ReputationDefender* ® (blog), October 3, 2017, www.reputationdefender.com.

86 Ganaele Langlois and Andrea Slane, "Economies of Reputation: The Case of Revenge Porn," *Communication and Critical/Cultural Studies* 14, no. 2 (2017): 13, http://doi.org/10.1080/14791420.2016.1273534.

87 See also Ann Bartow, "Internet Defamation as Profit Center: The Monetization of Online Harassment," *Harvard Journal of Law & Gender* 32, no. 2 (2009): 383–429.

88 Langlois and Slane, "Economies of Reputation," 132.

89 Teresa M. Senft, "Microcelebrity and the Branded Self," in *A Companion to New Media Dynamics*, ed. John Hartley, Jean Burgess, and Axel Bruns (Malden, MA: Wiley, 2013), 346–54; Alice Marwick and danah boyd, "I Tweet Honestly; I Tweet Passionately: Twitter Users, Context Collapse, and the Imagined Audience," *New Media & Society* 13, no. 1 (2010): 114–33.

90 Hearn, "Structuring Feeling."

91 See, for example, Henry Jenkins, Sam Ford, and Joshua Green, *Spreadable Media: Creating Value and Meaning in a Networked Culture* (New York: NYU Press, 2013); Adam Arvidsson and Elanor Colleoni, "Value in Informational Capitalism and on the Internet," *Information Society* 28, no. 3 (2012): 135–50.

92 On this point, see Banet-Weiser, *AuthenticTM*; Alison Hearn, "Insecure: Narratives and Economics of the Branded Self in Transformation Television.," *Continuum: Journal of Media & Cultural Studies* 22, no. 4 (2008): 495–504; Alice Marwick, "Instafame: Luxury Selfies in the Attention Economy," *Public Culture* 27, no. 1 (75) (January 2015): 137–60, http://doi.org/10.1215/08992363-2798379.

93 Citron, "Civil Rights in Our Information Age," 32.

94 Fertik and Thompson, *Reputation Economy*, 1–2.

95 Fertik and Thompson, *Wild West 2.0*, 3.

CHAPTER 6. THE BIG POWER OF SMALL DATA

1 For a detailed explanation of the personal data ecosystem landscape, see Ann Cavoukian and Shane Green, *Privacy by Design and the Emerging Personal Data Ecosystem* (Toronto: Information and Privacy Commissioner of Ontario, Canada, 2012), www.ipc.on.ca.

2 Maglena Kuneva, "Keynote Speech" (Roundtable on Online Data Collection, Targeting, and Profiling, Brussels, March 31, 2009), http://europa.eu; *Big Data, Big Impact: New Possibilities for International Development* (Geneva: World Economic Forum, 2012), www3.weforum.org.

3 Simona Jankowski, "The Sectors Where the Internet of Things Really Matters," *Harvard Business Review*, October 22, 2014, http://hbr.org.

4 Mark Andrejevic, *Infoglut: How Too Much Information Is Changing the Way We Think and Know* (New York: Routledge, 2013).

5 Andrejevic, 21.

6 Viktor Mayer-Schönberger and Kenneth Cukier, *Big Data: A Revolution That Will Transform How We Live, Work, and Think* (Boston: Houghton Mifflin Harcourt, 2013), 6.

7 See "The Growing Business of Marijuana; You Don't Know Me! 'The Dream Team' That Wasn't," *The Lead with Jake Tapper*, CNN, March 22, 2013, http://thelead.blogs.cnn.com.

8 Mark Andrejevic, "The Work That Affective Economics Does," *Cultural Studies* 25, nos. 4–5 (2011): 604–20, http://doi.org/10.1080/09502386.2011.600551.

9 John Hagel III and Arthur G. Armstrong, *Net Gain: Expanding Markets through Virtual Communities* (Boston: Harvard Business School Press, 1997), 106.

10 Hagel and Armstrong.

11 Hagel and Armstrong.

12 Personal changed its name to TeamData in May 2016. Shane Green, "Why Personal 'Graduated' to TeamData Today," *Medium* (blog), May 20, 2016, www.medium.com.

13 Sally Herships, "Taking Control of Your Personal Data.," *Marketplace*, American Public Media, June 2012, www.marketplace.org.

14 Zach Davis, "Personal, Your Private Network and Central Data Vault," *Tech Cocktail*, March 15, 2012, www.tech.co.

15 José van Dijck defines APIs as "a set of codes that specifies protocolized relations between data, software, and hardware." See van Dijck, *The Culture of Connectivity: A Critical History of Social Media* (Oxford, UK: Oxford University Press, 2013), 31.

16 Mark Sullivan, "Personal Data Vaults Put You in Control of Your Data Online," *PCWorld*, June 12, 2012, www.pcworld.com.

17 Sullivan.

18 Respect Network, "Prominent Internet and IT Analyst Gary Rowe Joins Respect Network as CEO," *Marketwired*, November 13, 2012, www.marketwired.com.

19 Respect Network.

20 Barrington Moore, *Privacy: Studies in Social and Cultural History* (Armonk, NY: M. E. Sharpe, 1984), 277.

21 Charles Duhigg, "Psst, You in Aisle 5," *New York Times Magazine*, February 19, 2012.

22 Frank Pasquale describes the issues of reputation aggregators that display a single, propriety score. See Pasquale, "Reputation Regulation: Disclosure and the Challenge of Clandestinely Commensurating Computing," in *The Offensive Internet: Speech, Privacy, and Reputation*, ed. Saul Levmore and Martha Craven Nussbaum (Cambridge, MA: Harvard University Press, 2010), 107–23.

23 Scott Peppet has referred to this idea of entwined privacy as "unraveling." Peppet argues that willingness to reveal information at the individual level threatens privacy at the social level. See Peppet, "Unraveling Privacy: The Personal Prospects and the Threat of a Full-Disclosure Future," *Northwestern University Law Review* 105, no. 3 (2011): 1153–1204.

24 Carole Cadwalladr and Emma Graham-Harrison, "Revealed: 50 Million Facebook Profiles Harvested for Cambridge Analytica in Major Data Breach," *The Guardian*, March 17, 2018, www.theguardian.com.

25 Zeynep Tufekci, "Facebook's Surveillance Machine," *New York Times*, March 19, 2018, www.nytimes.com; Nadeem Badshah, "Facebook to Contact 87 Million Users Affected by Data Breach," *The Guardian*, April 8, 2018, www.theguardian.com.

26 Third-party apps could access data on Facebook users and their friends until the platform tightened restrictions in 2015. Drew Harwell and Elizabeth Dwoskin, "Why Facebook Users' Data Obtained by Cambridge Analytica Has Probably Spun Far Out of Reach," *Washington Post*, March 22, 2018, www.washingtonpost. com.

27 Lior Jacob Strahilevitz, "Collective Privacy," in *The Offensive Internet: Speech, Privacy, and Reputation*, ed. Saul Levmore and Martha Craven Nussbaum (Cambridge, MA: Harvard University Press, 2010), 217.

28 Deborah Lupton, *The Quantified Self: A Sociology of Self-Tracking* (Cambridge, UK: Polity, 2016), 140.

29 Alice E. Marwick and danah boyd, "Networked Privacy: How Teenagers Negotiate Context in Social Media," *New Media & Society* 16, no. 7 (2014): 1051–67, http://doi.org/10.1177/1461444814543995.

30 The fact that the online dating site Match.com has incorporated a version of this into their mobile app to let people see if there are users with whom they frequently cross paths suggests that this developer was onto something.

31 Gary Wolf, "Know Thyself: Tracking Every Facet of Life, from Sleep to Mood to Pain, 24/7/365," *Wired*, June 22, 2009, www.wired.com.

32 Gary Wolf, "Data-Driven Life," *New York Times*, May 2, 2010.

33 For a detailed account of the movement, see Lupton, *Quantified Self*.

34 Wolf, "Know Thyself."

35 Wolf, "Data-Driven Life"; See also Melanie Swan, "The Quantified Self: Fundamental Disruption in Big Data Science and Biological Discovery," *Big Data* 1, no. 2 (June 2013): 85–99, http://doi.org/10.1089/big.2012.0002.

36 Wolf.

37 Gina Neff and Dawn Nafus, *Self-Tracking* (Cambridge, MA: MIT Press, 2016), 11.

38 Lupton, *Quantified Self*, 142.

39 E. B. Boyd, "Personal.Com Creates an Online Vault to Manage All Your Data.," *Fast Company*, May 6, 2012, www.fastcompany.com.

40 Hagel and Armstrong, *Net Gain*, 105.

41 *Unlocking the Value of Personal Data: From Collection to Usage* (Geneva: World Economic Forum, 2013), 11, www3.weforum.org.

42 Decisions not to share personal data may have particularly profound effects in the United Kingdom, where robust privacy laws give people more control over the collection and use of their personal information compared to other countries.

43 Quoted in David Budworth, "Is Data Mining Really Worth the Dig?" *The Times*, November 24, 2012, www.thetimes.co.uk.

44 Quoted in Budworth.

45 Mint is now part of Intuit's suite of business, finance, and tax software.

46 Enliken shut down in 2014.

47 Jessica Bruder, "What If Web Users Could Sell Their Own Data?" *New York Times*, October 4, 2012.

48 Frank Pasquale, *The Black Box Society: The Secret Algorithms That Control Money and Information* (Cambridge, MA: Harvard University Press, 2015).

49 Paul Ohm, "Changing the Rules: General Principles for Data Use and Analysis," in *Privacy, Big Data, and the Public Good: Frameworks for Engagement*, ed. Julia Lane, Victoria Stodden, Stefan Bender, and Helen Nissenbaum (New York: Cambridge University Press, 2014), 101.

50 Kate Crawford, Jessa Lingel, and Tero Karppi, "Our Metrics, Ourselves: A Hundred Years of Self-Tracking from the Weight Scale to the Wrist Wearable Device," *European Journal of Cultural Studies* 18, nos. 4–5 (2015): 494, http://doi.org/10.1177/1367549415584857.

51 Sophie Curtis, "How Much Is Your Personal Data Worth?" *Telegraph*, November 23, 2015, www.telegraph.co.uk.

52 Mark Little, an analyst for the technology and business research group Ovum, observes, "It's not just about blocking [data collection] because you are concerned about your data and how much people know about you. . . . People are also blocking because they are feeling like companies are getting rich on them. They're feeling exploited." Quoted in Antone Gonsalves, "Online Privacy: The Opt-Out Revolution Is Almost Here," *ReadWriteWeb* (blog), February 12, 2013, www.readwrite.com.

53 Quoted in "The Growing Business of Marijuana."

54 Hille Koskela, "Webcams, TV Shows, and Mobile Phones: Empowering Exhibitionism," *Surveillance & Society* 2, nos. 2–3 (2004): 209–10.

55 Steve Mann and Joseph Ferenbok, "New Media and the Power Politics of Sousveillance in a Surveillance Dominated World," *Surveillance & Society* 11, nos. 1–2 (2013): 18–34.

56 Mann and Ferenbok, 26.

57 Mann and Ferenbok, 27.

58 Mann and Ferenbok, 32.

59 Rachel Hall, *The Transparent Traveler: The Performance and Culture of Airport Security* (Durham, NC: Duke University Press, 2015).

60 Jonas Lerman, "Big Data and Its Exclusions," *Stanford Law Review* 66 (2013): 55–63.

61 Lerman, 56.

62 For a discussion of how surveillance technologies affect poor populations in the United States see Virginia Eubanks, *Automating Inequality: How High-Tech Tools Profile, Police, and Punish the Poor* (New York: St. Martin's Press, 2018).

63 "Reality Mining of Mobile Communication: Towards a New Deal on Data," in *The Global Information Technology Report, 2008–2009: Mobility in a Networked World*, ed. Soumitra Dutta and Irene Mia (Geneva: World Economic Forum, 2009), 75–80, http://hd.media.mit.edu.

64 Simon G. Davies, "Re-engineering the Right to Privacy: How Privacy Has Been Transformed from a Right to a Commodity," in *Technology and Privacy: The New*

Landscape, ed. Philip E. Agre and Marc Rotenberg (Cambridge, MA: MIT Press, 1997), 143–65.

65 In his book *From Counterculture to Cyberculture*, communication historian Fred Turner describes the centrality of the Homebrew Computer Club to the sociotechnical culture of the computer hobbyist community of the 1970s. See Turner, *From Counterculture to Cyberculture: Stuart Brand, the Whole Earth Network, and the Rise of Digital Utopianism* (Chicago: University of Chicago Press, 2006).

66 Shane Green, "About Shane," *Getting Personal: My Data and the Digital Me* (blog), n.d., www.rshanegreen.com.

67 Alex Fitzpatrick, "Transparency: The Key to Collecting and Using Customer Data," *Mashable*, May 16, 2012, www.mashable.com.

68 Katryna Dow, "The Meeco Manifesto," *Meeco*, 2012, http://meeco.me.

69 Bruder, "What If Web Users Could Sell Their Own Data?"

70 Quoted in Davis, "Personal, Your Private Network."

71 See, for example, Zizi Papacharissi, "Privacy as a Luxury Commodity," *First Monday* 15, no. 8 (2010), http://dx.doi.org/10.5210/fm.v15i8.3075.

72 Julia Angwin, *Dragnet Nation: A Quest for Privacy, Security, and Freedom in a World of Relentless Surveillance* (New York: Henry Holt, 2014).

73 Evgeny Morozov, "Why We Are Allowed to Hate Silicon Valley," *Frankfurter Allgemeine Zeitung*, November 11, 2013, www.faz.net.

74 Nora A. Draper, "From Privacy Pragmatist to Privacy Resigned: Challenging Narratives of Rational Choice in Digital Privacy Debates," *Policy & Internet*, November 2016, http://doi.org/10.1002/poi3.142.

75 Noam Cohen traces a version of this quote to a 2010 comment on the website MetaFilter See Cohen, "Silicon Valley Is Not Your Friend," *New York Times*, October 15, 2017.

CONCLUSION

1 E. F. Schumacher, *Small Is Beautiful: Economics as If People Mattered* (New York: Harper Perennial, 1989), 14.

2 Schumacher, 22.

3 Langdon Winner, *The Whale and the Reactor: A Search of Limits in an Age of High Technology* (Chicago: University of Chicago Press, 1986), 63.

4 Schumacher, *Small Is Beautiful*.

5 For a detailed outline of the shared ideologies between the environmental and privacy movements see Andrew Clement and Christie Hurrell, "Information / Communications Rights as a New Environmentalism? Core Environmental Concepts for Linking Rights-Oriented Computerization Movements," in *Computerization Movements and Technology Diffusion: From Mainframes to Ubiquitous Computing*, ed. Ken Kraemer and Margaret Elliot (Medford, NJ: Information Today, 2008), 337–58. See also, Colin J. Bennett, *The Privacy Advocates: Resisting the Spread of Surveillance* (Cambridge, MA: MIT Press, 2008), chapter 7.

6   Austin Hill, "A Road Less Travelled: Building Privacy by Design," keynote address at the Computers, Freedom, and Privacy Conference, 2000, www.youtube.com/watch?v=W2B718SObGA.

7   Bruce Schneier, "Architecture of Privacy," *IEEE Security & Privacy Magazine* 7, no. 1 (January 2009): 88, http://doi.org/10.1109/MSP.2009.1.

8   David Harvey, *A Brief History of Neoliberalism* (Oxford, UK: Oxford University Press, 2005).

9   Michael F. Maniates, "Individualization: Plant a Tree, Buy a Bike, Save the World?" *Global Environmental Politics* 1, no. 3 (2001): 33.

10 Maniates, 34.

11 Maniates, 33.

12 "About SVN: Our Vision," Social Venture Network, 2014, www.svn.org.

13 See Jeffrey Rosen, "The Right to Be Forgotten," *Stanford Law Review Online* 64 (2012): 88–92.

14 See Susan Krashinsky, "Publishers Bracing for the Brave New World of Internet Advertising," *The Globe and Mail*, April 14, 2016, www.theglobeandmail.com.

15 Helen Nissenbaum, *Privacy in Context: Technology, Policy, and the Integrity of Social Life* (Stanford, CA: Stanford Law Books, 2010), 71.

16 Priscilla Regan, "Privacy and the Common Good: Revisited," in *Social Dimensions of Privacy: Interdisciplinary Perspectives*, ed. Beate Roessler and Dorota Mokrosinska (New York: Cambridge University Press, 2015), 50.

17 Siva Vaidhyanathan, *The Googlization of Everything (and Why We Should Worry)* (Berkeley: University of California Press, 2011), 55.

18 Quoted in John Schwartz, "'Opting In': A Privacy Paradox," *Washington Post*, September 3, 2000.

19 Shane Green, "Why Personal 'Graduated' to TeamData Today," *Medium* (blog), May 20, 2016, www.medium.com.

20 Steve O'Hear, "Digi.me and Personal Merge to Put You in Control of the Nascent 'Personal Data Ecosystem,'" *TechCrunch* (blog), August 17, 2017, www.techcrunch.com.

21 Dan Primack, "Reputation.com Makes a CEO Switch," *Fortune*, August 28, 2015, www.fortune.com.

22 Winner, *Whale and the Reactor*.

23 Winner, 80.

24 Virginia Eubanks, *Automating Inequality: How High-Tech Tools Profile, Police, and Punish the Poor* (New York: St. Martin's Press, 2018).

25 Tim Wu, "The Intimacy of Anonymity," *T: New York Times Style Magazine*, June 15, 2014.

26 Wu, 26.

27 Natasha Baker, "Snapchat, Vine among Top Smartphone Apps of 2013," Reuters, December 31, 2013, www.reuters.com.

28 Wu, "Intimacy of Anonymity," 26.

29 Quoted in David Kirkpatrick, *The Facebook Effect: The Inside Story of the Company That Is Connecting the World* (New York: Simon & Schuster, 2010).

30 Brad Stone and Sarah Frier, "Facebook Turns 10: The Mark Zuckerberg Interview," *Bloomberg Businessweek*, January 30, 2014, www.businessweek.com.

31 Quoted in Stone and Frier.

32 Dave Lee, "Snapchat Secretly Saves Images Using App," BBC News, October 15, 2013, www.bbc.com.

33 Ryan Gallagher, "Watch Your Naked Selfies: Snapchat Can Turn Photos over to Government," *Slate's Future Tense Blog* (blog), October 15, 2013, www.slate.com.

34 Lily Hay Newman, "Open Secrets: The New Wave of Anonymous Social Networks Is Neither New nor Anonymous," *Slate*, March 21, 2014, www.slate.com.

35 Whisper Team, "New Addition to Team Whisper," *Whisper Blog* (blog), September 5, 2013, http://blog.whisper.sh.

36 Gina Neff and David Stark, "Permanently Beta: Responsive Organization in the Internet Era," in *Society Online: The Internet in Context*, ed. Philip N. Howard and Steve Jones (Thousand Oaks, CA: SAGE Publications, 2004), 175.

37 Nissenbaum, *Privacy in Context*, 127.

38 Isabel V. Sawhill, "Strengthening the Three-Legged Stool of Policy Analysis, Organization, and Leadership," *Journal of Policy Analysis and Management* 8, no. 3 (1989): 501, http://doi.org/10.2307/3324940.

39 For a detailed analysis, see Meg Leta Jones, *Ctrl-Z: The Right to Be Forgotten* (New York: NYU Press, 2016).

40 Catriona Mackenzie and Natalie Stoljar, eds., *Relational Autonomy: Feminist Perspectives on Autonomy, Agency, and the Social Self* (New York: Oxford University Press, 2000).

41 Mackenzie and Stoljar, 4. For a discussion of the application of relational theories to privacy, see Beate Roessler and Dorota Mokrosinka "Privacy and Social Interaction," *Philosophy and Social Criticism* 39, no. 8 (2013): 771–791, https://doi.org/10/1177/0191453713494968 and Dorota Mokrosinka "Privacy and Turonomy: On Some Misconceptions Concerning the Political Dimensions of Privacy," *Law and Philosophy* 37, no. 2 (2018): 117–143, https://doi.org/10.1007/s10982-017-9307-3.

INDEX

ABOUT THE AUTHOR

Nora A. Draper is Assistant Professor of Communication at the University of New Hampshire.